# Structured Finance

Stefano Caselli · Stefano Gatti
(Editors)

# Structured Finance

## Techniques, Products and Market

With 52 Figures and 28 Tables

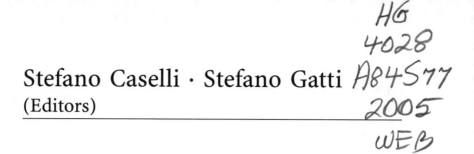

Springer

Professor Stefano Caselli
Professor Stefano Gatti
IEMIF
Bocconi University
Via Sarfatti 25
20136 Milan
Italy
stefano.caselli@unibocconi.it
stefano.gatti@unibocconi.it

Cataloging-in-Publication Data
Library of Congress Control Number: 2005927233

ISBN 3-540-25311-4 Springer Berlin Heidelberg New York

Springer is a part of Springer Science + Business Media

springeronline.com

© Springer Berlin · Heidelberg 2005
Printed in Germany

Hardcover-Design: Erich Kirchner, Heidelberg

SPIN 11407614        43/3153-5  4  3  2  1  0 – Printed on acid-free paper

# Foreword

Stefano Caselli and Stefano Gatti

"Giordano Dell'Amore Institute of Financial Markets and Financial Intermediaries – "L. Bocconi" University, Milan

Structured finance is a business area that encompasses a wide range of transactions. In this work, the authors opted to include securitization, project finance, leasing (as a transaction representative of asset based finance) and acquisition finance activities conducted by utilizing a deal design based on a strong debt component (essentially LBOs in all their contractual variations). This perimeter of analysis does not lend itself to meticulous theoretical or empirical debate. The evidence which emerges from observation of the managerial practices of international and domestic intermediaries that compete in this business (which are described in this work) substantially confirm this choice.

Though defining the boundaries of structured finance is not particularly problematic, the same can not be said of the position taken by Italian financial intermediaries in this business area. In actual fact, neither in national nor international literature can systematic studies be found which deal with both positioning of actors on the market (and in this context positioning of domestic intermediaries) as well as the choice of organizational structures at the basis of services offered. This was the primary motivation for drafting the present study.

The second reason that prompted the authors to address this topic lies in the transformation of the strategy that various Italian banks have begun to implement in recent years, reacting to pressure from changes in demand on one hand and in supervisory authorities on the other. These stimuli translate into the need for a more serious commitment to supporting financial policies of client companies by offering a complete range of services.

The shift from a logic of corporate lending to one of "full service", typical of corporate and investment banking, calls for change in two respects:

1. the range of financial services proposed;
2. the choice of organizational structure adopted to supply these services.

As for the first point, structured finance presents a unique situation. Unlike certain businesses which were for the most part unheard of among

Italian banks until a few years ago (for example, direct private equity or risk management to support customers' positions), structured finance transactions share many basic principles with medium to long term lending. In fact, in the past national banks have been participants in project finance, acquisition finance, and securitization. The novelty lies in the current need for national intermediaries to serve as direct interlocutors with customers in such transactions. In practice, this materializes in the need to integrate the offer of funding (which already exists) with consulting on modeling and assembling the transaction in question. Winning credibility in higher value added advisery and arranging activities has become the central objective for banks that wish to implement credible corporate and investment banking strategies.

As regards the choice of organizational structure, it is only natural to expect that adopting a higher profile in financial consultancy to support credit deals requires banks to rethink the way they interface with customers. Designing managerial practices to handle customer relations and, in this context, creating organizational roles for contact and transactions become critical elements in guaranteeing the effectiveness of the business proposal.

Within this framework of changes in transactional and commercial choices, various signals (confirmed by the results of this study) point to the family of structured finance as an attractive business area for Italian banks, most certainly in view of potential market size. In this regard, at least three examples can be given.

The first involves project finance. Now that the initial phase involving large projects which characterized the Nineties has come to a close, the market seems to have repositioned itself around smaller transactions with a stronger presence of public parties as concession awarders or buyers of services (a special case is partially self-financed projects). Beyond providing the foundation for consolidating business volumes, this opens the way for interesting opportunities not only for larger banks but for middle market players as well.

The second example refers to securitization. The market (despite some obstacles created by the regulations in Law 130/99) shows as of yet untapped potential in the segment of corporate originators. The dialectic role that even medium sized banks can play in this segment should not be underestimated.

The final example refers to LBOs in their many contractual variations. Such transactions underscore structural problems involved in family succession and governance transfer in the Italian business world. The development of the private equity industry, which has recently begun to reabsorb the recessive trends of the last three years, is apt to proliferate the possibilities of credit intervention in replacement phases in the future.

The evidence presented above provides a more accurate framework for the objectives of this research project. In fact, for each structured transaction, this work aims to do the following:

1. Analyze the key criticalities which emerge in the relationship between bank and customer. Critical success factors are then identified which enable banks to compete as credible service providers in this business area.
2. Examine the advantages which can be gained by originators/sponsors from each type of structured finance.
3. Quantify the current dimensions of the market and identify areas for development which as yet have not been completely exhausted by the competitive game.

In addition, a transversal objective in the study of transactions and business areas is to illustrate the macrostructural profiles that characterize business units tasked with advisery services and funding of structured transactions. This is particularly useful in research with an empirical bent so as to verify the existence of best practice benchmarks.

Lastly, from a methodological viewpoint this study has been conducted on two levels. First, considering the scarcity of literature dealing with the field of analysis in its entirety in any methodical way, every contributor reviews the best available literature on each single structured finance transaction. Secondly, to analyze its present and potential dimensions, an in-depth, empirical investigation is carried out to arrive at an accurate quantification of the current size of the domestic market. Wherever possible, qualitative and quantitative indications are also provided on the potential for development of this market.

The editors would like to thank Professors Paolo Mottura and Francesco Saita, respectively Director and Co-Director of Newfin Bocconi (Research Centre for Financial Innovation of Bocconi University in Milan), who have sponsored and funded the research on which this book is based. A special thank goes to Lorenzo Marinoni for the precious editing work. This book is dedicated by Stefano Caselli to Anna, Elisa and Lorenzo and by Stefano Gatti to the memory of his grandfather Giacomo.

# Table of Contents

# 1 Characteristics and Common Features of Structured Finance Operations

Stefano Caselli and Stefano Gatti

## 1.1 Introduction

This chapter gives a brief introduction to the characteristics that various structured finance transactions analyzed in the following chapters have in common. It is worthwhile to consider the entire set of such transactions in order to provide readers with a general framework and to focus attention directly on aspects which characterize each one.

After having described the basis of structured transactions, points of divergence with respect to usual corporate lending techniques are presented, highlighting the advantages that can be had from realizing a transaction following structured finance logic.

## 1.2 Typical features of structured finance transactions

Using the logic behind arranging financing on a structured basis, a transaction can be included in the business area of structured finance when the following conditions hold true:

1. The recipient of the funds raised is a separate entity from the party or parties sponsoring the transaction. This separation is achieved by creating vehicle companies (SPVs, Special Purpose Vehicles, or SPCs, Special Purpose Companies – the terms are synonymous) designated to take on the initiative and to secure cash receipts and payments which result.
2. Consequent to the previous point, since the initiative to be financed is undertaken by a legal entity set up for this specific purpose, all economic consequences generated by the initiative in question are attributed to this SPV. Financers, therefore, grant financing to the vehicle and not to the parties (sponsors or originators) who founded this company.
3. Since the SPV is the recipient of the financing, and considering that this vehicle has its own net worth, the assets instrumental to managing the project are separated from the remaining assets of the parties that

created the vehicle. Hence, along with the cash flow from the initiative, the SPV's assets become collateral for creditors.

The three conditions cited above explain why structured finance transactions are also called "off-balance sheet financing".

The presence of a separate vehicle company which is interested in obtaining financing for the realization of a specific initiative detached from other projects underway, implies that loan repayment is guaranteed primarily by the generation of cash by the assets tied up in the initiative in question. The net worth of the sponsors is, in theory, irrelevant in assessing the financial sustainability of the loans. This is due to the fact that creditors are dealing with no-recourse financing or limited recourse financing, in very specific cases, on the assets of parties that set up the vehicle company.

The use of ad hoc vehicles which encapsulate projects or asset portfolios finds a very wide range of applications; examples are plentiful.

1. In securitization, the Special Purpose Company (or securitization vehicle) issues bonds on the market against real or financial assets segregated in that same vehicle. The only source of reimbursement on capital and interest is the ability of the pool of assets to generate cash in equal measure. The cash flow profile is improved by means of internal and external credit enhancement techniques, which are discussed in Chapter 2.
2. In project finance transactions, industrial projects are segregated in an SPV. Financing is then awarded to this company, which is secured through a series of contractual agreements with key counterparts (contractors, purchasers, suppliers, operator agents, etc.) for the purpose of improving volatility profiles of free cash flows, as will be seen in Chapter 3
3. In leasing transactions (Chapter 4) – in particular big ticket deals, i.e. those involving complex, large-scale assets (airplanes, ships, large real estate projects) – the preference is to draw up the contract with an ad hoc legal entity as counterpart to allow better correspondence between cash outflow from payments on installments and inflow generated by the financed asset.
4. Lastly, in leveraged buyouts (Chapter 5) setting up a vehicle company facilitates capital budgeting of the initiative. Taking into account cash flow deriving from the target company (and only from that company), an assessment is made of the sustainability of the emerging financial structure based on the total liabilities of the target and the Newco (the vehicle utilized for the acquisition) with respect to the latter's equity.

## 1.3 The advantages of assembling a financing transaction in structured form

The advantages to be had through off-balance sheet forms of financing can be ascertained by analyzing the differences between on-balance financing logic (or corporate financing) and that based on the creation of ad hoc companies.

As explained in the preceding section, the goal in encapsulating an initiative or a pool of assets in an ad hoc organization is to isolate the fate of these assets in relation to those of the sponsor or sponsors of the transaction. This isolation works both ways. An initiative with poor prospects, even where default is a possibility, does not impact the performance or the survival of the company, due to the principle of limited shareholder responsibility set down in the regulatory framework of many countries. On the other hand, a project's worth should, at least in theory, remain untainted by business dealings that could negatively affect its shareholders. In this sense, a project's creditors continue to claim rights to the assets and cash flows of the initiative, even if its shareholders go bankrupt.[1]

The clear separation between the initiative and the sponsoring party also means that the two can have very different creditworthiness. One extreme may be strong sponsors and weak initiatives segregated in a vehicle. The other extreme (more commonly found in practice) could be cases where sponsors have rather low creditworthiness but nonetheless are able to make the initiative hinge on a vehicle company which, appropriately secured by credit enhancement mechanisms, can obtain a higher credit rating than its originators.

The first economic benefit of structured transactions lies in the cost of funding of new financial resources for the initiative. If the benefits of a reduced cost of funding are greater than the cost of credit enhancement (of whatever kind: a purchasing contract or a tranche-based bond issue, a pledge to pay penalties signed by a counterpart of the SPV, insurance coverage), realizing the initiative on a structured basis is advantageous for sponsors.

The second advantage in separating the initiative from the sponsor(s) lies in maintaining financial flexibility of this company or companies. In

---

[1] This situation, clearly described from a theoretical viewpoint in Brealey et al. (1996) is not what happens in actual practice. Often one of the events of default included in the loan agreement is precisely the default of one or more sponsors. If this occurred, it would also have repercussions on the initiative and thus on its creditors.

fact, financing is granted to a legal entity separate from the sponsor, which therefore does not tap into the latter's credit lines. A specially secured initiative is proposed to the pool of financers, for which a specific return/risk combination is offered in the face of new credit lines. Prior credit lines are not drawn on, nor are there any induced effects on the cost of already existing funding for the sponsor.

# 2 The Asset Securitization Activity in Italy: Current and Future Trends

Roberto Tasca and Simona Zambelli[1]

## 2.1 Introduction

The main object of this chapter is to analyze the basic characteristics and the market structure of the securitization activity, especially with reference to the Italian securitization market, which has rapidly developed in recent years.

In particular, this chapter intends to answer the following questions:

1. What is meant by securitization?
2. How is the transaction structured?
3. What is the role of financial intermediaries within the securitization process, especially in Italy?
4. What are the main characteristics of the Italian securitization activity?

At this purpose, we will first explain the basic components of a securitization transaction, describing the typical structure and the main players involved. Secondly, we will analyze the Italian securitization market, emphasizing its peculiarities through an international comparative analysis.

Generally speaking, the aim of securitization is to transform illiquid assets into securities. For the purpose of this chapter, the term securitization is used to represent the process whereby assets are pooled together, with their cash flows, and converted into negotiable securities to be placed into the market. These securities are backed or secured by the original underlying assets and are generally defined as Asset Baked Securities (ABS).[2]

---

[1] Even though this chapter is the result of a common effort by the authors, paragraphs 2.1, 2.2 and 2.3 have been written by Simona Zambelli, while paragraphs 2.4, 2.5 and 2.6 have been written by Roberto Tasca. The conclusive paragraph has been written jointly by the authors.

[2] An ABS represents a security backed by specific assets. This means that principal and interest repayment rely directly on the capability of the underlying assets to generate the expected cash flows. In the US it is common to distinguish between:

Theoretically, any financial assets producing cash flows (receivables, residential and commercial mortgages, credit card receivables, and other consumer and commercial loans) can be securitized.[3]

The concept of asset securitization was introduced in the US financial system in the 1970s, when the Government National Mortgage Association issued securities backed by a pool of loans, represented by residential mortgages.[4] During the last decade, it has rapidly developed within Europe, especially in the UK. Recently, the Italian securitization market has rapidly expanded thanks to the introduction of a specific regulation (Law 130/99).

Two main types of securitization transactions exist:

1. Cash flow based (CFB) securitization. The transaction is structured as a sale of assets by a company (Originator) to a special entity (Special Purpose Vehicle, SPV), which then issues securities backed by the underlying assets. The CFB securitization is also defined as Funded Securitization, because the Originator can raise money through the asset sale, diversifying its financing sources;
2. Synthetic securitization. It is a transaction through which the credit risk, associated with a pool of assets, is transferred to a separate entity (SPV). It is not a sale of assets, so the Originator does not receive any cash flow. The SPV in this case is not the owner of a pool of assets, but only the entity that carries the associated credit risk. It is realized through the use of derivatives instruments (total return swaps and credit derivatives).

---

- asset backed securities (ABS), which represent securities backed by specific assets (auto loans, credit card receivables, student loans, equipment leases). This definition does not include mortgages loans or corporate bond loans;
- mortgage backed security (MBS), which are securities backed by specific mortgage loans.

Outside the US, the definition of ABS may include deals backed by mortgages loans. For the purpose of this chapter, we will use the term of ABS to indicate all classes of securitized instruments. See: Bhattacharya and Fabozzi (1997), Saunders and Cornett (2004), Burton et al. (2003), Spotorno (2003).

[3] See, among others: AA. VV. (1999), Colagrande et al. (1999), Bontempi and Scagliarini (1999), Artale et al. (2000), Damilano (2000), De Angeli and Oriani (2000), Rumi (2001) Porzio et al. (2001), AA. VV. (2001), Galletti and Guerrieri (2002), Ferro Luzzi (2000), Gualtieri (2000), La Torre (2000), Caneva (2001), Navone (2002).

[4] See: Saunders and Cornett (2004), Burton et al. (2003), Spotorno (2003).

For the purpose of this chapter, we will only analyze the first type of transaction, since synthetic securitization has not been regulated by the Italian Securitization Law (Law 130/99).[5]

This chapter is organized as follows. Paragraph 2.2 describes the basic structure of the typical securitization transaction. Paragraph 2.3 discusses the securitization process and paragraphs 2.4 and 2.5 emphasize the particular role of financial intermediaries within this process, in view of the Law 130/99. Paragraph 2.6 highlights the current and future trends of the Italian securitization market, implementing a comparative worldwide analysis over the period 2001-2003 (first term). Paragraph 2.7 concludes the analysis of securitization activity in Italy.[6]

## 2.2 The typical securitization transaction scheme

Securitization is a financial instrument aimed at transforming a pool of assets into marketable securities, which are secured by the cash flow stream related to the underlying assets (Asset Backed Securities – ABS).

It is realized through a transfer of assets by a company (Originator) to a separate firm (Special Purpose Vehicle – SPV), which then issues securities, in the form of debt instruments, to be placed into the market through a private or public offering.

In order to analyze the basic structure of a securitization transaction, let us consider the following example. The Originator is a bank, willing to raise money by liquidating a specific pool of loans through securitization.

As Figure 2.1 shows, two basic deals are involved:

1. Asset sale;[7]
2. Issuance of Asset Backed Securities.

– Asset Sale. The first deal is represented by a sale of assets between two parties:

1. One party is the seller of the assets and is known as the "Originator". In our example it is represented by a bank;

---

[5] For a detailed analysis on the synthetic securitization transaction, see: Caputo et al. (2001).

[6] Notice that the international data on securitization market are from: www.abalert.com by Harrison Scott Publications, while the data on Italian securitization market are from www.securitisation.it by Talete Creative Finance. The two databases coincide with reference to the Italian market analysis.

[7] The example represented in Figure 2.1 considers a transfer of credits and receivables between the Originator and the SPV.

2. The other party is a separate entity, established for the purpose of buying the assets and transforming them into negotiable securities to be placed into the capital market. This entity serves only as securitization vehicle and so it is often defined as "Special Purpose Vehicle" (SPV) or "Special Purpose Company" (SPC). It may take the organizational form of corporation or limited partnership.

– Issuance of Asset Backed Securities. In order to finance the asset purchase, the SPV issues securities (usually debt obligation instruments), which are backed by the acquired assets (Asset Backed Securities – ABS). The cash flows originated by the acquired pool of assets are then used to pay the principal and interest on the securities sold to the final investors (holders of ABS securities).[8]

**Fig. 2.1.** Transactions involved and relative funds flow

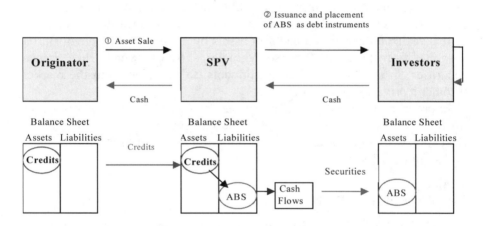

Source: the author

As a result of the securitization:

1. The Originator can liquidate assets and receive funds to use immediately for its business activity, without waiting for the maturities of each credits;

2. The underlying securities, issued by the SPV, are backed by a portfolio of assets, which allows a better diversification of risks;

---

[8] The payments collection related to the securitized portfolio is managed by a third party, the Servicer, which usually is represented by the Originator itself.

3. The issuance of Asset Backed Securities contributes to satisfy different investors' needs and to develop primary financial markets, allowing a transfer of certain risks to the final investors.

The risks carried by the investors depend mainly on the quality of the underlying assets, rather than the creditworthiness of the issuer or the Originator.[9] A careful evaluation of the assets' characteristics is then essential before performing any securitization transaction. The quality of the assets in fact will affect:

1. The creditworthiness of the related ABS, which is usually represented by a rating assigned by specialized agencies;[10]
2. The type and the amount of credit enhancement mechanisms, which might be necessary to lower the associated risk of the Asset Backed Securities and improve their rating.

A securitization differs from a traditional equity or debt financing for at least two reasons. First, it is not a loan. It implies an asset sale by the Originator to the SPV. Second, the buyers of Asset Backed Securities rely primarily on the cash flows generated by the underlying pool of assets, rather than the cash flows generated by the business activity of the issuer.

## 2.2.1 The role of the true sale of assets to the Special Purpose Vehicle (SPV)

Two important aspects of securitization needs to be emphasized. First, securitization is realized through a true sale of assets by the Originator to a separate company (SPV), which issues securities backed by those assets. The true sale mechanism allows a company to isolate a group of financial assets, separating the risk of the firm as a whole from the risk associated with the securitized assets.[11] Second, the SPV represents a critical actor within the securitization process: it servers as a vehicle to accomplish a securitization transaction.

---

[9] JCR-VIS Credit Rating Company Limited (2003), Nomura Fixed Income and Research (2002), Bond Market Association, (2002), Leixner (http://pages.stern.nyu.edu).
[10] Under the Italian Law, a rating is required only if the securities are sold to non professional investors.
[11] The expected return to investors depends mainly on the risk associated with the cash flows guaranteed by the securitized assets, rather than the default risk of the Originator.

In order to understand the crucial role played by the SPV, let us consider the following scenario. Imagine that the Originator could directly issue securities backed by a pool of assets, without selling it to an intermediate vehicle. In this scenario, the investors interested in buying the Asset Backed Securities would carry both the default risk connected to the entire business activity of the Originator and the risk related to the securities. In reality, in a securitization transaction investors are willing to assume only the risk related to the pool of assets they are investing in.

In order to protect final investors against the bankruptcy risk of the Originator, it is crucial to isolate the securitized assets from its business activity and its creditors. To guarantee this asset isolation, it is necessary to structure the transaction as a "true sale" of assets between the Originator and a third independent entity, the SPV, which is established exclusively for the purpose of facilitating the financing.

The SPV involvement provides an investor with greater protection against the credit risk of the Originator and the default risk of the issuer, for at least two reasons.

In the first place, the SPV is a separate company which is intended to generate an isolation of assets. In principle, once a pool of assets is transferred to a special independent vehicle, it is no longer available to the Originator or to its creditors. The subject assets are then "isolated" from the Originator activity and can only be used by the SPV to make payments to the final investors, willing to hold the Asset Backed Securities. In the second place, the SPV activity is strictly limited in order to increase the protection of the investors' rights. The vehicle can only hold specific assets and issue in turn securities backed by these assets. The SPV is not allowed to begin other business activities and to assume new obligations. By restricting its activity, then the operational and business risk can be minimized. This is why the vehicle is also called a "bankruptcy remote entity".[12]

With reference to the asset isolation effect, it is important to highlight a crucial difference between the Italian and the US regulation system.

In the US the assets sold by a borrower before falling into bankruptcy do not become part of the bankruptcy procedure. Consequently, the Originator is not allowed to reclaim the transferred assets and so, in case of default, its creditors cannot call on them to satisfy their claims.[13]

---

[12] JCR-VIS Credit Rating Company Limited (2002), Bond Market Association (2002).
[13] In the US there is no bankruptcy code provision regulating the legal status of securitized assets. Securitized assets are then considered as legally sold and are

By contrast, according to the Italian Securitization Law, the risk of reclaiming the sold assets is eliminated only if the sale occurred more than one year before the bankruptcy event (Figure 2.2).[14] Secondly, it is necessary to demonstrate that the assets have been sold to a fair price. If the above conditions are not satisfied, it is legally possible for the Originator (or its creditors) to reclaim the assets transferred to the SPV (art. 4 L. 130/99).[15]

**Fig. 2.2.** Asset Reclaim Risk, according to the Italian Securitization Law (L. 130/99)

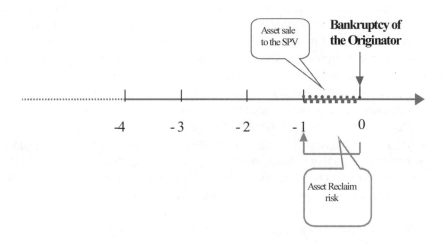

Source: the author

## 2.3 The securitization process: a basic analysis

In order to understand how it is possible to transform illiquid assets into marketable securities, let us describe the main steps that are required for

excluded from the eventual bankruptcy procedure of the Originator. For more information see: Nomura Fixed Income and Research (2002).
[14] Art. 4, Law 130/99.
[15] In case of bankruptcy of the SPV, the period in which it is possible to reclaim the sold assets is six months. See: Spotorno (2003).

accomplishing a typical securitization transaction.[16] As Figure 2.3 shows, a securitization process involves the following phases.[17]

- Selection of a pool of assets. In the first place, the Originator has to identify a pool of assets with similar characteristics. Theoretically, any asset producing cash flows (receivables, residential and commercial mortgages, credit card receivables, and other consumer and commercial loans) can be securitized, including non – performing loans, as we will emphasize in the course of the analysis of the Italian securitization market.
- Asset sale/True sale transaction. In the second place, it is necessary to guarantee the isolation of the pool of assets from the Originator. As noticed, this is achieved by structuring a true sale of the pool of assets by the Originator to an external entity (SPV), which has no business other than acquiring assets and issuing securities backed by these assets.
- Issuance of asset backed securities. To finance the acquisition of the assets, the SPV issues securities to be sold in the marketplace to investors. These debt securities are secured by the underlying assets acquired by the vehicle (Asset Backed Securities – ABS).
- Market placement. The SPV sells these securities on the capital market, through a private placement or public offering, with the help of underwriters. Usually, the ABSs are purchased by banks, insurance companies, pension funds and other institutional investors.
- Payment of the asset purchase. In the end, the funds raised by the SPV from the market placement are used to pay the pool of assets originally acquired by the vehicle.

As a result of the securitization process, funds will flow from the investors to the issuer (SPV) and from the issuer to the Originator.[18]

---

[16] Saunders and Cornett (2004), Burton et al. (2003), Spotorno (2003), Leixner (http:// pages.stern.nyu.edu), JCR-VIS Credit Rating Company Limited (2003), Nomura Fixed Income and Research (2002), Bond Market Association (2002).

[17] Paragraph 2.4 will analyze the specific role of financial intermediaries within the securitization process, emphasizing the conditions required by the Law 130/99.

[18] Saunders and Cornett (2004), Burton et al. (2003), Spotorno (2003), Leixner (http:// pages.stern.nyu.edu), JCR-VIS Credit Rating Company Limited (2002), Bond Market Association (2002).

**Fig. 2.3.** Basic securitization process

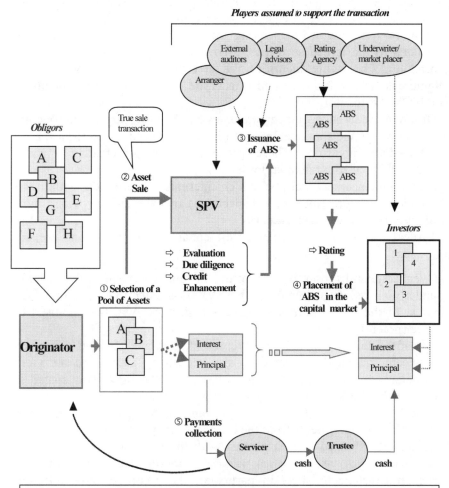

**Example**

Let as imagine that the loan originator is a financial institution, such as a bank. It wants to raise money by liquidating a pool of mortgage loans. A SPV is established for this purpose and a securitization transaction is then structured following several steps.
① A pool of assets is selected by the Originator (bank). The bank decides to sell a group of commercial and residential loans.
② A true sale transaction follows. The bank sells the selected pool of loans to a SPV.
③ After a detailed evaluation of the assets and a credit enhancement procedure, the SPV then issues securities backed by the acquired underlying assets (ABS). To make them more attractable, a rating is associated with the asset baked secur ities.
④ A placement in the market place follows. Underwriters and market placer will help the SPV to sell the securities into the market. Typical final investors are: mutual funds, banks, insurance companies and pension funds.
⑤ The servicer (usually repesented by the originator) then collects the monthly payments (in the form of interest and principal) associated with the acquired assets and then forward these cash flows to the Trustee. In the end, the Trustee forwards these payments to the final investors.

Source: the author

The securitization process summarized in Figure 2.3 is very basic. As we will analyze later, it actually involves more steps and additional players, especially financial intermediaries, to support the entire operation.

For example, in order to ensure marketability to the ABSs and to make them more appealing, a credit rating from specialized agencies is always associated to the issued securities, after evaluating the risk of the entire transaction. The rating identifies the creditworthiness, in term of the default risk, of the issuance and affects the cost of the entire operation, paid by the Originator.[19]

Different credit enhancement strategies can be necessary to improve the credit rating of the marketable securities and to reduce the risks that is transferred to investors. These procedures aim at creating specific mechanisms to absorb potential losses.

Credit enhancement can be either internally determined within the transaction structure (internal enhancement) or externally provided by a third party (external enhancement).

Typical examples of internal credit enhancement provisions are the following:

1. Over collateralization of the offer. In this case, the value of the underlying assets acquired by the SPV is greater than the total face value of the issued securities. Excess cash flows will then be used to cover potential losses;
2. Spread accounts. The spread is represented by the positive difference between: the yield generated by the underlying assets and the yield associated to the related securities, issued by the SPV. This spread is retained by the SPV in order to absorb potential losses;
3. Reserve Funds. A cash reserve fund might be created in order to cover potential underpayments from the original borrowers;
4. Senior/subordinated debt structure. With this provision, the SPV sells different types of securities (senior, subordinated) with different risk/return characteristics. In particular, the securities have different payment priority. Senior securities are characterized by a lower risk, higher rating and lower return. Conversely, junior securities are more risky. As a consequence, they are associated with: lower rating and higher expected return. In the worst-case scenario, senior securities give the holder the right to receive the related payments before the subordinated securities ones. Consequently, cash flows will be used to

---

[19] For more information: JCR-VIS Credit Rating Company Limited (2003), Nomura Fixed Income and Research (2002).

pay the senior securities and eventually, only if sufficient capital is left, to satisfy the subordinated securities.

External credit enhancement examples are the following:

1. Letter of credits by a bank or insurance company, to guarantee the security issuance;
2. Insurance contracts;
3. Special guarantees from a third party.

As Figure 2.3 shows, other two parties are involved into the securitization process: the Servicer and the Trustee.

The Servicer is responsible for the collection of receivables and other payments on the assets acquired by the SPV.

On the other hands, the Trustee is an independent third party (usually a bank) assumed to monitor the entire collection process and to make payments to the security-holders. Its aim is to protect the investors' interests, monitoring the regular payment-reports prepared by the Servicer.

Usually the Originator acts as a Servicer. In Italy, this occurs when the Originator is represented by a financial institution. In this situation, the obligors continue to make payments to the Originator, which will forward the cash flows to the Trustee. Then, the Trustee will forward the cash flows collected by the Servicer to the final investors.

## 2.4 The main players involved in a securitization transaction according to the Law 130/99

According to Law 130/99 a securitization transaction can be realized through any non gratuitous transfer of current or future credits, that are likely to generate ongoing periodic cash-flows. The Securitization Law specifies the following requirements:

1. The asset seller (Originator) shall be a company satisfying the requisites provided by the art. 3 of Law 130/99;
2. The sums paid by the assigned debtors shall be exclusively dedicated to the satisfaction of the debt service and principal payment of the securities issued by the special purpose vehicle and to the payment of the transaction-costs.[20]

---

[20] Law 130/99, art.1.

Credit derivatives, wholesale securitization and synthetic securitization transactions are not included into the above legal definition.[21] Law 130/99 does not discipline the securitization of future revenues, such as the expected EBIT.

As it is shown in Figure 2.4, the securitization process involves many players, with different roles: borrowers, loan Originator, special purpose company, rating agency, credit enhancer, underwriter and investors.

In particular, according to Law 130/99, the main actors of securitization can be summarized as follows:

1. The Asset Seller (Originator);
2. The Special Purpose Vehicle ("SPV"): according to the Law 130/99 the SPV is the entity specifically established to undertake particular securitization transactions (art. 3 Law 130/99), which would hold the legal rights over the assets transferred by the Originator. It can take the form of limited liability company (s.r.l.). A disposition of the Central Bank Governor also requires the SPV to be recorded into a special register (according to the provisions of the Legislative Decree 58/98 art. 107) and to satisfy minimum capital levels, depending on the volume of transactions managed;
3. The Arranger: the financial institution (bank or other) which agrees to structure a securitization transaction. The Arranger is responsible, alone or through a syndicate structure, for the issuance and the placement of the ABS;
4. The Servicer: entity which is responsible for the day-to-day collection. In many case the Originator also performs the role of the Servicer;
5. The Trustee: Institution (bank or other) which administers the securitization transaction, manages the inflow and outflow of moneys and does all acts needed for protecting the investors' rights.
6. Other actors: collection account bank, deposit account bank, cash manager bank e paying agent, letter of credit providers, liquidity facility provider, corporate Servicer, hedging counterparts. These actors play an important role in order to implement the collection, deposit, management and hedging of the cash-flows and risks related to the securitization process.

Moreover, other parties are usually involved into a securitization process (even though they are not identified by Law 130/99):

---

[21] See Caputo at al. (2001).

– Rating agencies: institutions which assign credit rating to debt obligations after analyzing the issuer and the transaction characteristics;[22]
– Legal consultants for the deal structuring;
– Auditors: institutions dedicated to the due diligence of the credit portfolio.

Other financial institutions might be involved in the securitization process, in order to guarantee collateral services, such as the hedging against the interest rate risk.

**Fig. 2.4.** Players involved in the securitization process

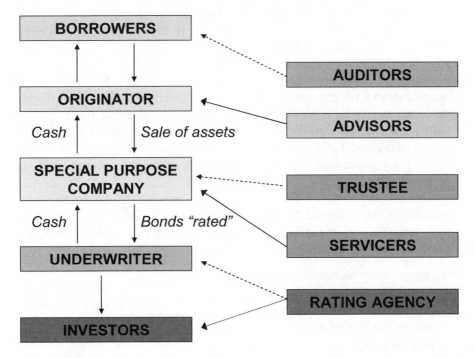

Source: the author

Law 130/99 requires that the activities indicated in number 2 and number 4 shall be realized by companies that are included into a special

---

[22] According to the provisions of Italian Securitization Law, a rating is required only of the ABS are sold to the private investors. However, in practice, any issuance of ABS is always accompanied by at least one rating by specialized agencies.

register, according to the legislative decree 385/93, art. 107 (New Bank Law). In particular, the SPV shall be a company satisfying the requisites provided by the Italian legislation of financial intermediation (articles 106 and ff. of the Legislative Decree n. 385/1993). The SPV shall also deal exclusively with one or more securitization processes (art.3, Law 130/99).

## 2.5 The role of financial intermediaries within the securitization process

According to the Law 130/99, financial intermediaries play a crucial role within the securitization process, which includes different steps.

The first step includes the identification of homogeneous financial assets, which can be securitized, according to the provisions specified by the art. 1 of Law 130/99 and the rating criteria used by specialized agencies. Informally, the Originator and the Arranger might contact rating agencies in order to receive general advices on the feasibility of the operation and on the entity of credit enhancements. The aim of credit enhancement is to enhance the security or the rating of the securitized instruments. Credit enhancement can be internal (subordination, over-collateralization, yield spread, excess spread, reserve funds), or external (third party guarantee, letter of credit, cash collateral account, collateral invested account).

The second step of the securitization process refers to the asset-evaluation implemented by rating agencies, on the basis of investigation and analysis of the transaction and the issuer's characteristics. In particular, rating agencies tend to evaluate:

- Assets characteristics;
- Credit tracking;
- Payment methods and timing;
- Diversification of the asset portfolio;
- Default rate;
- Recovery Timing.

According to the above assets characteristics, the chosen credit rating agency defines together with the Arranger the particular financial structure of the securities that will be issued into the market and backed by the assets. Credit rating agencies usually identify: collateral guarantees, "priority of payments", and those credit events that will imply an anticipated reimbursement.

If the analysis implemented by credit rating agencies is positive, a pre-sale report is then written. In the same time, external auditors implement a due diligence of the asset portfolio.

Once the pre-sale report has been completed, legal firms implement the deal structuring. The following contracts are involved:

- Transfer Agreement;
- Indemnity and Warranty Agreement;
- Corporate Services Agreement,
- Servicing Agreement,
- Cash Management Agreement e del Collateral Management Agreement;
- Trust deed;
- Deed of Pledge;
- Subscription Agreement by the pool of banks assuming the placement task.

After the deal structuring phase, it follows the marketing activity, including a road show aimed at presenting the transaction characteristics to institutional investors (usually assumed as target investors).

The fifth phase implies the issuance and the placement of the asset backed securities into the primary market. If the securities are sold to professional investors, it is important to design an Offering Circular, according to the provision of art. 2, Law 130/99. If the securities are sold to private investors, it is necessary to elaborate a particular information prospect, according to the Legislative Decree 58/98.[23] The underwriter works together with SPV and credit enhancer entity in order to arrange the placement of the securities into the primary market, usually offering to the Originator a service of acquiring those securities that remain unsold.

The next step of the securitization process is the acquisition of the securities by investors, usually represented by institutional investors. Once the placement of the securities into the primary market has been completed, the resulting net inflow is transferred by the SPV to the Originator. In this way, the debt obligation related to the asset sale initiated by the Originator is honored.

After the market placement, it is important to monitor and manage the cash flows payments that are related to the asset backed securities (service activity). Usually the Originator (or its subsidiary) is responsible for the collecting of the fee amounts due. Other times, a separate loan Servicer

---

[23] So far, the issuances of ABS in Italy have been directed to qualified investors and consequently no information prospects have been elaborated.

might be employed for the monitoring and management of the entire collection process.

The Servicer has to be recorded into a particular register, according to art. 107 of the Bank Law.

According to the Law, the Servicer must guarantee the respect of the maturity-payments related to the ABS.

Moreover, the Servicer must ensure that the SPV keeps the cash flows derived by the asset backed securities separated from the other SPV's assets. This "management and accountant isolation" represents a condition required by Law.

In order to better protect investor's interests, a Servicer must also have a sufficient own equity capital and should inform the monitoring Authority whenever irregularities in the payments-process occur.

### 2.5.1 Strategic business areas of activities

As anticipated, financial intermediaries play a crucial role within the securitization process and can be distinguished according to the different areas of activity:

1. asset selling and underwriting (primary market);
2. cash flow collection and asset management (secondary market);
3. market making (secondary market).

1 – The Arranger is the institution responsible for the asset placement into the primary market. The success and the costs of the whole transaction depend mainly on the placement skills of the Arranger. The choice of the Arranger is then very important and usually takes into account different elements: international experience; track record; business contacts (with investors and rating agencies); reputation; placement and underwriting capacity. There is a trade-off between reputation and cost of the deal of the Arranger: the greater is the reputation of the Arranger and the higher is the commission requested by him.

2 – The Servicer is the institution responsible for the cash-flows collection. If it is a financial institution, the Originator act as Servicer. The Servicer activity is usually played by the financial institutions which originated the securitization process, or by a subsidiary (captive organizational structure). Independent Servicer institutions play a marginal role (but increasing) within the Italian securitization market. Regarding the securitization process initiated by big-size corporate, the Servicer activity is usually done by a separate financial institution, who takes care of the all collection activity. Small-medium size firms, on the other hands, usually

sign a contract of sub-service with a financial institution, acting as a primary Servicer.[24]

3 – The marketing maker activity is currently limited to the transactions among qualified investors, especially institutional investors (gross market). Mainly asset backed securities are negotiated within: the MTS market (Table 2.1) and the OTC market.

**Table 2.1.** ABS listing within the MTS market and average monthly transaction volume

| Period | Volume of issuances (million euro) | | | | | Volume of transactions | % Volume negotiated over volume of issuances |
|---|---|---|---|---|---|---|---|
| | SCCI[25] | SCIP[26] | SCCPP[27] | INAIL | TOTAL | | |
| Jan-02 | 4,577,500 | 2,300,000 | 3,000,000 | 1,350,000 | 11,227,500 | 80,000 | 0.71% |
| Feb-02 | 2,246,300 | 2,300,000 | 3,000,000 | 1,350,000 | 8,896,300 | 77,500 | 0.87% |
| Mar-02 | 2,246,300 | 2,300,000 | 3,000,000 | 1,350,000 | 8,896,300 | 40,000 | 0.45% |
| Apr-02 | 2,246,300 | 2,300,000 | 3,000,000 | 1,350,000 | 8,896,300 | 50,000 | 0.56% |
| May-02 | 2,246,300 | 2,300,000 | 3,000,000 | 1,350,000 | 8,896,300 | 27,500 | 0.31% |
| Jun-02 | 2,246,300 | 2,300,000 | 3,000,000 | 1,350,000 | 8,896,300 | 12,500 | 0.14% |
| Jul-02 | 5,246,300 | 2,300,000 | 3,000,000 | 1,350,000 | 11,896,300 | 17,500 | 0.15% |
| Ago-02 | 4,710,000 | 2,300,000 | 3,000,000 | 1,350,000 | 11,360,300 | 35,000 | 0.31% |
| Sept-02 | 4,710,000 | 2,300,000 | 3,000,000 | 1,350,000 | 11,360,300 | 0 | 0.00% |
| Oct-02 | 4,710,000 | 2,300,000 | 3,000,000 | 1,350,000 | 11,360,300 | 15,000 | 0.13% |
| Nov-02 | 4,710,000 | 2,300,000 | 3,000,000 | 1,350,000 | 11,360,300 | 12,500 | 0.11% |
| Dic-02 | 4,710,000 | 8,937,000 | 3,000,000 | 1,350,000 | 17,997,300 | 70,000 | 0.39% |
| Jan-03 | 4,710,000 | 7,937,000 | 3,000,000 | 1,350,000 | 17,997,300 | 146,000 | 0.81% |
| Feb-03 | 4,710,000 | 7,937,000 | 2,000,000 | 1,350,000 | 15,997,300 | 82,500 | 0.52% |
| Mar-03 | 4,710,000 | 7,937,000 | 2,000,000 | 1,350,000 | 15,997,000 | 117,500 | 0.73% |
| Apr-03 | 4,710,000 | 7,937,000 | 2,000,000 | 1,350,000 | 15,997,000 | 190,000 | 1.19% |
| May-03 | 4,710,000 | 7,937,000 | 2,000,000 | 0 | 14,647,000 | 130,000 | 0.89% |
| Jun-03 | 4,710,000 | 7,937,000 | 2,000,000 | 0 | 14,647,000 | 55,000 | 0.38% |

Source: MTS SpA and www.securitisation.it

---

[24] In the US market, the servicer activity is usually played by auditing companies and not by financial institutions.

[25] See: Società per la Cartolarizzazione dei Crediti Inps Srl.

[26] See: Società per la Cartolarizzazione degli Immobili Pubblici Srl.

[27] See: Società per la Cartolarizzazione dei Crediti e dei Proventi Pubblici Srl.

Table 2.1 describes the volume of the transactions in the Italian MTS market over the period: January 2002 – June 2003 (first semester). Comparing the total transactions occurred in May 2002 with that of May 2003, it is evident that there is an increment of about 372%. Similarly, the volume recorded during the first four months of 2003 has increased by 142.18%, in comparison to the total volume recorded in the same period of 2002. This shows a good growth potentiality of the MTS market.

In order to operate as market maker in the MTS market it is necessary to satisfy the following requirements:

1. minimum capital requirement of 39 million of Euro;
2. in the previous year, it is necessary to have negotiated at least 38 billion Euro of bond obligations.[28]

The institutions that originated the securitization transactions are most likely to be able to work as market maker in the MTS context, guaranteeing also an underwriting service. This connection between market makers and financial institutions is crucial to ensure a future growth of the secondary market.

The Ministry of Economics and Finance Department seems willing to contribute to the development of the secondary market. In fact, with relative to the securitization of INPDAP credits, the Government required that the Arranger would also be able to offer a market making service.


## 2.6 The international and the Italian securitization market: current and future trends

The analysis of the competitive situation of the Italian Financial Intermediaries is seen with reference to the business areas identified before. It is important to note that, given the situation highlighted in table 1 and the absence of the public data on the volumes negotiated in the OTC market, the competitive positioning of the Italian Financial Intermediaries within the "market making" area cannot be exhausted in quantitative terms.

However, the purpose of this section is to provide an international comparative analysis of the Financial Intermediaries that operate within the primary market. A brief view is also devoted to the exam of secondary

---

[28] See: www.mtsspa.it.

market trend, for servicing activity. The analysis will cover the period from 2001 to 2003 (first term).

An analysis of the international securitization market is important to better emphasize the peculiarities and the growth of the Italian market.[29]

### 2.6.1 International securitization market

As Table 2.2 and 2.3 show, USA represents the most important securitization market in the world, because it covers about the 80% of total issuance within the examined period. The US leading role is explained by at least two reasons:

- its financial system structure, characterized by a very well development of investment banking activity;
- its experience: securitization has been developed more than 25 years ago.[30]

**Table 2.2.** Issuance of asset backed securities by country of origin over the period: 2001-2002

| (euro million) | 2002 Issuances | N. of Issuances | market share % | 2001 Issuances | N. of Issuances | market share % |
|---|---|---|---|---|---|---|
| U. S. | 694,343.12 | 1,601 | 80.1 | 539,358.24 | 1,263 | 78.5 |
| U. K. | 57,826.11 | 116 | 6.7 | 48,275.62 | 115 | 7 |
| Italy | 26,981.95 | 40 | 3.1 | 24,128.81 | 58 | 3.5 |
| Japan | 20,168.62 | 96 | 2.3 | 14,170.39 | 58 | 2.1 |
| Australia | 17,427.87 | 68 | 2 | 12,513.92 | 45 | 1.8 |
| Others | 50,463.87 | 143 | 5.8 | 48,636.20 | 129 | 7.1 |
| TOTAL | 867,211,54 | 2,064 | 100 | 687,083.27 | 1,668 | 100 |

Source: the author

The remaining 15% is shared among the following countries: United Kingdom, Italy, Japan, and Australia, while the left over 5% is covered by other nations. Particularly interesting is the position of Italy: in fact, over the first term of 2003, Italy covered the 20% of the total issuance of

---

[29] Notice that the international data on securitization market are from: www.abalert.com by Harrison Scott Publications, while the data on Italian securitization market are from www.securitisation.it by Talete Creative Finance. The two databases are consistent with reference to the Italian market analysis.
[30] See: Bhattacharya and Fabozzi (1997).

securities outside the US market. This confirms the Italian growth trend that started since April 1999.

**Table 2.3.** Issuance of asset backed securities by country of origin over the first term: 200-2002

| (euro million) | 1Q-03 Issuances | N. of Issuances | market share % | 1Q-02 Issuances | N. of Issuances | market share % |
|---|---|---|---|---|---|---|
| U. S. | 211,492.78 | 387 | 78.7 | 152,207.25 | 324 | 83.1 |
| U. K. | 26,385.29 | 32 | 9.8 | 11,823.17 | 18 | 6.5 |
| Italy | 11,172.17 | 17 | 4.2 | 3,451.63 | 10 | 1.9 |
| Australia | 5,345.54 | 15 | 2 | 5,789.94 | 22 | 3.2 |
| Japan | 3,266.83 | 13 | 1.2 | 5,724.22 | 36 | 3.1 |
| Others | 10,980.03 | 20 | 4.1 | 4,124.40 | 14 | 2.3 |
| TOTAL | 268,642.65 | 484 | 100 | 183,120.62 | 424 | 100 |

Source: the author

**Table 2.4.** Types of assets that originated securitization transactions over the period 2001-2002

| (euro million) | 2002 Issuances | N. of Issuances | market share % | 2001 Issuances | N. of Issuances | market share % |
|---|---|---|---|---|---|---|
| Residential mortgages | 202,346.03 | 501 | 23.3 | 128,156.86 | 376 | 18.7 |
| Home-equity loans | 89,933.07 | 186 | 10.4 | 36,800.09 | 84 | 5.4 |
| Commercial mortgages | 89,799.27 | 167 | 10.4 | 86,956.27 | 172 | 12.7 |
| Credit cards | 78,831.37 | 137 | 9.1 | 72,012.95 | 127 | 10.5 |
| Subprime mortgages | 75,782.46 | 176 | 8.7 | 58,053.57 | 133 | 8.4 |
| Non-U. S. mortgages | 67,389.45 | 136 | 7.8 | 55,212.54 | 126 | 8 |
| Corporate bonds | 62,572.89 | 250 | 7.2 | 57,190.90 | 202 | 8.3 |
| Auto loans (prime) | 60,113.83 | 58 | 6.9 | 45,162.86 | 53 | 6.6 |
| Auto loans (subprime) | 30,176.48 | 52 | 3.5 | 20,906.78 | 39 | 3 |
| Student loans | 24,463.80 | 36 | 2.8 | 9,897.34 | 21 | 1.4 |
| Equipment leases | 17,090.59 | 54 | 2 | 15,382.00 | 54 | 2.2 |
| Others | 68,712.31 | 311 | 7.9 | 101,351.19 | 281 | 14.8 |
| TOTAL | 867,211.54 | 2,064 | 100 | 687,083.27 | 1,668 | 100 |

Source: the author

As it is shown in Table 2.4 and 2.5, the typical securitized assets in year 2001-2002 have been the following: residential and commercial mortgages (most important), home equity loans, credit cards, collateralized bond obligations (CBO's), equipment leases. The trend illustrated in Tables 2.4 and 2.5 is confirmed in 2003 (first term).

**Table 2.5.** Types of assets that originated securitization transactions over the first term of 2001-2002

| (euro million) | 1Q-03 Issuances | N. of Issuances | market share % | 1Q-02 Issuances | N. of Issuances | market share % |
|---|---|---|---|---|---|---|
| Residential mortgages | 75,249.73 | 157 | 28 | 41,224.66 | 108 | 22.5 |
| Non-U. S. mortgages | 35,873.33 | 41 | 13.4 | 13,198.70 | 32 | 7.2 |
| Home-equity loans | 26,907.70 | 42 | 10 | 24,491.78 | 36 | 13.4 |
| Credit cards | 25,571.13 | 35 | 9.5 | 15,431.11 | 29 | 8.4 |
| Subprime mortgages | 20,160.97 | 40 | 7.5 | 16,714.82 | 36 | 9.1 |
| Commercial mortgages | 20,044.30 | 36 | 7.5 | 13,868.83 | 34 | 7.6 |
| Auto loans (prime) | 14,975.69 | 10 | 5.6 | 17,988.13 | 12 | 9.8 |
| Corporate bonds | 11,996.42 | 37 | 4.5 | 14,110.99 | 42 | 7.7 |
| Student loans | 10,456.12 | 11 | 3.9 | 5,144.58 | 6 | 2.8 |
| Auto loans (subprime) | 5,097.80 | 9 | 1.9 | 4,921.81 | 8 | 2.7 |
| Others | 22,309.34 | 66 | 8.3 | 16,025.40 | 81 | 8.8 |
| TOTAL | 268,642.65 | 484 | 100 | 183,120.62 | 424 | 100 |

Source: the author

**Table 2.6.** Who securitized the assets over the period 2001-2002

| (euro million) | 2002 Issuances | N. of Issuances | market share % | 2001 Issuances | N. of Issuances | market share % |
|---|---|---|---|---|---|---|
| Mortgage bank | 225,139.94 | 578 | 26 | 104,233.51 | 357 | 15.2 |
| Bank | 202,301.21 | 447 | 23.3 | 214,954.51 | 451 | 31.3 |
| Commercial mort. lender | 89,799.27 | 167 | 10.4 | 86,956.27 | 172 | 12.7 |
| Finance co. (diversified) | 76,918.00 | 176 | 8.9 | 55,991.29 | 151 | 8.1 |
| Investment firm | 75,857.26 | 264 | 8.7 | 59,890.69 | 204 | 8.7 |
| Finance co. (captive) | 67,080.72 | 72 | 7.7 | 54,864.77 | 65 | 8 |
| Securities firm | 29,208.59 | 110 | 3.4 | 10,946.48 | 52 | 1.6 |
| Credit-card bank | 26,949.90 | 52 | 3.1 | 18,623.73 | 34 | 2.7 |
| Sallie Mae | 13,335.24 | 11 | 1.5 | 5,661.37 | 5 | 0.8 |
| Auto lender | 11,825.63 | 25 | 1.4 | 10,030.61 | 18 | 1.5 |
| Altri | 48,795.97 | 162 | 5.6 | 64,930.04 | 159 | 9.5 |
| TOTAL | 867,211.54 | 2,064 | 100 | 687,083.27 | 1,668 | 100 |

Source: the author

Examining in details Tables 2.6 and 2.7, it is possible to understand that securitization represents an important instrument to raise money for financial institutions, above all within the market oriented financial systems. In English speaking nations the securitization is used also to ensure the financial equilibrium and for risk management purpose.

**Table 2.7.** Who securitized the assets over the first term of 2002-2003

| (euro million) | 1Q-03 Issuances | N. of Issuances | market share % | 1Q-02 Issuances | N. of Issuances | market share % |
|---|---|---|---|---|---|---|
| Mortgage bank | 89,483.61 | 178 | 33.3 | 57,879.44 | 125 | 31.6 |
| Bank | 59,586.22 | 98 | 22.2 | 40,064.63 | 96 | 21.9 |
| Finance co. (diversified) | 25,219.71 | 45 | 9.4 | 17,409.91 | 40 | 9.5 |
| Commercial mort. lender | 20,044.30 | 36 | 7.5 | 13,868.83 | 34 | 7.6 |
| Investment firm | 18,967.91 | 45 | 7.1 | 14,496.12 | 47 | 7.9 |
| Finance co. (captive) | 18,428.97 | 14 | 6.9 | 19,852.80 | 21 | 10.8 |
| Credit-card bank | 10,278.15 | 14 | 3.8 | 4,098.02 | 7 | 2.2 |
| Sallie Mae | 6,896.79 | 6 | 2.6 | 3,387.05 | 2 | 1.8 |
| Securities firm | 6,652.49 | 19 | 2.5 | 2,294.25 | 14 | 1.3 |
| Industrial company | 4,417.60 | 8 | 1.6 | 1,004.58 | 5 | 0.5 |
| Others | 8,666.68 | 21 | 3.2 | 8,765.00 | 33 | 4.8 |
| TOTAL | 268,642.65 | 484 | 100 | 183,120.62 | 424 | 100 |

Source: the author

Tables 2.8 and 2.9 represent the League Table of the Arrangers of securitization transactions in Europe, over the period from 2001-2003 (first term). As we can see, the market is very concentrated and the role of Italian institutions within this context is very marginal (they appear only after the twentieth position). In fact, the first 10 financial intermediaries in table 8 cover almost the 66% of the market and the turnover between them is very low. On the other hand, Italian institutions all together cover only the 4.4% of the entire volume of securitization transactions realized in Europe.

If now we connect the data of Table 2.2 with the data of Tables 2.8 and 2.9, we can deduce that Italian institutions in 2002 were active only within the local market context that represents the 28.2% of the issuances realized in Europe. Over the same period, the securitization transactions originated in Europe (considering UK, Italy and other European countries) have covered the 15.6% of the world securitization deals volume.

In the first term of 2003 the situation has improved, because the total quota of issuance realized by Italian institutions in Europe came up to about 20%. Within the Italian context, the local institutions over the first term of 2003 gained a significant share of the market, covering about the 50%.

**Table 2.8.** Bookrunners of European asset backed securities over the period 2001-2002[31]

|  | 2002 Issuances | N. of Issuances | market share % | 2001 Issuances | N. of Issuances | market share % |
|---|---|---|---|---|---|---|
| Salomon Smith Barney | 11,105.48 | 24 | 8.8 | 21,679.17 | 36 | 17.6 |
| Deutsche Bank | 10,806.87 | 34 | 8.5 | 8,865.93 | 27 | 7.2 |
| J. P. Morgan Chase | 10,592.13 | 26 | 8.3 | 5,810.94 | 23 | 4.7 |
| Morgan Stanley | 10,371.91 | 18 | 8.2 | 10,021.92 | 28 | 8.2 |
| Barclays Capital | 9,208.95 | 25 | 7.3 | 4,023.80 | 13 | 3.3 |
| ABN Amro | 9,161.67 | 17 | 7.2 | 10,283.09 | 16 | 8.4 |
| Credit Suisse First Boston | 5,452.84 | 15 | 4.3 | 11,877.67 | 42 | 9.7 |
| Lehman Brothers | 5,080.00 | 17 | 4 | 4,172.02 | 13 | 3.4 |
| BNP Paribas | 4,217.17 | 17 | 3.3 | 5,163.22 | 20 | 4.2 |
| Societe Generale | 3,921.20 | 12 | 3.1 | 139.09 | 2 | 0.1 |
| WestLB | 3,583.73 | 10 | 2.8 | 526.27 | 4 | 0.4 |
| HypoVereinsbank | 3,441.04 | 6 | 2.7 | 1,350.16 | 3 | 1.1 |
| UBS Warburg | 3,356.41 | 9 | 2.6 | 4,716.84 | 10 | 3.8 |
| Commerzbank | 3,181.01 | 8 | 2.5 | 1,335.92 | 3 | 1.1 |
| Merrill Lynch | 3,150.75 | 10 | 2.5 | 7,258.45 | 21 | 5.9 |
| Bear Stearns | 3,114.53 | 8 | 2.5 | 297.80 | 1 | 0.2 |
| Royal Bank of Scotland (Greenwich) | 2,859.23 | 9 | 2.3 | 2,902.38 | 10 | 2.4 |
| Dresdner Kleinwort | 2,206.40 | 9 | 1.7 | 1,814.37 | 6 | 1.5 |
| Fortis Bank | 1,934.74 | 5 | 1.5 | 1,214.21 | 3 | 1 |
| Credit Agricole Indosuez | 1,680.38 | 5 | 1.3 | 1,673.84 | 8 | 1.4 |
| Banca Nazionale del Lavoro | 1,570.69 | 1 | 1.2 | - | 0 | 0 |
| Rabobank | 1,100.74 | 3 | 0.9 | 1,024.06 | 2 | 0.8 |
| UniCredit Banca Mobiliare | 1,051.48 | 3 | 0.8 | 1,166.74 | 3 | 0.9 |
| Goldman Sachs | 1,036.25 | 3 | 0.8 | 1,573.53 | 6 | 1.3 |
| Banca IMI | 947.65 | 2 | 0.7 | 1,176.86 | 3 | 1 |
| DZ Bank | 925.91 | 6 | 0.7 | - | 0 | 0 |
| NIB Capital Bank | 857.54 | 2 | 0.7 | 1,239.46 | 4 | 1 |
| Mediobanca | 828.70 | 4 | 0.7 | 42.54 | 1 | 0 |
| CDC IXIS Capital | 799.86 | 3 | 0.6 | - | 0 | 0 |
| MPS Finance | 770.45 | 1 | 0.6 | 750.45 | 6 | 0.6 |
| Nomura International | 737.07 | 2 | 0.6 | 851.21 | 4 | 0.7 |
| Mizuho Securities | 722.32 | 5 | 0.6 | 1,500.99 | 9 | 1.2 |
| Bancaja | 713.53 | 2 | 0.6 | - | 0 | 0 |
| Bankinter | 689.99 | 1 | 0.5 | - | 0 | 0 |
| ING Barings | 674.10 | 1 | 0.5 | 64.40 | 1 | 0.1 |
| HSBC Bank | 570.09 | 3 | 0.4 | 1,140.76 | 5 | 0.9 |
| CIBC World Markets | 561.86 | 3 | 0.4 | 713.01 | 2 | 0.6 |
| Finanziaria Internazionale | 539.45 | 2 | 0.4 | - | 0 | 0 |
| Aborro | 532.64 | 2 | 0.4 | 110.07 | 1 | 0.1 |
| EBN Banco | 518.46 | 2 | 0.4 | 462.50 | 1 | 0.4 |
| Others | 2,336.70 | 22 | 1.7 | 5,955.22 | 38 | 4.8 |
| TOTAL | 126,911.07 | 267 | 100 | 122,898.62 | 288 | 100 |

Source: the author

---

[31] Notice that the Abalert.com database includes the bookrunners and not the arrangers. The difference is given by the fact that the arrangers usually play the bookrunner role, but it is not always true the opposite.

**Table 2.9.** Bookrunners of European asset backed securities in the first quarter of 2002-2003[32]

| (Euro Mil) | 1Q-03 Issuances | N. of Issuances | market share % | 1Q-02 Issuances | N. of Issuances | market share % |
|---|---|---|---|---|---|---|
| Salomon Smith Barney | 4,098.81 | 10 | 11.1 | 1,236.34 | 3 | 6.5 |
| Morgan Stanley | 3,674.82 | 8 | 10 | 1,833.75 | 4 | 9.7 |
| Lehman Brothers | 2,848.43 | 7 | 7.7 | 2,298.88 | 5 | 12.2 |
| Barclays Capital | 2,505.70 | 10 | 6.8 | 475.72 | 1 | 2.5 |
| J. P. Morgan Chase | 2,207.94 | 5 | 6 | 912.01 | 2 | 4.8 |
| Deutsche Bank | 1,882.39 | 6 | 5.1 | 2,269.47 | 6 | 12 |
| Societé Generale | 1,683.06 | 4 | 4.6 | 435.63 | 2 | 2.3 |
| Merrill Lynch | 1,677.48 | 5 | 4.6 | 1,627.14 | 3 | 8.6 |
| UBS Warburg | 1,600.09 | 5 | 4.3 | 1,045.80 | 3 | 5.5 |
| Fortis Bank | 1,402.26 | 1 | 3.8 | - | 0 | 0 |
| BNP Paribas | 1,293.85 | 4 | 3.5 | 415.39 | 2 | 2.2 |
| WestLB | 1,214.64 | 2 | 3.3 | 367.83 | 2 | 1.9 |
| Credit Agricole Indosuez | 1,202.83 | 3 | 3.3 | 255.02 | 2 | 1.3 |
| Credit Suisse First Boston | 1,199.82 | 4 | 3.3 | 548.15 | 2 | 2.9 |
| Royal Bank of Scotland | 1,161.93 | 3 | 3.2 | 422.67 | 1 | 2.2 |
| Banca Nazionale del Lavoro | 1,048.80 | 2 | 2.8 | - | 0 | 0 |
| ABN Amro | 883.18 | 2 | 2.4 | 1,193.60 | 3 | 6.3 |
| Caboto IntesaBCI | 783.03 | 1 | 2.1 | - | 0 | 0 |
| Nomura International | 753.08 | 1 | 2 | - | 0 | 0 |
| Mediobanca | 728.40 | 2 | 2 | - | 0 | 0 |
| Banco Santander | 633.29 | 1 | 1.7 | - | 0 | 0 |
| NIB Capital Bank | 573.61 | 1 | 1.6 | 659.44 | 1 | 3.5 |
| Bear Stearns | 571.15 | 1 | 1.6 | 257.95 | 1 | 1.4 |
| MCC | 427.63 | 3 | 1.2 | - | 0 | 0 |
| MPS Finance | 363.55 | 1 | 1 | - | 0 | 0 |
| UniCredit BancaMobiliare | 325.88 | 1 | 0.9 | - | 0 | 0 |
| RBC Dain Rauscher | 66.12 | 2 | 0.2 | - | 0 | 0 |
| Others | - | 0 | 0 | 2,660.37 | 10 | 14.1 |
| TOTAL | 36,811.35 | 60 | 100 | 18,914.98 | 38 | 100 |

Source: the author

---

[32] Notice that the Abalert.com database includes the bookrunners and not the arrangers. The difference is given by the fact that the arrangers usually play the bookrunner role, but it is not always true the opposite.

## 2.6.2 The Italian securitization market[33,34]

Tables 2.10 and 2.11 represent the typical securitizable assets in Italy. Comparing Tables 2.4 and 2.5 with Tables 2.10 and 2.11 we can see that, in contrast with what happened in the international context, in year 2001 the Non Performing Loans (NPL) represented one of the most used asset for a securitization purpose in Italy.[35] The situation has changed in year 2002 and 2003, aligned with the international trend. In fact, over the first term of 2003, this class of securitizable assets did not arrived at 4%. Today, the peculiarities of the Italian securitization market are more similar to the international context.

Another peculiarity of the Italian securitization market is represented by the high use of this financial technique by the Public Sector. In fact, the public sector used this financial tool to privatize many fixed assets, in order to raise money to fund its public pension-scheme.[36] Currently, the public sector continues to make a big use of the securitization tool. According to the Government financial law in Year 2003 (art. 84), even local public sector may use this technique to privatize its assts.

---

[33] The data on the Italian Securitization Market are taken from the website : Securitisation.it, owned by Talete Creative Finance.

[34] The international data on securitization market are taken from Albert.com database. Instead, the Itlaian data on securitization market are taken from a different database: securitisation.it. Even though the database are different, they coincide in the number of transactions and volumes. The only difference is that one operation recorded by Albert.com in 2001 has been inserted in 2002 by securitisation.it, while the total number of the operations recorded by the two database over the period 2001-2002 coincides (98 transactions). There is a small difference in volumes, because they have been recorded directly in euro by securitisation.it, while Albert.com recorded them in dollars and then converted into euro. There is another difference with reference the first term of year 2003. Infact, Albert.com recorded 17 transactions with a total volume of 11 milion euro, while Securitisation.it recorded 16 operations with a volume of 12 milion of euro. The variations in volume could be explained by the mechanism of conversation used by the two databases.

[35] See "Rapporto annuale sul mercato italiano della cartolarizzazione 1999-2001" chapter 3.

[36] Sometimes the public sector role has been too aggressive. Let us think about the securitization of future credits related to the Italian lotteries. A disposition by Eurostat infact stated that it is not possible to consider the debt obligation related to the securitization transaction as "off-balance" operation. See: Eurostat (2002).

**Table 2.10.** Types of assets that originated securitization transactions in Italy over the period 2001-2002

| Asset class | N. | 2002 | | N. | 2001 | |
|---|---|---|---|---|---|---|
| | | Issuance Volume | Market share % | | Issuance Volume | Market share % |
| NPLs | 3 | 1,301.0 | 4.25 | 17 | 7,088.40 | 21.51 |
| RMBSs | 12 | 6,577.7 | 21.49 | 16 | 8,138.10 | 24.69 |
| CDOs | 2 | 2,682.3 | 8.76 | 3 | 835 | 2.53 |
| GCs | 5 | 10,134.7 | 33.11 | 4 | 7,505.00 | 22.77 |
| LRs | 12 | 6,927.1 | 22.63 | 7 | 4,303.00 | 13.05 |
| CCs/PeLs | 4 | 1,606.3 | 5.25 | 7 | 3,396.70 | 10.31 |
| Others | 3 | 1,379.1 | 4.51 | 3 | 1,694.50 | 5.14 |
| TOTAL | 41 | 30,608.2 | 100 | 57 | 32,960.70 | 100 |

Source: the author

**Table 2.11.** Types of assets that originated securitization transactions in Italy over the first term of 2003

| Asset class | N. | Issuance Volume | Market share % |
|---|---|---|---|
| NPLs | 1 | 412,500,000 | 3.24% |
| RMBSs | 6 | 4,421,993,245 | 34.69% |
| LRs | 2 | 1,484,640,000 | 11.65% |
| PLs/CCs | 0 | 0 | 0.00% |
| CLO | 1 | 1,240,000,000 | 9.73% |
| TRs | 1 | 100,000,000 | 0.78% |
| GCs | 2 | 2,643,000,000 | 20.74% |
| Les | 2 | 1,845,900,000 | 14.48% |
| Others | 1 | 598,836,000 | 4.70% |
| TOTAL | 16 | 12,747,169,245 | 100% |

Glossary:
NPLs   Non Performing Loans
RMBSsResidentian Mortgages
LRs     Lease Receivables
PeLs/CCs        Personal Loans and credit cards
CLO    Financial Loans
TRs     Commercial credits
GCs     Government Credits
LEs     Local Public Sector Credits

Source: the author

Similarly to what happens in the international context, the players that generate the greatest volume of issuances in Italy are: banks, leasing firms, and personal lending firms. Instead, it is not remarkable the role of non financial institutions.

### 2.6.3 Competitive positioning of financial intermediaries within the primary market

Figure 2.5 indicates the competitive positioning of Arrangers within the Italian primary market, during the first term 2003.

**Fig. 2.5.** Positioning of arrangers, according to Law 130/99

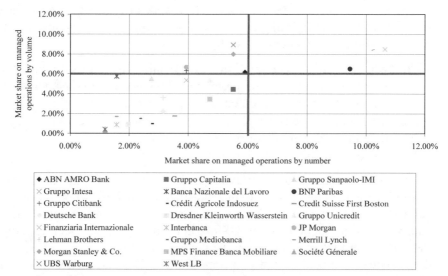

Source: the author

As we can see from the above table, in Year 2003 the leading role, in terms of number of issuance, has been played by Finanziaria Internazionale. This institution was the first that concluded securitization transactions in Italy, during earliest 90s, referring to others legislations. This probably contributes to explain its leading role in the Italian market.

In terms of volume of issuance, several institutions were leader: UBS Warburg, Morgan Stanley, JP Morgan, Citibank Group e ABN AMRO.

With reference to the Italian institutions, it is remarkable the role played by: MPS Finance Banca Mobiliare (Gruppo Monte dei Paschi di Siena), Mediocredito Centrale (Gruppo Capitalia), BNL, Sanpaolo-IMI, and Intesa Bank.

## 2.6.4 The competitive positioning of Italian financial intermediaries within the secondary market

Within the secondary market context, the most important activity is realized by the Servicer, which represents the entity that is responsible for the collection of payments on securitized assets, included the management of problematic loans.

As anticipated, Law 130/99 requires the Servicer to:

– receive a particular authorization by the Central Bank;
– satisfy minimum capital requirements, depending on the transaction-volumes.[37]

The server shall also be recorded into a special register, in accordance with art. 107 of the Banking Law (T.U.B). Moreover, a disposition of the Central Bank Governor requires to the Servicer:

– "to keep a separate accountability of the sums related to the payments on securitized assets. Those payments shall not be confused with the other assets eventually presented in the SPV's balance sheet";
– "to act in order to ensure the protection of the final investors' rights, avoiding any situation of conflict of interests";
– "to ensure the respect of each payment-maturity".

The above requirements make the Servicer similar to a financial institution. A peculiarity of Italian securitization market is that usually the servicer activity is realized by captive firms within a financial group, in contrast of what happens in the US market. So far, the Servicer activity in Italy has been realized mostly by the Originator. The only exception is for the issuances realized by the corporate system. Big companies in fact are most likely to employ a separate independent Servicer. Small companies instead usually sign a sub-servicing contract with a financial institution, which acts as a first sevicer.

Figure 2.6 examines the competitive positioning of independent Servicer within the Italian securitization market, over the period 2001-2003 (first semester).

---

[37] The minimum capital that has to be satisfied is the following:
  -   1 million €: for transaction-volumes <= 500 million euro
  -   1.5 million €: for transaction-volumes > 500 million euro.

**Fig. 2.6.** Positioning of independent servicer

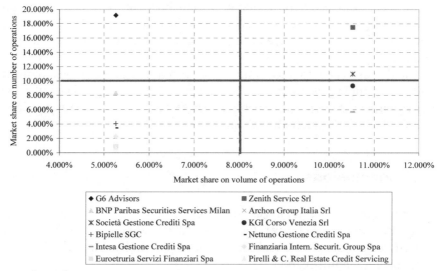

Source: the author

As we can see from the above table, there are few institutions that play a relevant role. Usually the majority of them manage one ore two securitization transactions. In terms of volume, we can see that the most active institutions are:

- G6 Advisors (which manage the public sector's assets);
- Zenith Service (which manages the transactions initiated by Fineco Group and operates mostly as corporate Servicer);
- Archon Group Italia & Società di Gestione Crediti (which are the result of a joint venture between an international software house – Archon Group Italia – and a Servicer institution operating for BNL group – Società di Gestione Crediti ).

The other institutions in the above table are part of a bank group. The only exceptions are:

- Finanziaria Internazionale Securitization Group (which plays a leading role in the primary market);
- Pirelli & C. Real Estate Credit Servicing (which is specialized in the securitization of residential mortgages and usually operates as Servicer).

As it is evident from Figure 2.6, there is not yet a structured environment for independent Servicer, which still play a marginal role in the Italian securitization market. However, if the corporate system will make a greater use of securitization technique in the future, the number and the competitive positioning of independent Servicer might grow. Currently, the corporate Servicers are exclusively working for international auditing firms, such as: Deloitte & Touche Tomatsu and Price Waterhouse Coopers.

With reference to the other credit-management activities (collection account banking, deposit account banking e cash management), the Italian environment is even less structured. These services are mostly provided by banks, especially international banks.

## 2.7 Conclusions

In this chapter we analyzed the securitization process and the Italian securitization market over the period 2001-2003 (first term). We also discussed about the role and the positioning of Italian financial institutions that operate in this market.

The securitization is a process through which illiquid assets are transformed into negotiable securities to be placed in the market.

The Originator pools together a set of assets with homogeneous characteristics, in order to sell them to a particular special purpose company (SPV), which buys the rights to receive the related future expected payments. Thanks to the asset sale to a SPV, the transaction becomes unaffected by the bankruptcy of the Originator. To finance the purchase of the assets, the SPV then issues asset backed securities (ABS), with the help of investment underwriters.

Many steps are necessary to accomplish securitization transactions. The credits are first transferred by the Originator to a SPV, and then transformed into marketable securities to be sold to final investors. The payments on the receivables are then collected by a servicing institution (Servicer), usually represented by the Originator. The funds are forwarded to a third party (Trustee) which forwards them to the security holders.

Regarding the future developments of the Italian securitization market, we can make at least two assumptions.

1. If the market would have to continue the actual trend, then we expect the captive financial institutions, such as banks, leasing and factoring firms and personal lending institutions, to maintain a massive role within the Arranger activity. In order to increase their weight, they have to become primary dealers in the secondary market context, given the strong international competition in the primary market.

2. A second alternative is that securitization would have to become an important financial instruments not only for financial institutions but also for corporate, especially for medium/big size firms, which could use this technique to raise money outside the traditional lending channel. In order to realize the above scenario, the bank system would have to offer to the corporate system an economic "full" service within the primary and secondary market context, especially for the credit management activity (Servicer), which could be handled by domestic lending banks. Italian financial institutions would increase enormously their active role, in spite of international intermediaries. This scenario is less realistic, given the current inability of Italian institutions to refund the bonds issued within the international context.

# 3 Project Finance

Stefano Gatti


## 3.1 Introduction

This chapter focuses on analyzing project finance transactions, centering on market analysis aspects for sectors in which such deals are mainly found both at international level and, in greater depth, at domestic level. It also looks at advisery and arranging services offered by consultants and intermediaries to the sponsors of these transactions. The aim is to identify market trends, the competitive situation for services offered and opportunities for Italian financial intermediaries in this business area. Instead, this chapter does not intend to give an exhaustive description of technical aspects involved in such deals or the evaluation process and assembly of project-based financing. Readers can obtain an overview of these issues by referring to works listed in the bibliography.

The chapter is structured as follows. Section 3.2 outlines the typical features of a project finance deal and compares it to traditional corporate financing, highlighting benefits sponsors can obtain by recourse to this structured finance technique. Section 3.3 analyzes those sectors in which the technique is mainly applied. First the topic is reviewed from an historical perspective, with an analysis focusing on European experience (European Union and non-EU countries) and then the domestic scene. Specifically as regards Italy, sectors are investigated that quantitatively represent over 90% of the country's total volume of syndicated transactions. Section 3.4 analyzes the offer of project finance advisery and arranging services. The overview starts with a review of competitors at international level and then moves on to look at the situation in Europe and Italy. The main conclusion emerging is that this business is firmly in the hands of a small group of competitors who are able to offer both advisery and arranging services according to an integrated intermediary model. Section 3.5 presents the main conclusions.


## 3.2 Distinctive features of the transaction

A rather widely agreed upon definition of project finance describes it as financing (by banks or, less frequently, in the form of bond issues) that as a priority doesn't depend on the reliability and creditworthiness of the sponsors, namely, parties proposing the business idea to launch the project and who often finance its working capital. Approval doesn't even depend on the value or solidity of assets the sponsors themselves are willing to make available to financers. Instead, it is basically a function of the project's ability to repay the debt contracted and allow for a remuneration of capital invested consistent with the degree of risk inherent in the initiative. It could also be said that project finance is the structured financing of a specific economic unit that the sponsors create by means of share capital, and for which the financer considers cash flow as the source of loan reimbursement, whereas project assets only represent collateral.

These are, in essence, the distinctive features of a project finance transaction.

1. The debtor is a project company set up on an ad hoc basis and is financially and legally independent from the sponsors. Such companies are often referred to as "SPVs – Special Purpose Vehicles".[1]
2. Financers have only limited recourse (or in some cases no recourse) to the sponsors after the project is completed. The sponsors' involvement in the deal is, in fact, limited in terms of: time (generally during the set-up to start-up period); amount (they can be called on for equity injections if certain economic-financial tests prove unsatisfactory); quality (managing the system efficiently and ensuring certain performance levels).
3. Project risks are allocated in an appropriate manner between all parties involved the transaction.
4. Cash flow generated by the enterprise must be sufficient to cover operating costs and service the debt in terms of capital repayment and interest. As the priority use of cash flow is to fund operating costs and service the debt, only after this is any residue used to pay dividends to the sponsors.
5. Collateral is allowed by the sponsors to financers as security written on revenues tied up in the project.

---

[1] Setting up an ad hoc vehicle company can, from a legal standpoint, be seen as both a positive and defensive move. Positive, because setting up an SPV completely isolates the initiative's cash flow from that of the originating company, so giving creditors full controllability. And defensive, because domiciling the project in a vehicle avoids commingling project equity with that of the originating company, consequently avoiding contamination of the two asset risks. See Esty (2002) and Novo (1999).

### 3.2.1 A comparison between project finance and corporate finance

The five points above summarize what can be gleaned from the many works on this issue, the authors of which are mainly in agreement. But in reality the majority of cases are very different. Considerations and evaluations made by financers are much more complex and in depth than a mere certification of the soundness of the sponsors and the project they intend to launch. In effect, a project-financed deal must first of all show that it has a balanced, viable allocation of risks between the various parties concerned, independent of whether they are from manufacturing, transport, telecommunications or any other sector. Apart from the risk in terms of the sponsors' economic-financial soundness, in project financing it is vital that financers also make a detailed analysis and evaluation of all other parties involved: plant and equipment suppliers, constructors, managers, suppliers of raw materials, purchasers or users of the end product or service. From a bank's standpoint project finance is above all seen as a question of credit, and so the long-term solvability of all parties gravitating around the Special Purpose Vehicle is of prime importance.[2]

The above comment, however, in no way detracts from the important differences between project financing and corporate financing. In the latter case, the bank concerned has to evaluate a project that will have a direct impact on a company's financial statements and so requires a combined project-company evaluation. This will certainly include an appraisal of the project in its own right, but also the balance sheet, the economic-financial situation of the company that will carry out the project, its past history and existence of longstanding customer relations (and, therefore, the company's business turnover with the bank).

This implies that corporate financing is based (perhaps even entirely) on being able to count on a much broader asset base than assets relating specifically to the individual project: if the latter fails, the financer can always count on the company's other assets. In the case of project finance this is not so. Financing is granted on a no-recourse or limited-recourse

---

[2] Intuitively, the financial soundness of parties involved in a project finance initiative should have a significant effect on the pricing of the transaction. However, there is very little evidence of this. Dailami and Hauswald (2001) found a strong negative correlation between the existence of a take-or-pay agreement (namely, long-term firm purchase contracts signed by a large buyer/offtaker) signed with sound counterparts and spreads recognized above leading rates for issue of project bonds. Furthermore, the authors demonstrated a strong correlation between project bond pricing and the rating trend, and the product or service purchaser's financial situation.

basis: these clauses – especially the first – mean banks have no recourse to assets of parties launching the project in the event that this should fail. Even if there is limited recourse instead of no recourse, the situation doesn't change. While it is true no absolute division exists between sponsors and project, the conditions under which banks could have recourse to collateral given by the vehicle company's sponsors are just possibilities, and in any event full enforcement of the guarantees would not enable full recovery of the sums loaned.

In Table 3.1 we have summarized the main differences between project as opposed to corporate logic behind granting financing.

**Table 3.1.** Main differences between project finance and corporate finance

|  | Corporate finance | Project finance |
| --- | --- | --- |
| Collateral for financing | Assets of the borrower | Project assets |
| Effect of financial flexibility | Reduces the borrower's financial flexibility | Non-existent or very reduced as regards the sponsor's flexibility |
| Accounting treatment | On-balance sheet | Off-balance sheet (the only effect is the cash outlay to subscribe the equity in the SPV or disbursement of subordinated loans) |
| Main variables considered when granting credit | Customer relations<br><br>Financial soundness<br><br>Profitability | Future cash flows |
| Sustainable leverage | Depends on the effects on the borrower's balance sheet | Depends on cash flow generated by the project (leverage is usually greater) |

Source: Gatti (2003)

## 3.2.2 Why use project finance: benefits for sponsors

In order to correctly assemble project-based financing the bank adviser must first understand the sponsors' reasons for wanting to completely separate the destiny of the project from that of the respective companies.

The reason is not necessarily always to cut costs. Normally project financing costs more than a regular medium-term industrial loan, bond issue or equipment leasing. Apart from the spread paid above interbank market base rates, project finance costs increase considerably as a result of technical and legal consultancy fees, which are fundamental to the successful outcome of the transaction.[3]

So reasons for recourse to project finance lie elsewhere. Usually when a venture is significantly larger than the borrower's current activities it is funded off-balance sheet by means of structured financing. In a structured transaction, in fact, the outcome of the venture doesn't affect the company or companies that want to launch the project, as it is segregated in a separate company, for which several legal systems recognize limited shareholder-sponsor liability. Isolating the project from the company works both ways: a project with poor prospects doesn't affect the company's performance nor its survival; conversely, default of the company shouldn't affect the project's performance nor, therefore, the possible claims of creditors financing it.[4]

Off-balance sheet financing therefore implies recognizing an important conclusion: if a venture is more creditworthy than the originating company then realizing the project by isolating it in a vehicle company provides certain benefits that could otherwise not be obtained. Naturally, superiority of the new enterprise compared to the merits of the originator means that risks must be identified in advance and covered by contractual credit enhancement-type instruments or insurance, as already indicated in point 3 of Section 3.2. Only in this way can the enterprise's creditworthiness be rated even higher than that of the sponsor company or companies and by virtue of this reduce the cost of obtaining financial resources for funding, in addition, of course, to increasing the degree of financial leverage utilized.

In essence, recourse to an off-balance sheet deal to realize and finance a project potentially enables sponsors to obtain several benefits, among which:

1. cost reductions as regards funding for the sponsor;

---

[3] Megginson and Kleimeier (2000) empirically showed a modest difference between pricing (measuring the spread above interbank base rates) for project loans and syndicated corporate loans. This, according to the authors, is because a project finance transaction isn't necessarily riskier than a corporate-financed project if the underlying contracts constitute a valid mitigant of the credit risk for the financers.

[4] Brealey, Cooper and Habib (1996), Shah and Thakor (1987), Leland and Skarabot (2002), Esty (2002).

2. sponsor's financial flexibility remains intact;
3. benefits for the sponsor in terms of "insurance" against any negative impact of the project.

The first benefit is achieved if the structuring cost for the initiative (that in any event is very high, especially if the deal is extremely complex) is less than the saving on funding cost, owing to the improved credit rating obtainable by the venture when compared to that of the sponsor. A cost benefit is therefore achieved if the structuring cost for the transaction and identification and allocation of risks is less than the lower cost of resources raised to realize the initiative.

As regards the second benefit – financial flexibility – it should be mentioned that if the project is particularly large (that is, represents a substantial part of the sponsor's assets and, therefore, financial structure), its realization would erode current credit lines, increasing debt and precluding possible future initiatives. Incidentally, it should also be remembered that an increase in indebtedness could also produce immediate side-effects on the future cost of any new funding. By using an off-balance sheet structured deal this effect is avoided: the funding concerns an ad hoc legal entity involving no or limited recourse to the sponsor/originator.[5]

The third is an "insurance-type" benefit against possible default of the initiative. Depending on how the initiative's risks have been foreseen and allocated, if the project fails the sponsor company or companies will still survive. On the other hand, a further "insurance-type" benefit is that if a company finances a project in-house (namely, includes the project in its own financial statements), banks can use total company assets as collateral and not just project assets. As mentioned in point 5 of Section 3.2, in project finance the only collateral is the project's assets, whereas the sponsor's assets remain unencumbered.

---

[5] The Special Purpose Vehicle's indebtedness has a real effect on sponsors when accounts are consolidated. The consolidated financial statements will, in effect, show an increase in indebtedness as a result of the debt of the subsidiary vehicle company. If, however, financing granted by the creditor is on a company and not a consolidated basis, then the off-balance sheet financing fully achieves its aim.

## 3.3 Project finance applications and sectors in which the transaction is most used

This section provides a market analysis of project-financed initiatives. The topic will first be examined from the standpoint of the way the market has developed over the years, identifying long-term trends and sectors mainly adopting the technique. Following this, the European and Italian situation will be reviewed in greater detail. Again in this case the aim is to identify the more attractive sectors in terms of adopting the technique and, as a consequence, opportunities for Italian financial intermediaries interested in operating in the structured financing business field.

### 3.3.1 Past development of project finance and market sectors

Modern examples of project finance date back to the Thirties in the United States when, in Texas, financing was granted for oil exploration and successive drilling of wells. Financing was granted based on the producer's ability to repay capital and interest using revenue from sales of crude, often counter-guaranteed by long-term supply contracts. Then in the Seventies project finance was also adopted in Europe, again in the oil sector: in fact it became the financial technique used for funding oil extraction off the British coast. Again in the Seventies, when the power production market was regulated in the USA (by means of the PURPA, Public Utility Regulatory Policy Act of 1978), Congress encouraged energy production from alternative sources by requiring that utility companies purchase all the power output from qualified producers (IPPs, Independent Power Producers). From then on, project finance began to be applied more and more to create power production plants using both traditional sources and alternative or renewable sources.

So from an historical standpoint, project finance was first launched in well-defined sectors marked by two salient factors:

1. the presence of a captive market, thanks to signature of long-term contracts in return for predetermined prices, involving large, financially sound buyers (so-called offtakers);
2. the absence of high-level technological risks when constructing plants.

In these sectors right from the early days the role of sponsor was covered by large international constructors/developers and multinationals in the oil sector.

Instead the growth trend seen in the Eighties and Nineties moved along two lines. The first expansion was when project finance was exported to developing countries. This was promoted by developers themselves who, faced with a progressive reduction in market opportunities at home, proposed the project finance technique to developing country governments as a means to rapidly create basic infrastructures and ensure a greater involvement of private capital, guaranteed by Export Credit Agencies in their own countries.[6]

But the second change in the project finance market took place in industrialized countries themselves, where the technique had initially been experimented in more traditional sectors. This expansion was the result of using project finance as a means to realize the following types of off-balance sheet initiatives.

1. Projects that had a lower or less effective market risk coverage: examples are sectors in which there was no one single large buyer, like toll motorway infrastructures, leisure facilities or urban parking solutions.
2. Projects in which the government intervened to promote realization of public works. In many cases these were works incapable of repaying investment costs, operating expenses and debt servicing by means of market tariffs; as such they had to be subsidized to a greater or lesser degree by recourse to public funds. In certain countries in Europe, first and foremost in the UK, adopting the project finance technique to realize public works reached considerable proportions on the wave of the PPP (Public-Private Partnerships) program, known as PFIs (Private Finance Initiative). In other countries – among which Italy – there has been an intensification of this phenomenon over recent years.

The reasons given can be summarized in the following figure (Figure 3.1).

---

[6] See International Finance Corporation (1999), Gatti (1998), Everhart and Sumlinski (2001).

**Fig. 3.1.** Project finance market trend by market and degree of underlying risk

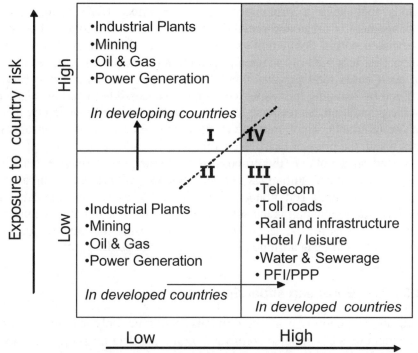

Source: the author, based on Esty (2002)

As can be noted, segment II constitutes the benchmark for project finance initiatives. The two arrows pointing towards segment I and segment III indicate market trends underway. It can also be seen that segment IV, while theoretically possible, represents an unfavorable combination of factors for project finance applications. In fact, faced with high uncertainty, a very inflexible contract structure and high financial leverage, it would be difficult for management to respond or adapt rapidly to change. In such circumstances recourse to a corporate finance approach is undoubtedly advisable.

The matrix in Figure 3.1 is also important from another standpoint. In fact a distinction is made between sectors in which project finance can be applied, depending on the initiative's capacity to sustain the attendant investments and costs from the cash flow it generates. In particular, it can be noted that while segments II and I include sectors in which the product can be sold at market prices based on long-term supply contracts (take-or-pay agreements or offtake agreements), projects in segment III (except for the hotel & leisure business) usually have problems in setting a market price capable of generating sufficient profit for sponsors. In fact these are goods that have a pronounced spillover effect (for instance, water management or urban and social development in depressed areas) or goods associated with a population's needs, the cost of which has a significant impact on less well-off segments (health and personal care, for example). In such cases total privatization of the sector would mean the service offered by realizing the works would not be accessible to certain segments of the population. So recourse has to be made to public financing by means of capital grants, which mitigate investment costs for private sponsors and, as a result, the price or tariff levels imposed on end-users.

Based on the above, the proposal is to divide project finance deals into fully self-financed initiatives (project finance as interpreted in a strict sense) and partially self-financed initiatives. As regards the first category, the basis for evaluation is the soundness of the contractual architecture and counterparts; as for the second category, apart from the factors indicated, bankability will be determined by the level of the public grant.

### 3.3.2 The European situation

Indications emerging from the previous section not only lead to theoretical considerations but are also confirmed by market data for project finance in terms of value. Here, reference will above all be made to the European context that will then be useful for providing more targeted evaluations as regards current and future major growth sectors in Italy.[7] The timeframe reviewed covers the five-year period 1998-2002. Data is also given for the first five months of 2003, although trend analysis is limited to the five

---

[7] Data referred to in this and the following sections are taken from Dealogic's ProjectWare database and include both new initiatives and the refinancing of previously syndicated transactions on a project finance basis. As will be seen in the case of league tables for advisery and arranging mandates in Section 3.4, recourse to this type of data must be weighed carefully because of the limitations of the databases themselves. More precisely, transactions recorded in ProjectWare don't cover the entire universe of project finance transactions assembled in any one year or in a certain country, given that input to the databases is provided by advisers or arrangers themselves. Normally this means data concerning the majority of smaller, probably not even syndicated, projects assembled at local level are not captured as they are structured directly by the promoting bank. This limitation becomes even more critical in more detailed surveys covering an individual country or geographical area.

complete years, given that annual and infra-annual data are not comparable.

From a quantitative standpoint the European project finance market shows a growing trend in the early part of the period considered (around 54,000 million dollars in 1998 to about 82,000 in 2000) but then declines significantly in the last two years (ending up in 2002 at 28,500 million dollars, about half the figure recorded at the beginning of the period).

The most representative sectors, in terms of average percentage of the total over the five years, are telecommunications (44.4% of the total), energy (14.6%), rail and infrastructure (12.09%), roads (7.31%), hospital construction and management (2.23%), water and sewerage (2%) and airports (1.96%). Details are shown in Table 3.2. An analysis of the data clearly indicates that sectors listed in segment III of Figure 3.1 (telecom, rail, roads and PPP/PFI) dominate in terms of amount financed compared with more traditional sectors, such as energy. This confirms a progressive move for the use of project finance from segment II to segment III as already highlighted previously.

In greater detail, it should be borne in mind that the important weight of the telecom sector is due to a technological acceleration witnessed in this sector in recent years. The significant increase in use of high capacity broadband networks for communications via web, together with the growing transformation of communications networks from mere voice carriers to transmitters of voice and data, are the most important factors. In addition there has been growth as a result of third-generation wireless technology and increased competition between operators following local loop unbundling[8] by traditional telecoms. In numerous countries, above all in Western Europe, the period under consideration has seen bids opened to award UMTS[9] licenses. Many operators financed their participation in these bids on a project basis considering future revenues that would accrue from exploiting the licenses themselves. In reality the high concentration of deals in the years 1998-2000 is largely the reason for the high percentage represented by the telecom sector. Moreover, the gradual decline in the number of these deals explains the trend after 2000, which starting in 2001 shows a progressive reduction in the volume of deals financed.

---

[8] The term can be translated as "disaggregated access" to the local network. This means that a national operator (for instance, Telecom Italia) provides a series of access services to one or several other operators, who can allow them to offer their own communications services directly to end-users.

[9] See Department of Trade & Industry (2001).

**Table 3.2.** Percentage breakdown of project-financed transactions in Europe

| Project sector | Financial close date | | | | | | |
|---|---|---|---|---|---|---|---|
| | 1998 | 1999 | 2000 | 2001 | 2002 | 2003 | Total 5 years |
| Airport | 2.03% | | 1.77% | 4.69% | | 4.74% | 1.96% |
| Bridge | 1.58% | | 0.48% | | 0.63% | | 0.53% |
| Commercial property | 2.23% | 1.68% | | 0.94% | 0.84% | | 0.99% |
| Defence | 1.65% | 0.13% | 1.37% | 1.05% | 1.53% | | 1.11% |
| Education | 0.41% | 0.27% | 1.61% | 2.38% | 4.06% | 1.27% | 1.51% |
| Gas Distribution | | | 0.10% | | | | 0.03% |
| Gas pipeline | 0.19% | | | 0.45% | | | 0.12% |
| Gasfield exploration and development | 4.60% | 0.83% | 0.24% | | 0.35% | | 1.17% |
| Government buildings | 0.15% | | 1.20% | 0.22% | 2.12% | 3.07% | 0.78% |
| Hospital | 4.15% | 2.38% | 1.16% | 0.96% | 3.54% | 2.18% | 2.23% |
| Hotel/resort/casino | 0.41% | 0.61% | | | | | 0.19% |
| Industrial/Commercial Zone | | 0.04% | | | | | 0.01% |
| Manufacturing | 0.54% | 0.79% | | | | | 0.25% |
| Mining | 0.10% | 0.29% | 0.68% | | 0.33% | 0.33% | 0.33% |
| Oil pipeline | | | | | 0.26% | | 0.03% |
| Oil Refinery/LNG and LPG Plants | | 0.40% | 0.70% | | | | 0.28% |
| Oilfield exploration and development | 0.39% | 0.81% | 0.08% | 0.29% | 1.77% | | 0.48% |
| Other Infrastructure Projects | 0.03% | 0.67% | 0.02% | 4.40% | 0.09% | | 0.91% |
| Other upstream | 0.84% | | | | | | 0.17% |
| Petrochemical/Chemical Plant | 1.85% | | 0.33% | | | | 0.47% |
| Police | | 0.23% | 0.13% | 0.58% | 0.89% | | 0.28% |
| Port | 0.34% | 0.27% | | | 0.53% | | 0.17% |
| Power | 22.98% | 14.71% | 11.24% | 2.23% | 25.74% | 22.12% | 14.58% |
| Prison | 0.47% | 0.75% | 0.36% | 0.40% | 0.36% | 1.28% | 0.50% |
| Processing plant | 0.23% | | | | | | 0.05% |
| Pulp and paper | 1.45% | | | | | | 0.29% |
| Rail - Infrastructure | 19.58% | 27.45% | 0.14% | 2.63% | 12.12% | 38.53% | 12.09% |
| Recreational Facilities | 1.41% | 0.63% | | | 4.62% | | 0.88% |
| Renewable fuel | 0.71% | 0.09% | 0.21% | 1.03% | 0.67% | | 0.47% |
| Residential property | 0.75% | | | 0.52% | | | 0.24% |
| Road | 3.65% | 7.62% | 4.73% | 10.47% | 10.67% | 20.61% | 7.31% |
| Steel mill | 2.19% | 0.08% | 0.26% | | | 1.18% | 0.57% |
| Telecom | 22.33% | 33.64% | 71.16% | 56.32% | 24.73% | | 44.44% |
| Tunnel | | | 0.40% | 0.47% | | | 0.20% |
| Urban railway/LRT/MRT | 1.49% | | 0.65% | 0.68% | 0.89% | 2.45% | 0.80% |
| Waste | 0.55% | 0.47% | | 0.04% | 0.81% | | 0.29% |
| Water and sewerage | 0.16% | 3.56% | 0.48% | 6.46% | | 1.05% | 1.99% |
| Wind Farm | 0.54% | 1.59% | 0.50% | 2.80% | 2.46% | 1.18% | 1.34% |
| Total | 100.00% | 100.00% | 100.00% | 100.00% | 100.00% | 100.00% | 100.00% |

Source: Dealogic – ProjectWare

The second sector showing a considerable weight at European level continues to be power generation (energy and power plants). In this regard, and intuitively given the sector has traditionally adopted the technique (it is one of the sectors appearing in segment II of Figure 3.1), a review of volatility in percentage share over the period considered shows that it is less pronounced than in the telecom sector. An indication that volumes for power generation have essentially been stable. It should also be borne in mind that during the period in question many power generation deals concluded in the early Nineties completed their start-up phase and were refinanced. So in order to interpret the trend correctly it should be remembered that the data not only includes new plants, or loans for the purchase and successive revamping of existing ones, but also funding granted following renegotiation of contract terms for financing agreed on previously.[10]

As for the third most important sector (rail and infrastructure), observing data for the five years, a progressively increasing trend can be noted for its weight, both in terms of absolute value and percentage share. Over recent years expansion of infrastructure has become a prime competitive factor at country system level, to the point that special attention is required when making economic policy decisions as regards the involvement of private capital.[11] A key factor in the case of transport infrastructure is also project finance deals linked to privatization of airports, among which Berlin airport in 2001 and Rome airport in 2000 are the most significant examples. These applications – in reality more like acquisition financing rather than true project financing, which instead would be linked to the realization of new airports – affect both the current size of the market (few deals for very substantial amounts) and volatility of data over the period considered.

Lastly it is worth mentioning the application of project finance in two quantitatively important sectors where partial self-financing of works is typical: hospitals and water treatment. As for the first, the figure for Europe is effectively explained entirely by data for the UK. In fact the UK was the first country to develop PFIs and has continued to use this approach in the hospital sector and, more recently, also in the prison and school construction sectors. In the case of water, on the other hand, this is an application area common to the majority of developed countries in Europe in response to increasing environmental degradation and growing concern over availability of water for industrial and domestic use.

---

[10] As regards techniques for refinancing project finance transactions, see Gatti (1999).
[11] Fisher and Babba (1999).

### 3.3.3 European Union and non-EU countries

Looking closer at the details of the analysis at European level, it can be noted that the average figure for the period is not always entirely indicative. As mentioned in the previous section, there is a wide swing in the incidence of individual sectors in the years considered and, furthermore, an aggregate figure doesn't take into account the different levels of economic development found in various regions of Europe. This means data must be broken down geographically into macro-areas. The aim of this part of the study is to make the analysis more meaningful by highlighting differences in the two contexts as regards application of project finance techniques. It is likely that a different degree of economic development has an important impact on the types of sector mostly applying the technique.

Consequently the decision was taken to break down data illustrated in the previous section into two groups: European Union countries and non-EU countries. As regards the latter, these are mainly ex-Soviet Union countries and those in the Balkans, therefore, countries that after the fall of planned economy regimes or periods of war and economic isolation found themselves faced with an infrastructure deficiency that couldn't be overcome by means of public financing alone. Moreover, these were normally countries with very significant potential in terms of natural resources that had still not been completely exploited.

As for the European Union, the global trend for transactions in terms of volume almost mirrors the result seen for Europe as a whole. There was an increase from 46,600 million dollars in 1998 to a peak in 2000 of 69,400 million dollars, followed by a downturn in volume to around 26,600 million dollars for 2002.

Some of the stronger sectors (see Table 3.3) were again telecommunications (43%), rail infrastructure and roads (overall about 20%), energy/power (15%), followed at a distance by hospitals (2.5%), airports (2%) and water and sewerage management (2%). Presence of basic industrial infrastructure sectors – manufacturing and production plants, natural resource exploitation, development of oil and natural gas fields – was decidedly lower. This indicates that, as might be expected, in more developed countries on the European continent the focus of project finance was on strengthening the existing industrial structure as opposed to creating new production capacity. There was further confirmation of indications emerging from Figure 3.1, namely, that countries that had pioneered industrialization utilize project financing in sectors falling within segment III.

**Table 3.3.** Percentage breakdown of project-financed transactions – European Union

| Project sector | 1998 | 1999 | 2000 | 2001 | 2002 | 2003 | Total 5 years |
|---|---|---|---|---|---|---|---|
| | | | Financial close date | | | | |
| Airport | 2.33% | | 2.09% | 4.89% | | 5.32% | 2.19% |
| Bridge | 1.82% | | 0.57% | | 0.67% | | 0.59% |
| Commercial property | 2.48% | 1.66% | | 0.98% | 0.90% | | 1.06% |
| Defence | 1.90% | 0.15% | 1.61% | 1.10% | 1.64% | | 1.24% |
| Education | 0.47% | 0.29% | 1.90% | 2.48% | 4.35% | 1.43% | 1.69% |
| Gas pipeline | 0.22% | | | 0.47% | | | 0.13% |
| Gasfield exploration and development | 5.30% | 0.90% | 0.28% | | 0.37% | | 1.31% |
| Government buildings | 0.17% | | 1.42% | 0.23% | 2.27% | 3.44% | 0.87% |
| Hospital | 4.78% | 2.58% | 1.37% | 1.00% | 3.79% | 2.45% | 2.49% |
| Hotel/resort/casino | 0.38% | 0.59% | | | | | 0.18% |
| Industrial/Commercial Zone | | 0.05% | | | | | 0.01% |
| Manufacturing | 0.13% | 0.46% | | | | | 0.11% |
| Mining | 0.05% | 0.08% | 0.36% | | | | 0.13% |
| Oil Refinery/LNG and LPG Plants | | 0.24% | 0.44% | | | | 0.17% |
| Oilfield exploration and development | 0.02% | 0.42% | 0.09% | 0.30% | | | 0.16% |
| Other Infrastructure Projects | 0.03% | 0.73% | 0.02% | 4.59% | 0.09% | | 1.02% |
| Other upstream | 0.96% | | | | | | 0.19% |
| Petrochemical/Chemical Plant | 0.19% | | 0.39% | | | | 0.15% |
| Police | | 0.25% | 0.15% | 0.61% | 0.95% | | 0.31% |
| Port | | 0.12% | | | 0.57% | | 0.08% |
| Power | 23.89% | 15.29% | 12.64% | 1.09% | 26.07% | 19.86% | 14.89% |
| Prison | 0.55% | 0.82% | 0.43% | 0.42% | 0.39% | 1.43% | 0.56% |
| Pulp and paper | 1.11% | | | | | | 0.21% |
| Rail - Infrastructure | 22.57% | 29.78% | 0.17% | 2.62% | 12.97% | 43.18% | 13.48% |
| Recreational Facilities | 1.63% | 0.68% | | | 4.94% | | 0.98% |
| Renewable fuel | 0.82% | 0.05% | 0.25% | 1.07% | 0.72% | | 0.52% |
| Residential property | 0.87% | | | 0.54% | | | 0.27% |
| Road | 2.68% | 8.27% | 4.48% | 10.93% | 11.42% | 17.65% | 7.33% |
| Steel mill | 0.45% | 0.08% | | | | | 0.10% |
| Telecom | 22.98% | 30.51% | 68.94% | 55.93% | 23.43% | | 42.84% |
| Tunnel | | | 0.47% | 0.49% | | | 0.23% |
| Urban railway/LRT/MRT | 0.12% | | 0.77% | 0.71% | 0.95% | 2.74% | 0.59% |
| Waste | 0.43% | 0.52% | | 0.04% | 0.87% | | 0.28% |
| Water and sewerage | 0.03% | 3.78% | 0.57% | 6.58% | | 1.17% | 2.14% |
| Wind Farm | 0.62% | 1.73% | 0.59% | 2.93% | 2.63% | 1.33% | 1.50% |
| Total | 100.00% | 100.00% | 100.00% | 100.00% | 100.00% | 100.00% | 100.00% |

Source: Dealogic – ProjectWare

As regards non-EU countries, instead, certain important aspects can immediately be observed.

The first concerns the size of the market, which was very small during the five years: considering the period 1998-2002, non-EU countries represented little more than 10% of the total European project finance market. This is consistent with indications at international level where less developed countries on the Asian and African continents have experimented with the technique for some time now with an obvious impact on the relative size of the markets themselves. As for the trend, again it first grew between 1998 and 2000 (rising from around 7,100 million dollars to 12,500) and then declined to a total of 1,900 million dollars for 2002.

A second aspect to highlight is that the number of application sectors was lower than in the case of European Union countries and also showed a different qualitative breakdown. Again in this case, the telecom sector was the largest, accounting for about 58% of the market, followed by the energy sector (12%) and road infrastructure (7%). Instead, as opposed to EU countries, industrial works occupied an important place: natural resource and petrochemical exploration (6.2%), steel and ferrous alloy production (4.6%), manufacturing plants and the mineral extraction sector (respectively 1.4% and 2%). So the data show a focus on use of project financing for setting up basic industrial infrastructure and exploitation of the considerable natural resources found, in the main, in the ex-Soviet block countries. Excluding energy, in fact, the positioning is in segment II of Figure 3.1, indicating significant opportunities but also a much higher overall risk compared with the situation seen for European Union countries. See Table 3.4 for details.

**Table 3.4.** Percentage breakdown of project-financed transactions – non-EU

| Project sector | Financial close date | | | | | | |
|---|---|---|---|---|---|---|---|
| | 1998 | 1999 | 2000 | 2001 | 2002 | 2003 | Total 5 years |
| Commercial property | 0.59% | 1.92% | | | | | 0.40% |
| Gas Distribution | | | 0.62% | | | | 0.27% |
| Hotel/resort/casino | 0.66% | 0.85% | | | | | 0.28% |
| Manufacturing | 3.22% | 4.71% | | | | | 1.43% |
| Mining | 0.43% | 2.81% | 2.46% | | 5.04% | 3.04% | 2.02% |
| Oil pipeline | | | | | | 3.93% | 0.26% |
| Oil Refinery/LNG and LPG Plants | | 2.28% | 2.14% | | | | 1.24% |
| Oilfield exploration and development | 2.81% | 5.36% | | | 26.81% | | 3.18% |
| Petrochemical/Chemical Plant | 12.74% | | | | | | 3.19% |
| Port | 2.57% | 2.01% | | | | | 0.91% |
| Power | 17.04% | 7.88% | 3.50% | 28.44% | 21.01% | 40.86% | 11.93% |
| Processing plant | 1.77% | | | | | | 0.44% |
| Pulp and paper | 3.68% | | | | | | 0.92% |
| Rail - Infrastructure | | | | 2.84% | | | 0.20% |
| Renewable fuel | | 0.48% | | | | | 0.06% |
| Road | 10.02% | | 6.11% | | | 45.11% | 7.08% |
| Steel mill | 13.54% | | 1.68% | | | 10.99% | 4.59% |
| Telecom | 18.13% | 70.69% | 83.50% | 65.19% | 43.21% | | 58.01% |
| Urban railway/LRT/MRT | 10.44% | | | | | | 2.62% |
| Waste | 1.32% | | | | | | 0.33% |
| Water and sewerage | 1.04% | 1.00% | | 3.54% | | | 0.64% |
| Total | 100.00% | 100.00% | 100.00% | 100.00% | 100.00% | 100.00% | 100.00% |

Source: Dealogic – ProjectWare

### 3.3.4 The Italian market

The Italian market essentially shows a growth trend throughout the entire period analyzed, except for a drop in 1999. The effective volume of projects recorded rose from 1,744 million euros in 1998 to over 9,200 million euros in 2002.

In terms of percentage breakdown, data recorded by ProjectWare indicate the telecom sector in first place (52%), followed by energy and renewable sources (32%, including wind-farmed energy), airports (12%) and water treatment and management (3.5%).

It should be emphasized that, as indicated at the beginning of Section 3.3.2, this is not exactly the whole picture as data recorded also include deals organized on a project basis that are often more similar to acquisition finance transactions. The most emblematic cases are the privatization of Rome airport with the Leonardo operation in 2000-2001 and the acquisition of the three Genco units (Elettrogen, Eurogen and Interpower) sold by ENEL (the previous Italian National Electricity Board monopolist) as a result of the Bersani Decree 79/1999.

For this reason the following part of this work will provide information on the most significant sectors as regards application of project financing in Italy, not only based on market data but also on several other information sources, news gathered from financial publications, official reports and discussions with operators in the sector. The specific sectors analyzed are:

1. energy, cogeneration and gas;
2. telecommunications;
3. transport;
4. water treatment;
5. hospital construction.

#### *3.3.4.1 Energy and cogeneration*

Right back in the early Nineties, Italy's electrical power sector was the laboratory for analysis, research and development as regards major project-financed deals, thanks also to regulations in force and considerable grants made available to promoters by measures known as CIP 6/92.

The situation in this sector in the early Nineties was marked by construction of large-sized power production plants with sale of power to ENEL based on the subsidized facilitated tariff established by CIP 6/92 (Table 3.5). By the end of the Nineties the situation had changed radically as a legislative decree was passed to liberalize Italy's power market

(Decree 79 of 16/03/1999, known as the Bersani Decree), with a consequent impact on ENEL's management and operating strategies.

**Table 3.5.** Cases of project-financed cogeneration plants in Italy

| Special Purpose Vehicle | Locality | Type of project | Value of plant (lire/billions) | Contractor |
|---|---|---|---|---|
| Isab Energy (Erg Petroli and Edison Mission Energy) | Priolo Gargallo | Cogeneration plant (512 mwt) | 1,885 | Snamprogetti-Foster Wheeler |
| API Energia (API and ABB Sae Sadelmi) | Falconara Marittima | Cogeneration plant (276 mwt) | 1,003 | ABB Sae Sadelmi |
| SARLUX (Saras SpA and Enron Netherlands Holding BV) | Sardinia | IGCC plan (551 mwt) | 1,802 | Snamprogetti-Turbotecnica (GE) |
| ROSEN (Powerfin SA, Solvay SA) | Rosignano | gas-fired cogeneration plant (350.8 mwt) | 731.8 | Ansaldo |

Source: Gatti (1999)

With the approval of the Bersani Decree to liberalize Italy's power sector, the country came into line with EU Directives, in particular Directive 96/92, so giving a strong boost towards improvements in terms of the effectiveness and efficiency of the electrical power production, transmission, distribution and sale system.

Clearly this legislation was a move towards the privatization of ENEL and therefore tended to encourage the development of a free market and strengthen competitive mechanisms in the power sector, achieved by abolishing the power production monopoly in favor of ENEL itself.

Starting January 2003 provisions were introduced stating that no domestic operator could produce or import more than 50% of the total power produced in or imported into Italy. Again in 2003, ENEL was forced to divest a minimum of 15,000 MW of its production capacity to third-party operators, whereas the expansion or modification of these divested plants was authorized by means of specific Ministry of Industry regulations.

In reality this ban on exceeding 50% of power produced in or imported into Italy meant ENEL had to carve out three NewCo's (Genco's) –

Eurogen, Elettrogen and Interpower – sale of which began at the end of 2000. A joint venture led by Endesa and ASM Brescia was awarded Elettrogen in August 2001; a second joint venture led by Edison, EdF, Fiat and certain municipal operators (AEM Milan and Turin) acquired the largest Genco, Eurogen, in March 2002. Lastly, in February 2003 a group formed by Electrabel, Energia (Cir Group) and Hera formalized the acquisition of Tirreno Power (Interpower). All three deals were realized on a project finance basis. As already indicated, this explains the high percentage incidence of the power sector on total project finance deals realized in Italy.

Today, therefore, production, importing, exporting, purchase and sale of power can be freely exercised in Italy, even by private producers. Instead the State still retains control of certain activities, which it assigns to the National Transmission Network Operator (GRTN)[12] based on a specific concession covering:

- transmission (namely, transfer and transformation of high tension power so it can be made available to users);
- dispatch (namely, activities required to issue instructions concerning the coordinated use and operation of production plants, the power transmission network and ancillary services necessary for its functioning).

The network Operator can, in turn, make agreements for the maintenance and expansion of the network with other companies that have transmission networks interlinked with the national network.

The Bersani Decree also introduced important changes as regards the structure of the electrical power market.[13]

Purchasers were broken down into two categories:

- eligible customers (namely, customers who can stipulate supply contracts with any domestic or foreign power producer, distributor or

---

[12] The National Transmission Network Operator is a joint stock company born from a carve-out of the parent company, ENEL, and then sold to the State. The carve-out concerned assets necessary to manage transmission and dispatch activities, the staff and part of the debt. Its basic mission is network management: it must guarantee that all parties who request to do so can be connected to the domestic transmission network. The Operator is remunerated based on a fee established by the Electrical Power and Gas Authority, paid by those requesting to access and use the network.

[13] See Freshfields et al. (2002), GME – Power Market Manager (2003), Infrastructure Journal – Power News (2003).

wholesaler – these are parties with an annual consumption of at least 50,000 kWh);
– locked-in customers (namely, end-users who are not part of the previous category, which utilize power for their own industrial or domestic purposes and can only buy power by stipulating contracts with the distributor in their local territory).

Locked-in customers pay a single tariff for power supplies and this tariff must be established according to principles that ensure the same treatment for all users throughout Italy.

This objective was achieved by setting up a joint stock company – created by the National Transmission Network Operator – designated as the "sole purchaser" (Acquirente Unico). The sole purchaser is, in effect, a broker between electrical power producers and distributors. In particular:

1. it buys power from producers under long-term supply contracts based on its forecast for level of demand over the following three years;
2. it sells this power to electricity distributors at non-discriminatory conditions to ensure application of the single tariff to locked-in customers at national level.

For customers who purchase large quantities of power, in June 2000 the National Transmission Network Operator formed a joint stock company – Gestore del Mercato Elettrico SpA (GME) – to service them. In essence the power market framework created by the Bersani Decree can be summarized as shown in Figure 3.2.

The new framework outlined above has had, and will probably continue to have, a significant impact on the project finance market in the power sector:

1. First, as can be seen, a considerable number of Italian and foreign operators participated in the bids for sale of the Genco's by setting up joint ventures in the form of Special Purpose Vehicles financed on a project basis. The intention of these operators was to acquire a substantial share of the market once liberalization is finally completed.
2. Secondly, as not all the power stations ENEL will sell to private operators are in a completely efficient state, in addition to the investment required to purchase them there will also be a considerable revamping cost to replace obsolete plants and equipment to reinstate their original efficiency or even improve it. Achieving high productivity standards will be vital for operators in the new market: high operating efficiency will be the key competitive factor in what is expected to be a very crowded, tough market situation.

**Fig. 3.2.** Structure of the power market in Italy

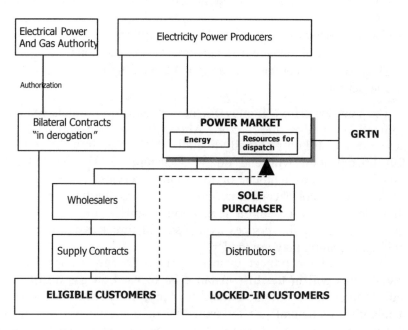

Source: Gestore Mercato Elettrico SpA

### 3.3.4.2 Gas

In addition to the electrical power sector and end of ENEL's monopoly, the other sector that has undergone a significant transformation in recent years is gas supply. Starting 1 January 2003, with the definitive launch of liberalization of the natural gas market introduced by Legislative Decree 164/2000 (the so-called Letta Decree), all consumers were free to stipulate supply contracts with any Italian or foreign producer, importer, distributor or wholesaler. All natural gas consumers, whether for industrial or domestic use, became "eligible" customers, whereas before the Decree only those whose annual consumption exceeded 200,000 $Sm^3$ were considered as such.

Before the Letta Decree the gas market was virtually a monopoly situation in the hands of SNAM. Distribution and delivery[14] of gas at local

---

[14] Distribution and sales activities are not defined by the Letta Decree. In general, distribution activities can be defined as those concerning management of the

level effectively took place on an almost exclusive basis as a result of four key principles:

- Local bodies assigned management of the service directly to subsidiary companies.
- Management was assigned on an exclusive basis.
- The duration of management agreements was very long.
- The expiring operator had a right of pre-emption over potential new competitors.

The new legislative framework has created the grounds for increased competition within the sector. Although gas transport and dispatch activities are still only partially liberalized (the transition period to achieve full liberalization will end on 31 December 2005) the Letta Decree establishes that assignment of distribution services must take place by tender and cannot exceed a period of 12 years. Furthermore, companies that, de facto or based on legislation, administrative act or contract, manage local public services as a result of direct assignment or a non-public procedure, may not tender.

In terms of the project finance market, the new set-up indicates that investments will in the first instance be focused on gas distribution and sales rather than on extraction. In Italy, in effect, the issue is not availability of natural gas for industrial or domestic use, but rather the heavy concentration of supply in a few producer countries (Russia, Algeria, the Netherlands and Norway). The incentive for private parties to enter the market will be (together with locating alternative sources to traditional supply markets) the search for more efficient, economic distribution systems in an attempt to keep down the end-consumer price, which by its very nature is bound to increase given the constant growth of domestic demand. The investments forecast will again in this case be considerable and will fuel a strong demand for funding, which will be raised in the market according to a typical project finance approach.

distribution network, its expansion, strengthening and renewal; management of plants to connect up users and relevant maintenance; control over safety; carrier business and contractual transactions. As regards sales activity, this includes purchasing gas within the national territory, marketing operations, business management (billing and providing information to users), regulations, excluding performance as regards safety. For more details see Butti and Chilosi (2003).

### 3.3.4.3 Cogeneration waste-to-energy

In the power sector, production of energy from waste provides interesting opportunities for applying the project finance technique if forecasts based on analyses made by banks should hold true. The reason for this is firstly the permanent state of emergency as regards collecting and disposing of waste, which is a particularly serious problem in large urban areas in northern Italy.

In 1999 waste treated in Italy represented only 25.6% of total waste collected (differentiated or otherwise). Furthermore, compared to other European Union countries the Italian situation is an anomaly as disposal still takes place in waste dumps due to opposition to construction of technologically complex treatment or destruction plants. See Tables 3.6 and 3.7 in this regard.

**Table 3.6.** Final destination of urban waste in Europe (data for 1997)

|  | Incineration | Dumps | Composting and recycling | Total |
|---|---|---|---|---|
| Austria | 16.3 | 55.0 | 28.6 | 100 |
| Belgium | 30.3 | 54.9 | 14.8 | 100 |
| Denmark | 56.2 | 22.5 | 21.4 | 100 |
| Finland | 2.4 | 71.4 | 26.2 | 100 |
| France | 48.8 | 50.1 | 1.1 | 100 |
| Germany | 26.3 | 70.1 | 3.6 | 100 |
| Greece | 0.0 | 92.8 | 7.2 | 100 |
| Ireland | 0.0 | 92.4 | 7.6 | 100 |
| Italy | 5.2 | 88.9 | 5.9 | 100 |
| Luxembourg | 57.8 | 38.1 | 4.1 | 100 |
| Netherlands | 26.0 | 34.0 | 40.0 | 100 |
| Portugal | 0.0 | 88.0 | 12.0 | 100 |
| Spain | 4.4 | 83.2 | 12.4 | 100 |
| Sweden | 40.6 | 37.5 | 21.9 | 100 |

Source: CRS Proaqua, 1999

Secondly, mention should be made of the mounting attention competent Ministries, especially the Ministry of Industry and above all the Ministry for the Environment, have begun to dedicate to the issue of waste, also because Italy needs to come into line with EU Directives. In particular, Decree 22 of 5/2/97 (the Ronchi Decree) completely redefined the general principles for waste management and disposal.

A significant factor is that waste disposal and consequent energy production is an activity that will continue to benefit from Government incentives, similar to those prescribed in CIP 6/92, together with other natural renewable sources (biomass, water and wind).

In our opinion numerous plants will be built in Italy over the coming years and all of them will be funded on a project finance basis because of the evident financial benefits new initiatives in this sector will enjoy.

In fact the objectives imposed by the Ronchi Decree can only be achieved by significantly increasing the number of plants for incinerating waste. A survey conducted by ANPA in 1999[15] reported 41 functioning incineration plants. Even taking into account improvements during 1999, these would only be able to handle 2.1 million tons of waste annually against an objective of a total potential of 3 million tons (see Table 3.7).

**Table 3.7.** Situation for incineration plants in Italy – 1990

|              | Number | Tons of waste | %    |
|--------------|--------|---------------|------|
| North        | 28     | 1,692,284     | 80%  |
| Center       | 10     | 242,610       | 11%  |
| South        | 3      | 185,949       | 9%   |
| Total Italy  | 41     | 2,120,843     | 100% |

Source: ANPA, 2001

Furthermore, several Italian regions totally lack incineration plants (see Figure 3.3). The scope for constructing new destruction and energy production plants is therefore considerable.

A typical feature of project-financed initiatives as regards waste management and energy production from solid urban waste is the cash flow benefit for the project thanks to the waste disposal gate fee paid by the municipality or consortium of municipalities for use of the service. The margin level is therefore interesting for a potential financer.

However there are two factors that complicate the picture outlined above. The first is that it will not be possible to take for granted availability of waste for cogeneration in years to come. In fact, while waste disposal is still a problem today, proliferation of plants and extensive differentiated waste collection could mean that in the future waste will become a commodity for which plants may even have to compete. So solid waste could undergo a transformation from being a positive cash flow item to becoming a raw material cost. Moreover, cash flow stability could be partly compromised by the impossibility to sign put-or-pay contracts capable of covering a significant percentage of the raw material required.

---

[15] ANPA-ONR (2001), ANPA (1999).

**Fig. 3.3.** Percentage of urban waste incineration by region – 1999

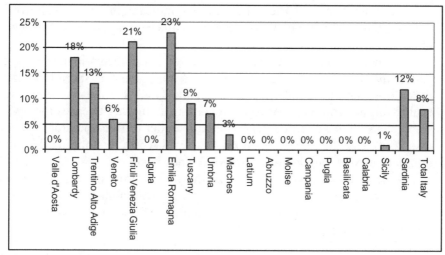

Source: ANPA (2001)

The doubt concerning growth of the waste-to-energy sector in Italy is that there continues to be considerable resistance on the part of the population in municipalities where plants are to be constructed. The immediate perception of public opinion is the negative impact of these plants on the environment, even though latest advances in engineering offer good possibilities to control emissions, fumes and unpleasant odors. This is undoubtedly less of a problem in the case of certain types of biomass (timber waste, for instance). Sponsors in the renewable sources' sector are moving more and more towards projects that use the same biomass as a raw material to utilize for combustion: in fact, if this is not pre-treated with chemical additives or bonders then the environmental impact is only slight.

### 3.3.4.4 Telecommunications

Starting in 1998 Italy began a process of full competition for provision of fixed-line telephony services, a project already designated for some time at European level as the Open Network Provision. A Telecommunications Guarantee Authority was also set up as the body appointed to guarantee a clear division between regulators and operators in the sector. On the wave of liberalization numerous licenses were issued during these years for providing public telephone services. As regards fixed-line telephony, 198 licenses were issued to 151 operators. In the mobile phone field based on second-generation technology (GSM – DCS) today there are four competitors: Telecom Italia Mobile, Omnitel Pronto Italia, Wind Telecomunicazioni and Blu. The numbers indicate the interest shown by the previous monopoly operator Telecom Italia's competitors to participate in the new free market.

A further reason for interest in this sector is the technological progress underway that over the next few years will see the spread of third-generation mobile telephony based on the UMTS standard, which will enable full integration of voice and data traffic. In Italy licenses for UMTS were awarded in January 2001 by private tender to five operators: Andala, Ipse 2000, Omnitel, TIM and Wind. It is well worth mentioning that these transactions were funded on a project finance basis.

The new rules imposed by the Authority in terms of interconnection, unbundled access to the local loop (ULL, unbundling of local loop), operator selection/preselection and portability of telephone numbers, have effectively broken Telecom Italia's monopoly of the domestic market, even though the full effects of liberalization are still not entirely evident. A recent report prepared by the Authority[16] indicates that the market share of the Italian incumbent compared with the average share for other European incumbents in their local markets is higher in terms of local calls, indicating that Telecom Italia is still a power in the largest voice transmission segment of the market. Furthermore, in the mobile telephony field, if the C2 index (sum of the market shares of the two largest operators) is considered then the figure for Italy is 83%, against an average considering the UK, France and Germany of 72% (Table 3.8). In summary, numerous interventions are still required to ensure a perfectly transparent market in which any operator intending to enter can effectively compete. In particular, given existing shortcomings in terms of infrastructure newcomers will have to rely on Telecom Italia's systems and structures quite considerably for some years to come.

Lastly it should be remembered that from the standpoint of the figures Italy presents an evident contradiction: while for fixed-line telephony the country is the least advanced (the voice telephone market versus GDP is 1.18% against a European average of 1.22%) in mobile telephony it is undoubtedly one of the leaders (again see Table 3.8). In our opinion this means that convergence of fixed-line/wireless telephony will be the winning solution for new operators intending to enter and succeed in the Italian market. Clearly, once again the key factors in the competitive battle will be to reduce costs, offer new products, propose new standards and technological innovations. In the future we believe this sector can offer

---

[16] See Alfano et al. (2002).

some interesting opportunities for applying the project finance technique, even though as in the case of other sectors in which services are sold to the general public, the critical point will remain the difficulty to estimate user volumes.

**Table 3.8.** Indicators of competitive status in the TLC sector – 2001

| Incumbent Market Share | | |
| --- | --- | --- |
| | Italy | European Average |
| Local calls | 93% | 90% |
| Long Distance calls | 76% | 77% |
| Mobile phone calls | 48% | 48% |
| ITZ calls (international trafic) | 60% | 75% |
| Mobile telephony market | | |
| | Italy | European Average |
| Mobile service penetration rate | 82% | 73% |
| Main incumbent market share | 48% | 48% |
| C2 index | 82,90% | 71,80% |

(*) C2 index is calculated as the average for data re the UK; France and Germany

Source: Alfano et al. (2002)

### 3.3.4.5 Transport

The transport sector can include a wide range of ventures. Here are a few examples:

- toll road infrastructure;
- urban transport;
- light subway transport;
- courtesy buses linking with airports and train stations;
- exit road tunnels and bridges.

Generally speaking, a license is granted to a private company (which can be an ad hoc SPV) for the construction and management of these infrastructures on a BOT (Build, Operate and Transfer) basis. Costs for the works are therefore repaid by tolls that the management company charges to users during the validity period of the license. Currently, licenses to build and manage in Italy are governed by Articles 19 and 37-bis of the Merloni Law and successive modifications.

The transport sector represents an extremely high total turnover, especially as regards road building, for two basic reasons. First, Italy's toll road/freeway system is small compared with the European average. Secondly, for this very reason numerous large-scale works are considered "priority investments" by the Italian Government, with equally numerous pledges by politicians to streamline procedures for authorizations and licenses as far as possible.

**Fig. 3.4.** Extent of road networks (December 2000); data in kilometers

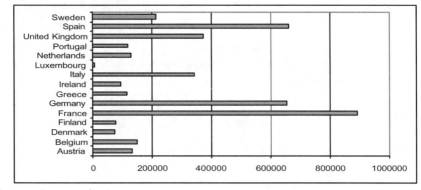

Source: Autostrade

As for the first of these two points, certain data covering the 1999-2002 period is well worth mentioning. In terms of road networks in European Union countries, as of December 2000 Italy stood in fifth place based on total length (about 340,000 km). However, this figure should be compared with countries like France and Germany that have networks measuring 892,000 km and 656,000 km respectively. See Figures 3.4 and 3.5 in this regard.

**Fig. 3.5.** Kilometers of freeway/tool road in the European Union (data as at 31/12/2000)

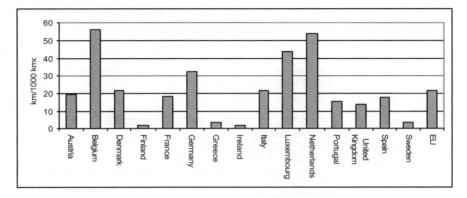

Source: Autostrade

**Fig. 3.6.** Freeway/Toll road density in EU countries (1999-2002)

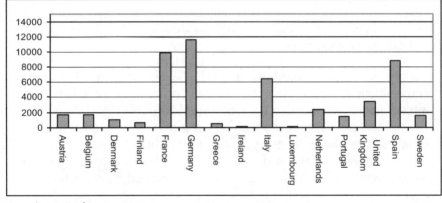

Source: Autostrade

At European Union level, countries with the highest freeway/toll road density (number of kilometers per 1,000 square kilometers) are Belgium (56.5), the Netherlands (53.8), Luxembourg (44.1) and Germany (32.3). The ratio for Italy is only 21.4 (see Figure 3.6).

Road network density shows a similar picture to that seen for the freeway/toll road system, and again Belgium and the Netherlands have the highest density (respectively 4,855.1 and 3,029.1) against a figure for Italy of 1,128 km/1,000 square kilometers. This low normal and toll road density clearly affects crowding on the roads, measured as the ratio between total number of vehicles and kilometers of road. While the European Union average is 45 vehicles/km, Italy shows the highest ratio with 104 vehicles/km (see Figure 3.7).

**Fig. 3.7.** Vehicle density index in EU roads (1999-2002)

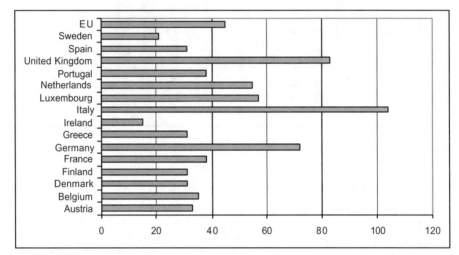

Source: Autostrade

Certain recent decisions should be mentioned concerning the Government's favorable attitude to private involvement in road infrastructure works. On 21 December 2001, CIPE (Interdepartmental Committee for Economic Planning) approved the first national strategic infrastructure plan calling for a total expenditure of around 24,200 million euros for basic public works during the four-year period 2003-2006, of which about 6,000 million euros will be financed by recourse to private capital.

Again with reference to the Italian Government's encouraging stance on project finance, the 2003 Budget instituted the FROP (Rotating Fund for Public Works) and by means of Legislative Decree 190 of 20 August 2002 (the so-called Obbietivo Law), introduced a more favorable legislative framework to speed up the start of construction on infrastructure and strategic production sites, and those considered to be in the national interest.

This heralds the launch of numerous initiatives in this sector in the near future; see Table 3.9 for a list of priority works. Note that normal and toll road works account for a significant percentage of the total figure.

**Table 3.9.** List of priority works indicated by the Government for the period 2003-2006

| Strategic infrastructure projects | Progress on project | 3 years expenditure forecast (€/millions) |
|---|---|---|
| Frejus Pass Railroad | 30% | 149.77 |
| Sempione Pass Railroad | 20% | 22.23 |
| Brennero Pass Railroad | 20% | 50.00 |
| Turin – Trieste Railroad (corridor 5 Lyons – Kiev) | | 1,962.54 |
| Turin – Novara | 100% | 955.45 |
| Novara – Milan | 90% | 516.46 |
| Milan – Verona | 50% | 180.76 |
| Verona – Venice – Mestre | 40% | 309.87 |
| Medium-length Toll Roads | | 877.97 |
| Mestre By-pass | 40% | 568.1 |
| Brescia – Bergamo – Milan | 80% | 309.87 |
| Ventimiglia – Genoa – Novara – Milan Railroad | | 224.12 |
| Ventimiglia – Genoa | 80% | 118 |
| Genoa – Milan | 60% | 106.12 |
| Brennero – Verona – Parma – La Spezia Railroad | 30% | 568.1 |
| Brennero – Verona – Parma – La Spezia Toll Road | 40% | 98.13 |

**Table 3.9.** (cont.)

| | | |
|---|---|---|
| Project to safeguard the lagoon and city of Venice | 60% | 609.42 |
| New Romea | 20% | 90.9 |
| Marches – Umbria Raod Link | 20% | 320.2 |
| Cecina – Civitavecchia Toll Road | 30% | 438.99 |
| | | |
| Integrated Transport System in Rome area | | 1,032.59 |
| Ring Road | 100% | 307.29 |
| Castelli Area | 10% | 129.12 |
| Line C | 70% | 340.86 |
| Line B1 | 100% | 255.32 |
| Naples Junction | 60% | 1,154.28 |
| Bari Junction | | 79.02 |
| Catania Junction | | 70 |
| Salerno – Reggio Calabria – Palermo – Messina – Siracusa – Gela Toll Road | | 3,653.93 |
| Salerno – Reggio Calabria | 90% | 2,687.13 |
| Palermo – Messina | 100% | 485,8 |
| Messina – Siracusa – Gela | 50% | 481 |
| Salerno – Reggio C. – Palermo – Catania RailRoad | 40% | 404.39 |
| Genoa Normal/Toll Road Junction | 10% | 150 |
| Bridge over Strait of Messina | 40% | 356.36 |
| Emergency waterwork projects in southern Italy | 60% | 2,478.48 |
| | | 22,542.57 |

Source: Treasury Department

Readers must remember, however, that the list of possible initiatives in the transport sector includes cases that, while being of considerable interest from the standpoint of their complex financing requirements, lie within segment III of the matrix in Figure 3.1. Therefore, these are not the most interesting type of project (at least from the standpoint of financers) for assembling project finance transactions. This situation is by no means a prerogative of Italy as many similarly negative cases can be found at European level. It will come as no surprise that in periodic League Tables prepared by the financial press, road and infrastructure projects financed on a structured basis are always found near the bottom of the table.

The low attractiveness for financers of transport-related projects is a result of two important factors. First (as can be noted in Section 3.3.1) in the case of transport the uncertainty as regards user volume would represent a risk for the SPV and, therefore, for its financers. Sponsors can only attempt to forecast this variable based on historical or even simply hypothetical data. The second factor is the tariff level (ticket or toll fee) to be applied to users. Certain services mentioned at the beginning of this section are considered as socially useful by local authorities. It is therefore very difficult to imagine that tariffs can be sufficiently remunerative to make management of such projects economically viable. In reality the price charged for the service would have to be high and so would end up being too onerous for certain segments of the population.[17]

### 3.3.4.6 Water treatment

In this context, for water treatment we refer to a basic cycle that includes:

- conveying water from reservoirs;
- water distribution to users;
- sewerage and water treatment.

In Italy reservoir management is still highly fragmented in terms of structures and operators. There are about 13,000 aqueducts and 6,000 operators – almost all public bodies – supplying water to around 8,000 Italian municipalities. Apart from generating low economies of scale in management terms, over time fragmentation has created a vicious circle in which low operator efficiency has led to a drop in water quality and a decidedly low price/quality ratio for the service. Water loss for Italy's

---

[17] Certain estimates for building toll road sections developed by simulation models can be instructive in understanding the problem. The estimated cost to build one kilometer of toll road in Italy ranges from 20 to 25 million euros, and can even be as high as 35 million in the case of ring roads around large metropolitan areas. Using current toll levels as the price variable, the break-even traffic volume would be between 100-120,000 vehicles per day, evidently an unrealistic figure for the majority of sections. Instead, if it is assumed normal traffic volume remains stable, this mean tolls would have to be increased to an unsustainable level for the average user.

aqueducts, for instance, stands at 27%, against a figure for Germany and France of respectively 13% and 24%. In addition, about 70% of the population in southern Italy suffers a lack of water supply.

For many years the issues of Italy's water treatment sector and hydrological reserves were not addressed by any radical reform. Only from the mid-Nineties, with a series of regulatory provisions, first and foremost Law 36/1994 (the so-called Galli Law), did the authorities start to demonstrate a new sensitivity towards the issue of water resources. The Law mentioned, in fact, defined certain basic principles that are particularly favorable as regards involvement of private capital in the sector:

- integrated management of water treatment to overcome the past fragmentation of operations;
- management of the service on the basis of optimum size at an ATO (Optimum Territorial Unit) level;
- separation of the planning, policy and control functions for integrated water treatment (attributed to the AATOs – Optimum Territorial Unit Authorities) from service operations management;
- recognition of the need to ensure capital investments made by sector operators are adequately remunerated by defining a tariff sufficient to cover investment costs and at the same time provide satisfactory increases in terms or productivity and service quality.[18]

In early 1999 the Government approved the outline of a legislative decree concerning water with the intention of adopting EU Directives 91/271 on urban waste water and 91/676 on pollution caused by nitrates used in agriculture. The text is in harmony with EU policy on water and sets two specific objectives. The first concerns "environmental quality", defined as the capacity for water courses to maintain their natural self-cleansing processes and sustain plant and animal life. The second is to achieve "quality for a specific purpose", whether this be industrial or domestic. In essence the aim is to ensure users receive a resource meeting the minimum quality standard necessary for their water consumption needs.

The water treatment sector represents a substantial annual turnover. In a study made by the Supervisory Committee for Water Resource Use,[19] based on the analysis of a sample of 10 Territorial Plans, the required

---

[18] For a detailed review of the reference regulations and standard method for calculating tariffs to provide remuneration for integrated water treatment plant operators, see Gatti (1999).
[19] See Supervisory Committee for Water Resource Use (2001).

investment was estimated at approximately 5.5 million euros over the coming 23 years. Extrapolating from the sample data to cover the entire resident population, the estimate for Italy as a whole will amount to over 51.6 million euros. See Table 3.11 in this regard.

**Table 3.10.** Forecasts for all ATO plans for Italy

| ATO | Total Investiment (€ millions) | Duration of plan (n. years) |
|---|---|---|
| Chiampo Valley | 34.65 | 30 |
| Tuscany North | 345.97 | 30 |
| Lower Valdarno | 671.45 | 20 |
| Middle Valdarno | 823.06 | 20 |
| Upper Valdarno | 216.54 | 23 |
| Tuscany-Coast | 319.17 | 25 |
| Ombrone | 418.84 | 25 |
| Latium Latina | 363.78 | 30 |
| Latium Frosinone | 341.82 | 30 |
| Sarnese | 1,895.45 | 20 |
| Totale | 5,430.73 | |

Source: Nicolai (2002)

The size of this sector in Italy has already caught the eye of large foreign operators, such as Générale des Eaux and Suez Lyonnaise des Eaux (foreign water management on an industrial basis has already been a practice abroad for some years now). These companies have bought shares to create a privileged observatory of the Italian market. Know-how acquired in an international context enables them to participate with their own capital in one or more of the following roles:

1. Integrated water operator. In this case the operator is entrusted with management of the service, either by forming a company with local public participation or by obtaining a license. Integrated water service management includes the entire water supply chain and therefore payment for the service is by means of invoicing end-users in the relevant catchment area.
2. Performer of specific activities in a given segment of the water supply chain on a build, operate and finance basis under license. In this case it is very much nearer to being a project finance technique. The licensee builds a specific part of the water service facilities (for instance, the water capture structure, treatment plant, etc.) and manages it for a

certain number of years, recovering the investment by selling the service wholesale to the other business party.

Even though there are factors that would favor introduction of project finance techniques in the water treatment sector, as discussed previously, there are other aspects that could limit private capital investment considerably. On the one hand there are unfavorable institutional factors. For example, as of today only eight of the 89 ATOs have issued licenses for Integrated Water Services (see Table 3.11). In addition, local authorities have shown strong resistance to the consolidation process of current operations.

**Table 3.11.** ATOs in Italy: status of implementation of the Galli Law

| ATO | Region | Population | Method of assigment | Operator |
|---|---|---|---|---|
| Upper Valdarno | Tuscany | 296,226 | Direct | Società Nuove Acque Spa |
| Lower Valdarno | Tuscany | 777,385 | Direct | Società Acque Spa |
| Latina | Latium | 563,739 | Direct | |
| Middle Valdarno | Tuscany | 1,205,198 | Direct | Pubbliacqua |
| Ombrone | Tuscany | 352,199 | Direct | Acquedotto del Fiora Spa |
| Sarnese | Campania | 1,462,613 | Direct | Gori Spa |
| Terni | Umbria | 220,000 | Direct | |
| Chiampo Valley | Veneto | 53,350 | Direct | Società Acque del Chiampo Spa |

Source: Nicolai (2002)

Other factors, instead, concern the industrial management of the water cycle. The sector as a whole requires heavy investments; there is a need for rapid re-qualification, and a transparent system for establishing tariffs; demand is quite stable not too elastic to price. Despite these characteristics, however, the sector shows a very high fragmentation of investments. Apart from a limited number of large treatment plants included in regional plans, single transactions involve a relatively modest amount. So, given the high initial costs to assemble this financing technique, project finance can only be applied in the case of composite projects for which the overall value is rather substantial and, above all, where the returns are sufficient to justify these costs.

Also the cost of renovating individual urban sewerage networks planned by the end of 2005[20] will involve quite modest amounts. For this reason the authors believe it will be difficult to adopt techniques as sophisticated as project financing.

### 3.3.4.7 Hospital construction

Similar to experience abroad (in particular in the UK as part of the PFI program) over recent years Italy too has begun a process that sees private participation in projects in the hospital and health fields. This process is linked to the radical reform of the National Health Service launched by Legislative Decree 502/92, which placed the accent on rationalizing and re-qualifying public expenditure in the health sector. Among other objectives, this rationalization calls for the reorganization of the system in the light of a new concept for health services and the role assigned to organizations charged with the responsibility of safeguarding health. Specifically as regards hospitals, the new functional approach foresees an ongoing reduction in use of these facilities by patients with a short term prognosis, giving more emphasis to day hospital and day surgery facilities, which for a number of pathologies can provide more appropriate and more efficient treatment than recourse to hospitalization.

The breakdown of services transforms hospitals de facto into high-technology facilities for treating patients who recover rapidly (maximum 3-4 days) and for certain other specific pathologies. In parallel a network of complementary facilities will be developed for specific situations requiring less intense assistance intended as an alternative to hospitalization, such as long-term patient facilities, hospices and RSAs (assisted in-patient services).

The planned objectives based on current legislation are a direct consequence of the above approach and can be summarized as follows:

– average annual utilization of beds not less than 75%;
– beds available for patients whose symptoms are overcome rapidly equal to 5 per thousand inhabitants, of which 1 per thousand is reserved for long-term patients and rehabilitation;

---

[20] These initiatives were covered in Art. 141, paragraph 4 of Law 388 of 23 December 2000 (the 2001 Budget). One of the specific provisions was that, while waiting for AATOs to be set up, the Italian provinces could organize urgent works on a transitional basis for sewerage and treatment systems. These transitional works can also involve private capital, to be remunerated by application of tariffs.

- introduction of LEA (Essential Assistance Levels) and transfer of certain important pathologies for which hospitalization is "inappropriate" to more suitable out-patient facilities;
- closing down or reconversion of facilities with less than 120 beds.

The new regulatory framework means that Italy's health service is no longer anchored to a strictly welfare-type regime. The hospital is conceived as a facility that also embodies certain business characteristics, but in which the role of health control and management remains the competency of the Health Agency acting as the reference organization for the National Health Service. However, private-funded ventures can be effective for the construction or renovation of buildings or for providing hospital services and those of a business nature.[21] And so it is possible to imagine hospitals as facilities capable of generating revenue flows over time that would enable project financing techniques to be applied, even in a sector with a strong social orientation.

As regards the market size in Italy, currently there is no systematic survey which establishes what initiatives that have been proposed, approved and implemented. Data presented have been gleaned from various information sources based on ASSR (Agency for Regional Health Services) data, the OICE (Italian Organization of Civil Works Contractors) observatory and notices appearing in the financial press. The overall picture is that recourse to project finance in Italy for new construction or modernization of hospitals is still in its infancy, however, the data show a constant growth trend. As of April 2002, for instance, statistics published by ASSR reported 11 project-financed transactions to build and manage

---

[21] There are essentially three sources of revenue for a private sponsor that derive from the building and management of a health care structure. 1. Grants for work in progress. 2. Annual rent. 3. Revenue from management of commercial and service areas. This revenue structure has been experimented with success in the UK but is also found in hospital construction projects launched in Italy. In greater detail, grants for work in progress and annual rent (points 1 and 2) are paid to the concession holder by the Hospital Agency and/or Local Health Agency; tariffs for managing commercial areas (point 3) are instead paid directly to the licensee by private lessees of the areas concerned or by service operators. As regards the annual rent, this is the determining factor. It is paid from the time the new structure is operative and is broken down into a number of components: an availability payment linked to the available floor space of the hospital; a service fee linked to the quality level of services rendered compared to a contractually defined benchmark; and lastly, a volume fee proportionate to the volume of services rendered (payment for usage, volume or demand). For further details on this subject see Gatti and Germani (2003), Amatucci (2002).

health facilities and hospitals for an average of 40 million euros per transaction. See Figure 3.8 in this regard.

**Fig. 3.8.** Project finance in the hospital sector. Procedure initiated in the four years 1999-2002

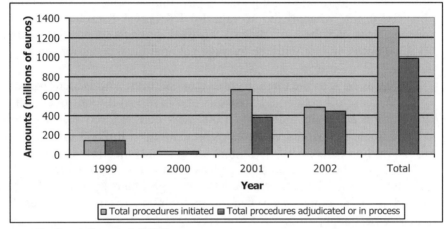

Source: Gatti and Germani (2003)

The data show that for the four years 1999-2002 there were a total of 20 procedures initiated on a project finance basis for hospitals and RSAs, for an overall value of around 1,300 million euros. Of these, as of 31 December 2002, 14 had been adjudicated or were in process for a total investment of 985 million euros. Therefore in terms of value the mortality was around 25% of all procedures initiated. This figure can be considered acceptable given the difficulties encountered by project-financed procedures to date in Italy and the distinctive nature of the health sector (characterized by high partially self-financed investments) which doesn't make 100% application of the technique easy. Furthermore, the data confirm an almost exclusive preference for recourse to Art. 37-bis of the Merloni Law (project finance with promoter procedure), chosen by the authorities concerned in 86% of the cases, and also recourse to project financing for new construction, which alone represented 50% of all cases. The evidence gathered therefore confirms a generalized recourse to the sponsor procedure as a consequence of the public administration's interest in proposals submitted by private operators, for which the plan's originality and organization in the management phase can be evaluated. According to the data the option based on Art. 19 (projects designed initially by the public administration and then proposed to private parties) seems less attractive. In effect a new construction project holds less constraints for a private party proposing to completely manage the facility; in such a case one would be free from constraints found in already existing operational facilities.

Of the 14 initiatives existing at the end of 2002, 12 concerned hospitals and 2, RSAs. The average investment for hospitals was about 80 million euros per project, confirming that single transactions are substantial in financial terms, whereas the average for RSAs was 8 million euros. The average cost per bed of the 12 hospital projects was approximately 211,000 euros, in line with the average national investment for this type of facility.

Lastly, as regards the three licenses that had been adjudicated by the end of 2002, these all concerned hospitals and involved a total investment of 267 million euros for more than 1,000 new beds. Moreover, two further project-financed hospital ventures were announced in 2003 for a total cost of 370 million euros, while two more are at an advanced study stage.

In essence the Italian hospital construction market is moving out of the start-up phase and becoming statistically significant in terms of size. It should also be emphasized that currently none of the initiatives have reached the start-up of construction stage.

## 3.4 The offer situation: Positioning and opportunities open to Italian intermediaries

The structure of offer in the project finance market is rather difficult to analyze precisely. The reason is the very nature of the product this financing technique represents, made up of a package of services comprising many possible parts, modeled on the needs of individual clients. In a way it is a unique "product" that doesn't lend itself to standardization and is difficult to identify in an unambiguous manner for a number of reasons.

- While financing can apply to any project, this doesn't mean that the specific approach adopted will automatically be project financing in the true sense of the term. In fact, as can be seen in previous sections, many transactions organized on a project basis are in reality very much more like other corporate finance transactions (especially highly leveraged acquisitions).
- Often a project-financed transaction is offered for subscription to a relatively limited number of investors, who will not find any organized "secondary market" in which it can be traded. The intermediaries,

however they might be involved in the initiative, are not subject to provisions requiring mandatory disclosure of certain information.
- Cooperation from intermediaries is indispensable in order to gather data. It is reasonable to assume that details of all transactions effectively closed are not made available to the market, especially if these are small and closed at domestic level by operators with little standing at an international level.

Given this, gathering data concerning both advisory or arranging services for financing has to rely entirely on "self-certification" by the intermediaries themselves, who normally announce news about their project finance activities in the specialized press or through information providers. One particularly reliable source is ProjectWare, the database managed by Dealogic, which constantly updates quantitative data for the global project finance market. Data included in this database can be a source for preparing so-called League Tables, which constitute the basis for our analysis spanning the period from 1999 to the end of 2002.

These League Tables show which commercial and investment banks or financial consultants have been most active at global level during a given year. For this purpose we have decided to divide the analysis into its two component parts: financing activity, referred to as "arranging", and consultancy or so-called "advisory" services.

Advisers are classified based on the total value for projects in which they provided consultancy services, whereas arrangers are ranked based on the amount of bank lending they have been appointed to manage as mandated (lead) arrangers. This latter criterion has been chosen as opposed to merely using the amount of financing effectively disbursed. The reason is that every project will necessarily have a lead arranger (or more than one if the size of the project warrants it) who then "transfers" small or large parts of the syndicated loan to other participants. A League Table based on the amount of financing arranged leaves the total resources effectively invested unchanged while offering the advantage of highlighting the most active intermediaries in what is the most significant role for the success of the transaction.[22]

---

[22] It can also be said that a League Table based on amount financed could distort the view of competition as regards arranging in the international syndicated loan business. In fact, there would be a risk of finding banks with little specific competency in arranging near the top of the table because of their considerable financial strength (pure lenders) whereas less "robust" banks from a financial standpoint, but with the necessary expertise to assemble these transactions, would be lower down the League Table.

A last point worth mentioning concerns the timeframe used. The decision was to use a four-year period (therefore, a medium timeframe) to show that while the international project finance market has a sufficiently stable core of competitors, it is also true that over time the leaders' positions are threatened by new competitors, especially as regards pure advisory activities. This means that the situation for leading positions is quite fluid. The last advantage of a four-year period is that trends for concentration or fragmentation of the advisery service or lending offer can be viewed from a structural standpoint, without distortion caused by effects of the economic cycle, which would instead emerge if the analysis had covered fewer years.

### 3.4.1 Advisers

Figure 3.9 gives the League Table for the top 20 advisers for the four-year period considered (by value of projects in which they were consultants) at global and European level. For the period analyzed this represents over 70% of the mandates given. Hence, the market is somewhat concentrated, even though this percentage shows a downward trend in response to growing fragmentation within the sector.

At global level Citigroup is unquestionably the leader as it occupied one of the top two positions in the League Table in all four years. Instead other leading positions show a much greater turnover, with a presence of both pure advisers (typically the corporate finance divisions of major audit firms) and integrated service commercial banks such as Deutsche Bank AG, ABN Amro, Societé Generale or Royal Bank of Scotland. The position of independent investment banks (Merrill Lynch) or affiliates of integrated service banking groups (Credit Suisse First Boston) is even more unstable. Finally, it can immediately be noted how competitors in the leading group are very heterogeneous.

Furthermore, two trends would seem to clearly emerge. The first is the progressive rise of the corporate finance divisions of major audit firms (PriceWaterhouseCoopers, KPMG Corporate Finance, Ernst&Young and Deloitte&Touche) as credible rivals to financial intermediaries. The second is that well-known names in the international investment banking field (Morgan Stanley, JP Morgan, Lehman Brothers, Credit Suisse First Boston, Merrill Lynch), found in the top positions of the League Table in the first half of the Nineties, are now challenged strongly by the group of large integrated service commercial banks. This situation would seem to confirm the competitive superiority of the integrated service intermediary model illustrated in Section 3.4.4.

**Fig. 3.9.** Global Advisers for project finance transactions (1999-2002)

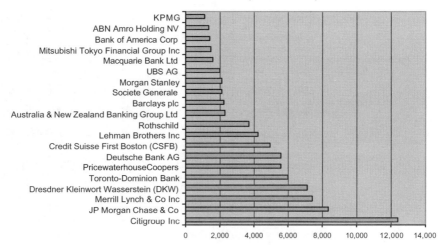

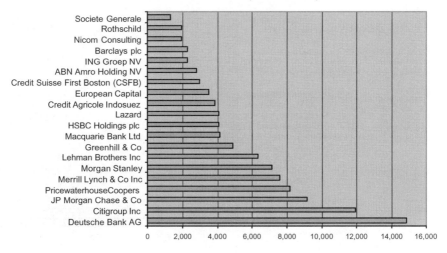

**Fig. 3.9.** (cont.)

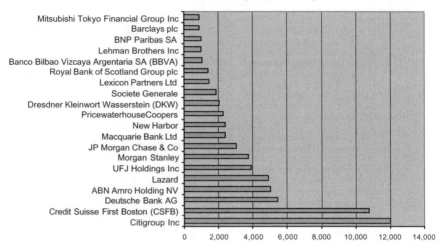

2001 - Global Advisers (US$ millions)

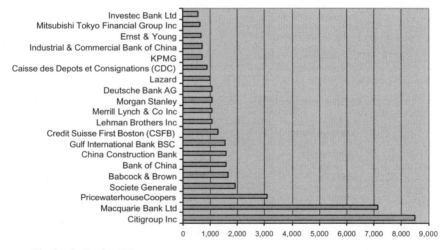

2002 - Global Advisers (US$ millions)

Source: Dealogic ProjectWare

**Fig. 3.10.** Advisers for project finance transactions in Europe (1999-2002)

## 1999 - Advisers for European Projects (US$ millions)

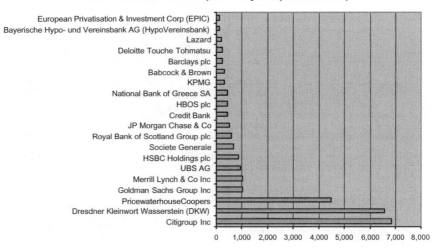

## 2000 - Advisers for European Projects (US$ millions)

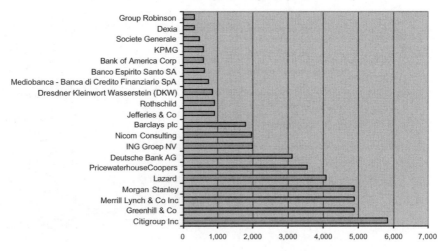

**Fig. 3.10.** (cont.)

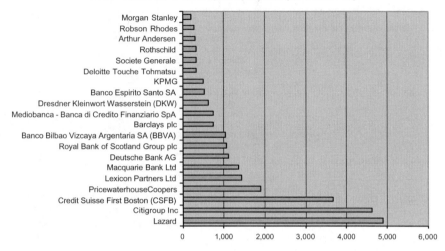

2001 - Advisers for European projects (US$ millions)

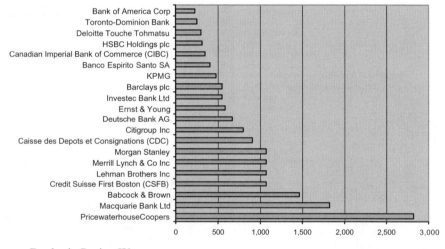

2002 - Advisers for European projects (US$ millions)

Source: Dealogic ProjectWare

The situation seen at global level is confirmed when the analysis focuses on advisery mandates awarded for projects on the European continent. Figure 3.10 shows the trend for the top 20 positions during the period 1999-2002. Compared to the global situation, the domination of large integrated service commercial banks in the top positions of the League Table is even more pronounced. As one would expect, there is a stronger presence of European banks. In fact, in addition to Deutsche AG, ABN Amro, Société Generale and Royal Bank of Scotland mentioned above, there are also ING Groep NV, UBS, Barclays and Banco Bilbao Vizcaya Argentaria.

### 3.4.2 Arrangers

Again in this case we have taken the top 20 arrangers, classified according to the amount of arranging done. Over the period 1999-2002 their share of the total arranging market ranged from 60% to 80%, although also on the lending side there is the same progressive fragmentation seen in the case of consultancy services. This means the market is growing faster than the possibility for traditional intermediaries to expand their activities, meaning conditions are favorable for new competitors to enter the sector. Contrary to the situation for advisers, the group of top arrangers is much more homogeneous, since the majority of them are clearly commercial banks or, once again, the investment banks divisions of large banking groups (Figure 3.11).

**Fig. 3.11.** Global Arrangers for project finance transactions (1999-2002)

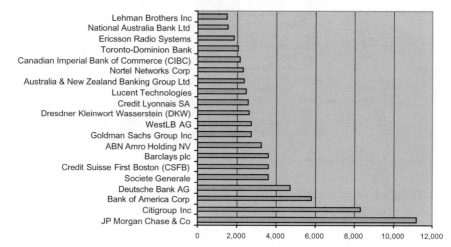

**Fig. 3.11.** (cont.)

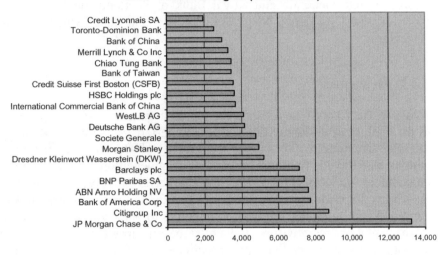

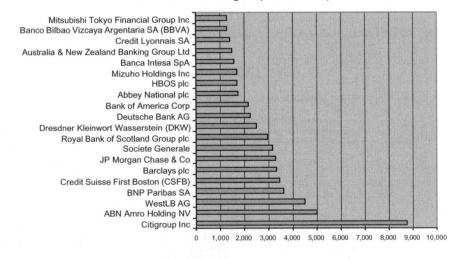

Another aspect worth noting is that unlike in the case for advisers, the top positions are much more stable. Considering the top ten, all the arrangers considered were in the top half of the League Table in two of the four years. Instead positions for advisers were much more fluid. In fact, Citigroup was the market leader, consistently occupying the first or second position for mandates awarded during the period considered. However, European banks are well entrenched in the upper positions and number more than the American intermediaries.

**Fig. 3.11.** (cont.)

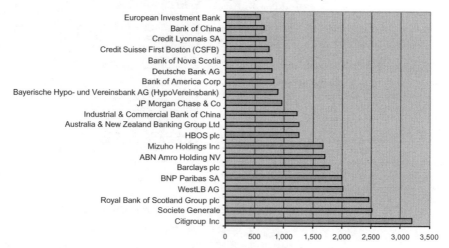

Source: Dealogic ProjectWare

The considerations made in terms of mandates for arranging at global level can be repeated for mandates for projects awarded in Europe (Western and Eastern Europe). In this case, if possible it would seem the presence of large European banking groups is even more marked and shows that American intermediaries find it very difficult to increase their market share in Europe. It should be noted, however, that it is rare to find any one intermediary in the same position in the League Table in all four years considered. This indicates a certain instability of market share, clearly due to the different weight project financing transactions had over the years in the various Western and Eastern European countries (Figure 3.12).

**Fig. 3.12.** Arrangers for projects finance transactions in Europe (1999-2002)

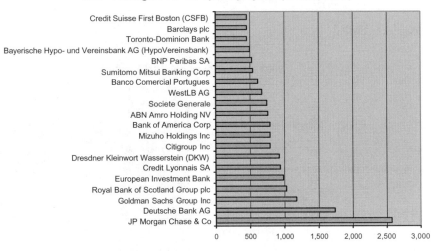

### 1999 - Arrangers for European projects (US$ millions)

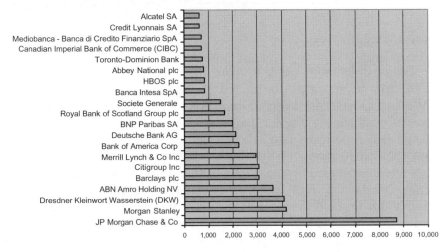

### 2000 - Arrangers for European projects (US$ millions)

**Fig. 3.12.** (cont.)

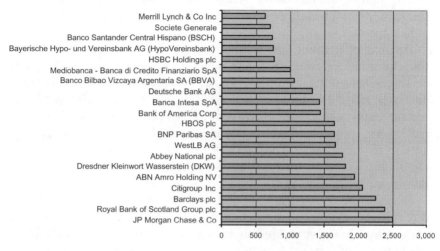

**2001 - Arrangers for European projects (US$ millions)**

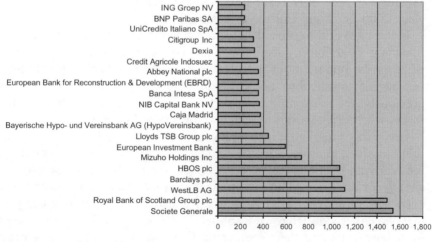

**2002 - Arrangers for European projects (US$ millions)**

Source: Dealogic ProjectWare

### 3.4.3 Italian intermediaries

The considerations above refer exclusively to the international situation at global and European level. Italy only launched structured financing transactions in the early Nineties, often based on requests coming from the public sector.

Because of tradition and legislative constraints, in Italy it is difficult to find domestic intermediaries that operate like the investment banks found in English-speaking countries. Those that are somewhat similar have a narrower range of activities and only in rare cases – above all seen in recent years – are they involved in project finance in other than a participant bank role. Commercial banks, on the other hand, only began to appear in the League Tables starting 1996 and have only participated marginally in the explosion of business in Italy, where the scene has been dominated by foreign banks.

During the 1999-2002 period the League Tables highlight the difficulties experienced by Italian banks to make their mark as credible competitors in the structured financing transaction advisery and arranging field outside of national boundaries. In fact there is only one Italian adviser (and only for transaction mandates closed in Europe) which was Mediobanca in 2000 and 2001. On the arranging front, apart from Mediobanca, the only other Italian names are Banca Intesa in the three years 2000-2002 and Unicredito Italiano in 2002.

In the light of the above data we are convinced Italy's role in the project financing field for transactions of an international size will be limited, whereas the opportunities are greater in an area comprising a significant number of transactions not exceeding 50/100 million euros. As noted previously, the more promising sectors often see private operators joining forces with public parties to realize project-based initiatives.

Given this situation, it is to be hoped that Italian banks will first try to be fully involved in projects led by foreign intermediaries so they can become familiar with the issues involved in project finance transactions. Moreover, already existing contributions made by Italian banks (as co-arrangers or even just co-underwriters) is of great assistance to foreign banks, given that the latter don't have consolidated business relations with potential local borrowers and therefore cannot approach them directly. Bearing in mind that the majority of future projects will involve a public counterparty (either acting as licensor or sponsor), the participation of local intermediaries who are already known would even seem to be indispensable.

In essence, Italian banks have the opportunity to consolidate their presence in the project-financed business area by using consultancy and arranging services as the lever in smaller projects. This, because they have an advantage over large foreign banks who don't find such projects sufficiently remunerative or, even if they are, find it difficult to gain the necessary confidence of borrowers, above all when these are local public parties.

As is the case internationally, we are convinced the most appropriate and effective intermediary model for Italy is again the integrated service approach. Given that projects are small, risks are low because of the technology employed, and the fact that a public party acts as licensor or sponsor, this should lead to a reduction of all-in financing costs and participation of a limited number of parties, which at the same time should avoid problems in terms of conflict of interest. In short, what can be called a "one-stop shopping approach" would seem to be the answer.

As part or their organizational restructuring of dealing with corporate clients in general, several Italian banks have adopted the above approach, even though as of today this is only a start of what will certainly be quite a long process. Furthermore, it can be noted that this approach has already been adopted by foreign intermediaries operating in the structured finance field in Italy.

### 3.4.4 The integrated service bank as the dominant model and trend for the offer

A review of the market data leads to certain important conclusions. To help illustrate these we have constructed a matrix grouping operators active in project financing into one of four broad categories based on their success in the two fundamental activities of consultancy and lending (Figure 3.13). The horizontal axis reports the amount of transactions arranged, defined qualitatively (decreasing moving from the left to the right segment); the vertical axis indicates the value of mandates received (decreasing from top to bottom).

The main result of the survey is that a growing number of banks are operating in the dual role of adviser and arranger, offering their clients integrated consultancy and lending services, and abandoning extreme specialization. As can be seen in Table 3.12, data contained in the League Tables for advisers and arrangers are matched to see the number of arrangers who also figure among the leaders in the advisery market. Considering the top 20 positions, with the exception of 2002 the match between advisery and arranging roles is always from 50 to 60%. The group of integrated service intermediaries includes a more or less stable core of operators (between 10 and 12) who account for the considerable share of

50% and 55% respectively of the global arranging and advisory markets. Moreover, the integration between commercial and investment banking also seems to benefit activities in the capital market: many of the integrated service operators also occupy leading positions in the project bond book runners League Table and are making inroads in a market segment traditionally dominated by investment banks, which have less experience in the financ ial intermediation field.

**Fig. 3.13** Competitive models in the project finance sector

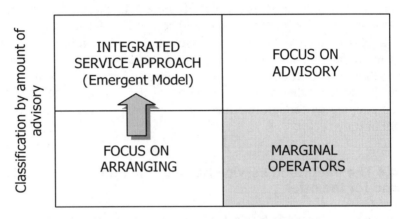

Classification by amount of arranging

Source: Gatti (1999)

The narrowing of the gap between the advisery and arranging business areas seems to be more pronounced for banks with a strong commercial background, traditionally focused on lending activities and therefore relatively more competitive for arranging services. In fact, it is much less costly for the latter to extend the range of their services to include consultancy than it is for investment banks to increase their lending potential.[23]

As regards intermediaries focusing on the advisery role, it can be said that they are almost entirely what is today a limited number of American investment banks and British merchant banks (again see Table 3.12). Non-

---

[23] As regards American intermediaries, in addition there is the impact of the recent abolition of the Glass-Steagall Act, which for many years had prohibited commercial banks from undertaking investment banking business. This legislative reform has in effect accelerated the trend towards integration.

financial intermediary-type consultants, already discussed in Section 3.4.1, are not considered here.

**Table 3.12.** Strategic groups of financial intermediaries involved in the project finance business (1999-2002)

| Year | | | |
|---|---|---|---|
| 1999 | 2000 | 2001 | 2002 |
| Number of 20 Arrangers in position among the top 20 advisers | | | |
| 12 | 10 | 12 | 6 |
| Integrated Intermediaries | | | |

JP Morgan Chase & Co.
Citigroup Inc.
Bank of America Corp.
Deutsche Bank AG
Societe Generale
Credit Suisse First Boston
Barclays plc
ABN Amro Holding NV
Dresdner Kleinwort Wasserstein (DKW)
Australia & New Zealand Banking Group Ltd
Toronto-Dominion Bank


Focused on arranging
Canadian Imperial Bank of Commerce
Credit Lyonnais
National Australia Bank
WestLB AG
BNP Paribas
ING Group
Royal Bank of Scotland
Focused on advisory services
Macquarie Bank Ltd
Merrill Lynch & Co. Inc.
Morgan Stanley
Rothschild
Lehman Brothers Inc.

Source: authors' table based on Dealogic, ProjectWare data

Lastly, the category we have defined as marginal operators covers a group of heterogeneous operators who are highly specialized by geographical area or by business sector. These occupy niches in the global market although they are often leaders in their specialist sector.

The conviction that banks offering integrated services (now more and more common in the sector) have a competitive edge over both "pure" investment banks and commercial banks is also borne out by the operators themselves and depends on a number of factors. Compared with the former, integrated service banks:

- normally have lower funding costs as they can rely on gathering stable, low-cost retail deposits. This means they can offer very competitive pricing;
- have much less extreme levels of leverage, given that their balance sheets are more solid, which means their underwriting policies can be more aggressive. For the borrower this means there is much less uncertainty as regards raising financial resources. In fact, if the bank arranging the financing is also willing to underwrite a substantial part of the total amount (and therefore pratically guarantees an exact amount of proceeds from the loan) then the borrower doesn't run the risk of being unsuccessful in the syndication phase;
- can often appeal to their long-term relations with the borrower. This factor can be particularly important in cases where, as often happens, the borrower explicitly wants the involvement of banks with which it normally conducts its business.

Instead, compared to commercial banks, those that adopt the integrated service approach normally have superior expertise in terms of consultancy, acquired either by a traditional presence in the sector or as a result of targeted acquisitions of merchant or investment banks.

And lastly, compared with both types of intermediary, the integrated service bank can offer sponsors all the benefits of so-called "one-stop shopping", so avoiding the burden in terms of time and expense of having to interact with two different counterparties in various stages of the project's lifecycle.

## 3.5 Conclusions

The analysis of data conducted in the previous pages means that certain overall conclusions can be drawn, particularly with reference to the Italian situation.

The first conclusion concerns the development of the project finance market over the past ten years. Starting in the early Nineties when initial experiments in project financing concerned the power sector (especially for cogeneration projects), over time the project finance technique has spread to other sectors, often because of the public sector's need for a more substantial involvement of private capital in partially self-financed projects. Today project financing covers a very wide number of application sectors. This has also brought about a change in the essential features of the transaction, especially as regards risks remaining with the SPV and, consequently, for its financers. In our opinion current market trends favor projects in which the market risk is not completely excluded and, therefore, left (at least in part) as a risk for the vehicle company. Intermediaries should take this factor into account when setting adequate pricing given the risk a particular transaction involves.

The second conclusion, instead, concerns the trend on the offer side. It has been seen that the market is based on an oligopolistic competitive model, especially at global and European levels. As regards Italy, it is reasonable to assume there will be a clear-cut division of market share based on transaction size. For larger transactions it can be assumed there will be a consolidation of today's financial intermediary positions in the League Tables, as operators take positions as co-lead arrangers in cooperation with major European and American competitors. As for smaller transactions, foreign banks or international advisers don't find the service offer particularly remunerative. Especially in the public works sector involving local public parties, strong territorial presence and client relations are two important assets for domestic and, to a lesser degree, local banks. Proximity to and knowledge of the client means even not particularly large deals can be assembled at generally acceptable costs. It is more difficult to imagine a presence of these intermediaries in transactions involving large amounts, unless simply in a participant role.

# 4 Structured Leasing Transactions

Stefano Caselli

## 4.1 Introduction

The aim of this chapter is to investigate and highlight the typical features of the transactions and market covering a family of instruments known as structured leasing deals, namely, complex, intricate deals assembled ad hoc, with an organizational and contractual framework that is grafted onto a leasing transaction.

Given the tenor of the definition, the first task is to establish the boundary between conventional and structured leasing transactions in a clear and correct manner. This would seem to be very complicated given both the novel nature of these instruments and the objective difficulty of establishing distinctions that may then prove arbitrary and excessively theoretical. In this sense the decisive factor is to examine what options and practices have been adopted by financial intermediaries at a global market level and, above all, what the most advanced organizational-contractual forms are. This, in order to survey on a supply-and-demand basis the needs behind the demand for structured transactions and the characteristics of products proposed by operators in the sector.

To achieve the above, this chapter has been structured in four parts.

The first part tackles the issue of defining structured leasing deals by examining their characteristics within the broader context of the structured finance and leasing market, both in terms of indications coming from the international financial market and the limited scientific references available. The second part, instead, focuses on the market set-up, highlighting basic trends, its size and internal organization, and the types of financial intermediary operating within it. This necessarily means looking at the international scenario, both because this is a new issue and, above all, because of the very nature of the transactions themselves, which in terms of size and intrinsic features are such that it would not be easy to refer to one single, specific domestic market.

The third part looks at the leasing transaction from a tax standpoint, examining its distinctive features and possible room for maneuver, which is fundamental when assembling a structured transaction. At this juncture it would appear significant to conduct a sensitivity analysis to measure the effects on cost of capital produced by changes in the basic components of the leasing contract and tax implications for the lessee. Lastly, the fourth part examines the issue of classifying and analyzing structured leasing transactions in order to provide an initial classification scheme, illustrating their characteristics from a standpoint of the transaction's basic set-up, tax and financial architecture and main results achieved.

## 4.2 Basic characteristics of structured leasing transactions

A detailed definition of structured leasing transactions is hampered by a series of factors that limit possibilities to outline the significant characteristics in a sufficiently clear manner. These factors are the combined result of a number of situations, above all linked to the initial development phase of structured leasing and low diffusion of the necessary operational know-how required to manage this instrument. As for the first point, structured leasing is essentially a new type of transaction, confirmed by the fact that there were very few references to it or analyses in specialized publications until early in 2000. Initial considerations on this subject – have only appeared recently, together with the first accounts of transactions assembled by specia lized financial intermediaries.[1] As a result structured leasing was recognized as a new transaction and an independent form of leasing within the structured finance and asset finance sector. On the second point, a certain reticence of operators who have acquired significant expertise in the sector seems to be justified by their need to safeguard know-how believed to constitute an essential competitive edge and by the considerable level of financial resources involved. With specific reference to the Italian financial market, it should also be mentioned that

---

[1] Works published on the subject of structured leasing transactions appear to be few and far between, and so reference has to be made to studies carried out in the research environment and activities in closely associated operational areas. For this reason there is one type of material that covers the subject directly and another, broader category of material that, when referring to conventional and project leasing, deals with the issue of "structuring a leasing transaction". The first two publications in the first category date from the Nineties: Bernstein (1993)and Keating (1996). Later, starting with the proceedings of the 18th World Leasing Convention (2000) and in those covering the three following editions, specific reference is made to "structured leasing" in debates and published as a defined, independent type of deal. References in this regard are: Keating (2003), IFC (2003), Leaseurope (2002). In the second, broader category of publications, "benchmark" reference works on project leasing are: Grant and Gent (1992), Ascari and Albisetti (1996), Nevitt (1997), Ruozi et al. (1997).

structured leasing is in its infancy and only slowly making inroads, as can be seen from continuing recourse to the conventional form of leasing, above all for extremely large transactions.

Examining transactions about which there is news, above all those that have taken place in more progressive financial markets as regards the use of financial leasing (USA, UK and, in part, France and Germany), certain essential elements can be pinpointed that enable reasonably accurate identification of structured leasing transactions, distinguishing them from conventional leasing and, in part, from project finance leasing, with which they can often overlap.

While there is still no precise, accepted definition at international level, structured leasing is intended as those transactions that, to differing degrees, develop an organized synergy between funding policy, asset and risk management of the underlying asset and tax-based finance. The aim being to manage the need for complex financing in a creative manner, as opposed to just raising funds by mobilizing a party's wealth by means of recourse to the leasing instrument (see Figure 4.1). It follows that the very essence of such transactions is the existence of an asset and the simultaneous and indispensable presence of the above three distinctive elements, which can be combined in different manners depending on the specific need profile. This very possibility to exploit a different interaction between the factors concerned makes structured leasing a highly versatile tool. So versatile that its use can range from transactions in the corporate finance context – with a view to financing the company – to those in high-profile private banking.

In analytical terms, a structured leasing deal formally comprises a financial leasing contract concerning various types of underlying asset. In this sense, at first sight structured leasing would not seem to be an original, distinct type of financial transaction but instead a type of financing lease referring to a very clear category of assets.[2] The structure of the transaction calls for a succession of installments over the entire duration of the operation and a final one-time payment made as a call option on the underlying asset. As in all leasing contracts the structure of the installments can vary based on whether there is a fixed or variable interest rate, a larger first installment and indexing to a specific foreign currency. The very presence of the final option call means the user can link the leasing transaction to a later financing transaction to cover cash required in the event of purchase at the end.

---

[2] For a review of the basic features of leasing transactions see Carretta and De Laurentis (1998).

**Fig. 4.1.** Distinctive elements of structured leasing transactions

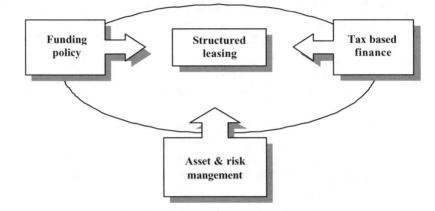

Source: the author

The conventional nature of a leasing transaction makes it particularly effective if the value of the underlying asset is high compared to the financial situation of the intended user, given that in the event of outright purchase this would create a financial strain and also a need to govern risks inherent in the asset's characteristics. This, inasmuch as a leasing transaction can:

– enable contract terms to be modulated in relation to the lessee's cash flow structure;
– generate governable tax benefits, with a different sequence and structure than is achieved by depreciating the asset and covering attendant financial costs arising from the funding policy adopted to purchase the asset;
– finance the possible call option at the end of the leasing transaction.

The three factors mentioned make a leasing contract a very flexible instrument that enables the lessee to position the deal in an optimal manner in relation to cash flow structure, its sustainability over time and the distribution of tax benefits.

While these considerations remain valid whatever the type of underlying asset, it should be emphasized that the assembly of a structured transaction is much more significant when the value of the asset is considerable (whether in absolute terms or relevant to the lessee's potential) and when tax benefits accruing from the leasing transaction are potentially greater and more flexible than those obtained by depreciating the underlying asset and considering financial costs associated with the funding source. This is also consistent with tax-based financing techniques, in which the aim when assembling the transaction is to maximize available financial maneuvering room with reference to tax variables by analyzing the sensitivity of the transaction itself. As a result, assets typically found in structured leasing transactions are, in order of decreasing importance:[3]

– real estate of various types and uses
– industrial plant and equipment
– ships and aircraft

The decreasing importance of the three asset classes for big-ticket leasing is linked to the versatility and potential represented by utilizing the structured leasing instrument. If in the case of real estate the underlying asset could refer to various types of corporate needs or private purposes (with a view to mobilizing a business person's wealth) in the case of industrial plant and equipment and, above all, ships and aircraft, the need in question tends to be exclusively corporate. Furthermore, real estate can be utilized independent of the asset's use for any given business or personal purpose, in that it represents a form of investment in its own right, utilizable merely as a means to produce value.

The organizational methods and objectives of the transaction can effectively be modeled bearing in mind the nature and role of the asset from the standpoint of:

– its nature in terms of product category
– its nature from a legal standpoint

In fact, the underlying asset can have different product-category and legal profiles, which condition the financial flows and risk set-up for the leasing transaction. In the first case (product-category profile), real estate can be residential, administrative, commercial, industrial or even infrastructural. In the second case (legal profile), the asset can already exist and be owned by the lessee, can already exist but be owned by a third party or may even not yet be built. By overlapping the two profiles a map of possible structured leasing transactions is obtained that highlights the complexity and level of internal differentiation of such deals (see Figure 4.2).

---

[3] On this subject see: World Leasing Convention (2000), Leaseurope (2002).

**Fig. 4.2.** Map of structured leasing transactions based on the nature of the underlying asset

| | | | LEGAL PROFILE OF UNDERLYING ASSET | | |
| --- | --- | --- | --- | --- | --- |
| | | | Existing and owned by lessee | Existing and owned by a third party | To be built |
| **PRODUCT-CATEGORY PROFILE OF UNDERLYING ASSET** | Real estate | Residential | | | |
| | | Administrative | | | |
| | | Commercial | | | |
| | | Industrial | | | |
| | | Infrastructural | | | |
| | Plant & equipment | | | | |
| | Ships & aircraft | | | | |

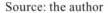

| Pure sale & leaseback or structured leasing | Leasing or structured leasing or project leasing | Leasing or mainly project finance |
| --- | --- | --- |

Source: the author

   In particular it can be observed that while the asset's product category heavily conditions the nature and intensity of financial and equity risks associated with the transaction, the legal profile, if the asset already exists, conditions the financial structure and overall arrangement of the transaction itself.[4] For instance, residential, and to a degree, administrative real estate, ships and aircraft represent, all things being equal, a lower financial and equity risk because they tend to have a better defined market value. This, because there is a much wider secondary market and often, as in the case of real estate, few or even no factors that can generate a negative impact on the asset's value. Vice versa, commercial, industrial and infrastructural real estate, and above all industrial plant and equipment represent an increasing financial and equity risk because of a progressive reduction of the role played by the secondary market and an increase in factors generating risks of an equity nature. Looking at the transaction from a legal profile standpoint highlights that, given the same asset product-category profile, an already existing asset owned by the lessee technically makes it a sale and leaseback, as the purpose of the transaction

---

[4] In this regard the interpretation in terms of legal profile and product-category profile can be extended and broken down further by considering size and whether the deal is of a domestic or international nature. This latter distinction has a significant effect inasmuch as it introduces the aspect of country risk, which interacts with the various other risk aspects of the transaction .

has an impact on liquidity of the lessee's assets. The case of an asset owned by a third party is entirely different: if the asset is residential or administrative real estate then in essence it is just like any other financial leasing deal. Instead if it is commercial, industrial or infrastructural real estate, industrial plant and equipment or ships and aircraft, the leasing transaction progressively becomes an integral part of the lessee's business. Hence installments must be structured in such as way as to increasingly take cash flows produced by the asset underlying the leasing transaction very closely into account, making it de facto more like project leasing.[5] In the case, instead, of real estate or plant to be built (so-called "to-be-built leasing"), the leasing transaction can take the shape of project leasing. This, because the weight of the "project" element in the transaction (linked to a project still to be realized over a number of stages) must be seen together with the overall planning, construction and post-construction risks associated with the asset concerned. In these terms, the distinctive element of the transaction is its "project" nature, which encapsulates the equity and financial impacts throughout the various stages of completion.[6] In this sense, the transaction is undoubtedly like a true project financing deal.

## 4.3 Structure of the structured leasing transaction market

### 4.3.1 Basic trends and the international market set-up

In Europe leasing transactions in the real estate, plant and equipment and, partially, ship and aircraft sectors are substantial (Table 4.1) and growing strongly both in absolute and relative terms, namely, in relation to overall investment in individual geographical areas (Table 4.2). The reasons for the expansion of big-ticket leasing and growth of its importance depend on certain general and specific factors. The former are linked to big-ticket leasing per se, regardless of the lessee's objective and the specific product-category or legal nature of the real estate or other underlying asset. The second are specifically linked to the asset's legal profile and therefore to the type of leasing transaction – conventional, sale and leaseback, project or structured – it is intended to assemble. Clearly, in addition to the above

---

[5] On this issue see evaluations made in Ruozi et al. (1997).
[6] Particularly as regards project finance transactions, see considerations made in the study of this specific issue.

there are other country-specific, occasional or structural factors that add to the convenience of leasing transactions and fuel their growth[7].

With reference to general factors, those stimulating demand for big-ticket leasing transactions can be summarized as follows:

- transfer of the risk and risk management of the asset
- exploitation of tax benefits and in-country and extra-country tax loopholes
- overall investment financing, even including a full-service technique
- progressive extension of the average term for leasing transactions, with a consequent expansion of the types of project and parties that can be financed

**Table 4.1.** Size of the European leasing market (leased assets at en of 2002; data in billions of euros)

| COUNTRY | REAL ESTATE LEASING | EQUIPMENT LEASING | SHIP & AIRCRAFT LEASING |
|---------|---------------------|-------------------|-------------------------|
| Austria | 3.5 | 7.5 | 1.3 |
| Belgium | 0.5 | 5.0 | 0.2 |
| Denmark | 0.5 | 4.7 | 0.2 |
| Finland | 0.5 | 3.5 | 0.1 |
| France | 12.5 | 18.0 | 7.6 |
| Germany | 8.7 | 38.5 | 4.7 |
| Ireland | 0 | 4.5 | 0.1 |
| Italy | 7.7 | 22.0 | 2.1 |
| Netherlands | 1.0 | 8.0 | 1.1 |
| Portugal | 4.0 | 9.0 | 1.2 |
| UK | 18.5 | 35.0 | 4.9 |
| Spain | 6.5 | 12.6 | 2.1 |
| Sweden | 0.5 | 7.0 | 0.2 |

Source: authors' table based on European Commission (2002), Leaseurope (2002, 2004)

Risk transfer is an intrinsic characteristic of leasing transactions and, in cases where the lessee is capable enough, there can also be the further, broader and more complete service of asset risk management. If this is true in general for any type of leasing transaction, the presence of significant

---

[7] The above maneuvers have been used widely in the past, above all in Eastern European countries, to attract foreign investors and sustain growth of the investment process at aggregate level. Moreover, similar actions can also be seen in the US market in terms of tax-based leasing transactions that offer strong tax incentives for certain specific real estate leasing transactions. In this regard see Caselli (1996).

risks in the case of real estate, plant and equipment or ships and aircraft means this aspect has added value and so makes it a factor contributing to market growth. This emerges in a significant manner, for instance, in the case of to-be-built leasing, where the lessor shoulders the entire risk structure associated with the transaction, de facto taking on the role of risk manager. In this sense, with an eye to exploiting risk management as an integral service element of the transaction, numerous lessors coordinate their activities with other parties, such as insurance companies or industrial operators, in order to offer a long-term integrated service. Indeed, this is a characteristic feature of project finance transactions, a field with which big-ticket leasing overlaps in the form of project leasing.

**Table 4.2.** Penetration level in the European leasing market (leased assets at the end of 2002; data expressed as the percentage of leased assets to total investments at country level)

| COUNTRY | REAL ESTATE LEASING | EQUIPMENT LEASING | SHIP & AIRCRAFT LEASING |
| --- | --- | --- | --- |
| Austria | 8% | 16% | 25% |
| Belgium | 3% | 10% | 16% |
| Denmark | 5% | 12% | 16% |
| Finland | 2% | 12% | 11% |
| France | 8% | 15% | 29% |
| Germany | 10% | 19% | 27% |
| Ireland | 0% | 26% | 16% |
| Italy | 30% | 16% | 20% |
| Netherlands | 2% | 13% | 18% |
| Portugal | 9% | 21% | 15% |
| UK | 15% | 24% | 25% |
| Spain | 3% | 14% | 18% |
| Sweden | 2% | 26% | 16% |

Source: authors' table based on European Commission (2002), Leaseurope (2002, 2004)

Exploitation of tax benefits refers to taking advantage of possible differences in tax treatment between leasing and other sources of financing, with the aim of significantly reducing the net tax liability produced by the deal, or in other words the impact on the lessee's cost of capital. The above tax benefits can be either in-country or extra-country. For instance, in the first case tax legislation in the country where the transaction takes place most likely grants a considerable tax benefit for real estate leasing transactions, so making them attractive. In the second case, independent of the in-country benefit the deal is structured in a way that it (also or in alternative) takes advantage of tax benefits in a country other than that in which the transaction takes place. This is achieved by using a vehicle company domiciled in the other country, which assumes the role of lessee and then proceeds to rent the underlying asset to the effective lessee.

While the above considerations can apply to any type of underlying asset, in the majority of countries at international level three significant factors can be noted that make real estate leasing particularly attractive.[8]

- The minimum duration for real estate leasing is always significantly shorter than the depreciation period prescribed by tax legislation for the underlying asset. As this differential is normally greater than for other asset classes, this means real estate leasing has a significant potential for reducing the net tax effect of the transaction.
- The tax effects of the leasing transaction can be governed based on the duration of the lease, the amount of the one-time first installment and cost of the call option. This enables the lessee to combine benefits deriving from the tax reduction as regards costs with accurate financial planning.
- Often real estate leasing enjoys ad hoc tax benefits created by legislators to enable companies to undertake substantial but risk-free investment programs. This has been and still is the case in Eastern European countries and in other development areas where, moreover, these concessions interact with the development programs of international financial institutions such as, for instance, International Finance Corporation.

Overall financing of the investment itself is also a structural and, in a sense, traditional feature of leasing transactions. However, as already mentioned in the case of risks, the high average value of real estate, plant and equipment or ship and aircraft deals makes this specific aspect particularly attractive and in effect boosts the growth of demand in this market. In addition, more and more frequently proposals offer a full-service solution, in which the lessor provides a series of ancillary services to asset management that supplement and enhance the financing service. Examples of these ancillary services are maintenance, insurance, placement of the redeemed asset in the secondary market or, in the case of real estate, overall management of the asset.[9]

---

[8] In this regard see Walton (1999).

[9] As regards growth of ancillary services based on the full-service technique for big-ticket deals, see the international market survey and review of possible models presented by Equipment Leasing Association (2002).

**Table 4.3.** Average duration of leasing transactions in Europe (average data at end of 2002)

| COUNTRY | REAL ESTATE LEASING | | | |
|---|---|---|---|---|
| | UP TO 8 YEARS INCLUSIVE | FROM 9 TO 16 YEARS INCLUSIVE | FROM 17 TO 20 YEARS INCLUSIVE | OVER 20 YEARS |
| Austria | 4.6% | 37.1% | 45.4% | 12.9% |
| Belgium | 0.3% | 93.8% | 3.1% | 2.8% |
| Denmark | 53.4% | 28.6% | 5.7% | 12.3% |
| Finland | 100.0% | 0.0% | 0.0% | 0.0% |
| France | 10.0% | 90.0% | 0.0% | 0.0% |
| Germany | 11.4% | 29.5% | 29.5% | 29.5% |
| Ireland | 0.0% | 0.0% | 0.0% | 0.0% |
| Italy | 100.0% | 0.0% | 0.0% | 0.0% |
| Netherlands | 0.0% | 100.0% | 0.0% | 0.0% |
| Portugal | 8.9% | 89.4% | 1.2% | 0.4% |
| UK | 0.0% | 0.0% | 100.0% | 0.0% |
| Spain | 0.0% | 85.0% | 15.0% | 0.0% |
| Sweden | 38.5% | 61.5% | 0.0% | 0.0% |
| Total Europe | 46.7% | 33.5% | 10.9% | 8.9% |

**Table 4.4.** (cont.)

| COUNTRY | EQUIPMENT LEASING | | | |
|---|---|---|---|---|
| | UP TO 2 YEARS INCLUSIVE | FROM 3 TO 5 YEARS INCLUSIVE | FROM 6 TO 10 YEARS INCLUSIVE | OVER 10 YEARS |
| Austria | 10.0% | 76.4% | 11.1% | 2.5% |
| Belgium | 9.2% | 79.9% | 10.8% | 0.2% |
| Denmark | 6.3% | 71.3% | 21.6% | 0.8% |
| Finland | 18.7% | 68.1% | 12.8% | 0.4% |
| France | 0.3% | 87.8% | 10.0% | 1.9% |
| Germany | 14.7% | 70.7% | 10.7% | 4.0% |
| Ireland | 0.0% | 95.0% | 5.0% | 0.0% |
| Italy | 4.8% | 93.5% | 5.0% | 0.0% |
| Netherlands | 0.0% | 100.0% | 0.0% | 0.0% |
| Portugal | 5.6% | 89.0% | 4.6% | 0.7% |
| UK | 21.1% | 58.2% | 9.5% | 11.2% |
| Spain | 2.2% | 93.7% | 4.1% | 0.0% |
| Sweden | 12.0% | 71.7% | 8.5% | 7.8% |
| Total Europe | 11.3% | 76.7% | 8.0% | 4.0% |

Source: authors' tables based on European Commission (2002), Leaseurope (2002, 2004)

Lastly, extending the average duration of big-ticket leasing deals is a basic trend found typically in the international leasing market and responds to two different requirements to create growth.

The first is a thrust to broaden the market by "type of customer": in fact, creating long-term leasing contracts makes recourse to leasing transactions more accessible to a larger number of parties, who appreciate the improved financial sustainability this solution offers.[10]

The second instead concerns the drive to broaden the market "by type of asset": long-term contracts mean both the lessor and lessee can proceed to finance projects that, given their big-ticket size, could not have been repaid over a "conventional" timeframe. Examples of this are the real estate leasing transactions developed in Germany, which have a duration ranging from 25-30 years against a conventional duration of 8-12 years (see Table 4.3).

With reference to specific factors, aspects that stimulate growth in demand for big-ticket leasing must instead be differentiated according to the legal profile of the underlying asset.

In the case of existing real estate, plant and equipment or ships and aircraft already owned by the lessee, apart from general factors, the specific boost in demand is stimulated by the lessee's objective to modify the combination of risk and return. In fact, the sale and leaseback technique allows the owner of the asset to sell it, obtain substantial liquid resources available for investment and obtain increased tax benefits – above all in the case of real estate – when compared to depreciation, and then to reacquire the asset at the end of the leasing transaction. The sequence of these effects highlights how a leasing deal competes both by offering securitization alternatives as opposed to a closed real estate fund investment and also enables the lessee to use such a transaction as support for achieving highly differentiated objectives. In this second case the factors stimulating demand can be summarized as follows:[11]

– acceleration of tax benefits by transforming depreciation into leasing installments

---

[10] See Lasfer and Levis (1998).

[11] The stimulus to demand mentioned represents the "virtuous" factors that encourage users to apply the sale and leaseback framework to big-ticket assets. There are undoubtedly also other stimuli, for instance the need to reduce company debt by using financial resources coming from real estate rather than plant and equipment. In this case the transaction can involve considerable margins of risk as, on the one hand, the company doesn't acquire resources to sustain an investment and growth process and, on the other, it loses ownership of part of the company's net worth dedicated to business growth.

- increase in company structural margin and freeing up of financial resources to sustain investment and growth processes
- investment of wealth and net worth in a private banking mode

In all cases mentioned the sale and leaseback technique can be used in a conventional or unconventional manner. In the former case the owner of the asset becomes the lessee as a result of the leasing transaction; in the latter, the owner can nominate an associated third party as the lessee. This is done when the third party has a more favorable tax profile (either inherent or based on the tax system under which it operates) than the asset's owner.

Apart from normal factors, in the case of an existing asset owned by a third party or real estate to be built, the specific boost for demand is above all the availability of a flexible instrument that can be modeled (in tax and financial terms) to match the typical requirements of large-scale transactions and, above all, in to-be-built projects.

### 4.3.2 State of the art as regards offer

The many types of deal that can be assembled in the big-ticket leasing field de facto leads to a many-faceted segmentation of the market. This can not only be seen in terms of the breakdown used in Figure 4.2 based on the characteristics of the underlying asset, but also as regards the geographical positioning of the deal, which can either be domestic or international. This means a framework for analysis comprises the asset product-category, the asset's legal status and the relevant geographical context, which effectively impacts the characteristics of financial intermediaries in terms of choice of positioning and specialization.

The structure of competition found in the international market and within individual domestic markets is complex. In general terms the following profiles can be identified for intermediaries active in developing this market:

- international merchant and investment banks
- leasing companies
- intermediaries specialized in real estate financing, equipment financing and ship and aircraft financing
- private banking boutiques
- family offices
- supranational financial institutions

The international merchant and investment banks operate on a global scale (Merril Lynch, Morgan Stanley DW and Goldman Sachs) or over large geographical areas (Deutsche Bank, UBS, Credit Suisse, Nomura and Mitsubishi) with an offer that covers the entire spectrum of corporate finance services.[12] Banks always have a dedicated real estate division whose mission as presented to customers is their ability to satisfy all financing and associated management needs in relation to real estate business rather than other big-ticket assets (although in certain cases there is also a plant and equipment or ship and aircraft division). Positioning is both at international and domestic level, given that there are regional banks operating in individual country markets. In the majority of cases the transactions assembled by these banks in the real estate field are big-ticket deals and cover all the various types of transaction examined. In terms of innovation, this is above all their ability to react to changes in the legislative and tax fields within the various countries concerned, where the aim is to prepare contractual solutions with tax profiles that are attractive for customers.

Leasing companies are a highly heterogeneous group inasmuch as it includes large operators competing on a global scale and more marginal operators who do business within specific areas of a single domestic market. In any event (with only rare exceptions like, for instance, CommerzLeasing und Immobilien AG) leasing companies address the market as universal operators specialized over the entire spectrum of leasing transactions. But in fact only the very largest operators can assemble leasing deals for all "product-category type and legal type" combinations for real estate, plant and equipment or ship and aircraft assets, and so to a degree resemble the international merchant and investment banks. Instead small and medium-sized operators occupy less complex and lower-risk market segments, limiting themselves to leasing deals for already existing residential and administrative real estate. In the latter case the ability to innovate appears to be low.

Specialized real estate financial intermediaries are instead a small, more homogeneous group, inasmuch as the focus on the real estate segment requires a substantial critical mass and normally a coverage at national level. A review of the market reveals that while merchant and investment banks cover the international, mainly big-ticket market, and leasing companies span a wide size range, specialized intermediaries are domestic-

---

[12] In this regard see Forestieri (2003).

sized national operators.[13] Furthermore, there are almost no operators specialized in only the plant and equipment or ship and aircraft segments.

From a company standpoint, specialized financial intermediaries tend to be independents (for example, Depfa Bank) or are part of the real estate construction and sale sector (e.g. KG Allgemeine Leasing GmbH & Co) or yet again, financial group product companies (e.g. Deutsche Immoblien Leasing GmbH). Generally speaking, given their basic strategic focus specialized intermediaries cover the entire spectrum of real estate leasing transactions and are market leaders and innovators. However, in the big-ticket deal area and at international level they meet tough competition from international merchant and investment banks.

Private banking boutiques only entered the real estate leasing scene recently. This, because they wanted to offer customers an all-in management service for that part of their wealth invested in real estate assets. Inevitably the positioning of private banking boutiques is almost exclusively in the segment comprising existing assets owned by the lessee (normally residential or administrative and, in some cases, commercial real estate), where the aim of transactions assembled is rationalization and tax optimization or investment and value creation by utilizing the unconventional sale and leaseback formula.[14]

As regards the mission of family offices, this is completely in line with that of private bankers, given the overlap of business areas in which both operate.

Supranational financial institutions operate in the real estate leasing sector to provide support for economic growth in developing countries. In this sense transactions mainly fall within the to-be-built, big-ticket area, in particular for infrastructure projects (hospitals, bridges, power stations, etc.). The leading institution in the sector is IFC (International Finance Corporation) The World Bank Group, which continually uses the leasing technique in the real estate and plant and equipment sectors because it can:[15]

---

[13] On this point it should be observed that the presence of specialized intermediaries in the real estate financing segment is particularly strong in Germany. In fact, the League Table prepared by Leaseurope in 2002 covering the main operators in the leasing sector (by asset and by volume) showed that in the top 100 positions at European level there were as many as six German operators specialized in real estate. No other European country shows such high-profile performance.

[14] On this issue see considerations in Caselli (to be published).

[15] On this issue see considerations in Albisetti (2001).

– guarantee adequate management of risks throughout the entire lifecycle of a project;
– enable IFC to be in direct charge of the project because of ownership;
– enable the future owner to learn how to realize and manage a project.

So presence of supranational institutions plays a critical role and significantly boosts the big-ticket leasing market and in particular promotes innovation in the risk and legal management fields of transactions, which are typically of a project type.

Specifically as regards the Italian market, there is only a trace of the breakdown reported above, given that the majority of the offer is in the hands of leasing companies owned by the major national banking groups. While in terms of size many of these are substantial at European level, their offer is mainly focused on small and medium-ticket leasing. Looking specifically at structured leasing, the basic traits that emerge compared with trends found in the international market are as follows:

– Asset transfer and risk management is not a factor that the offer exploits as a priority.
– There tends to be exploitation of tax differences and in-country loopholes, but there is almost none at an extra-country level.
– Exploitation of full-service platforms is almost exclusively geared to the retail market, using a technique that is more similar to operating rather than big-ticket leasing.[16]
– Progressive extension of leasing duration in a big-ticket sense is still not underway, although the real estate leasing market is showing strong growth.

### 4.3.3 Considerations on certain critical aspects found in the market

While the big-ticket leasing market is experiencing a substantial growth trend and significant diversification as regards type of user situations and needs, there are a number of factors that pose obstacles to its growth and diffusion. The above factors refer to both elements concerning demand and, above all, to critical management junctures on the offer side. In particular, on both sides factors representing obstacles increase in importance with the size of the transaction and as regards certain more complex types of real estate (industrial, infrastructural) and to-be-built deals. Referring back to the framework proposed in Figure 4.2, this means

---

[16] See Carretta and Fiordalisi (2000).

the complexity of the transaction and constraints when assembling it increase with a move from the upper left corner (residential real estate – already existing real estate owned by the lessee) to the lower right corner (infrastructural real estate and plant and equipment – asset to be built).

With reference to the demand side, the main factor putting a brake on requests for big-ticket leasing deals stems from two elements.

Firstly, the strong tax acceleration generated by leasing deals and limited duration of the deal itself require a stable level of taxable profits over time and a financial position consistent with the succession of installments. This means that only companies with good liquidity (and the ability to plan and manage it), but above all the ability to generate profits, can organize a big-ticket leasing transaction to good effect. In the absence of these two conditions the leasing transaction may generate a dangerous boomerang effect on the company's overall management equilibrium and even solvency.

Secondly, exploitation of in-country and extra-country tax differences makes tax benefits the center of gravity for the deal. Any changes for the worse in tax legislation over time will not only reduce the transaction's economic justification but, above all, may jeopardize the lessee's ability to sustain the transaction itself. In other words, the tax risk in terms of legislative volatility becomes an obstacle to the growth of these transactions. This is even more probable the more such transactions grow by using the leverage of extra-country tax differences with an eye to assembling frameworks to exploit loopholes and maximize available financial maneuvering room.

With reference instead to the offer side, there are three management constraints that limit or even kill an inclination to participate in the big-ticket leasing market.

First, the substantial size of assets involved in such transactions represents a rigidity factor in the asset side of financial intermediary balance sheets. This, both because of an impact on structural margin and eligible capital ratio, but above all because of risks associated with the asset. From this standpoint, if the financial intermediary doesn't have a sufficient networking capability with other operators, either enabling it to organize offer pools or, above all, contracts for risk sharing and transfer, then the expected remuneration profile would not appear to be consistent with the type and size of the risks taken. This aspect becomes unacceptably critical in to-be-built leasing where, in addition to an increase in the number of risks, there is also the issue of the intermediary's civil and criminal liability as regards the construction site for the work concerned.

Secondly, as the real estate asset is owned by the financial intermediary/lessor, in the event of the lessee's insolvency, all things being equal, this increases the loss given default (LGD) value underlying the financing. This, because even if the market value of the asset is substantial, the recovery rate value relevant to real estate leasing is particularly low. This means that in the overall transaction framework, capital absorption for the lessor is significant both because of the size of the deal and its LGD value. The end result is a rationalization impact within the financial intermediary's portfolio that affects the amount or cost of the transaction.

Lastly, in the specific case of sale and leaseback transactions, the lessor's purchase of an asset owned by the lessee can generate dangerous setbacks in the event the lessee should become insolvent. This, in terms of the impact on withdrawal of bankruptcy and also possible liability, issues that the financial intermediary may be summoned to demonstrate before the court from the standpoint of acceleration of the lessee's insolvent status.[17]

## 4.4 Analysis of the tax profile for leasing relevant to value creation in structured operations

### 4.4.1 Overview of tax variables relevant to capital structure

The review of factors behind the growth of the big-ticket leasing market highlighted the centrality of taxation. This is the pivot in transactions that enable a lessee to achieve significant tax savings, in any event much more than by using other financing and investment strategies, above all in real estate. In other words, the tax variable becomes a powerful tool for creating economic maneuvering room to reduce the cost of capital for its users. This means lessees can use the tax benefit this transaction provides in the most appropriate manner to achieve their objectives, bearing in mind their financial and balance sheet profile.

An understanding of this economic maneuvering room can be gained by reviewing the taxation framework in force in the country concerned, examined in terms of tax deductibility of costs for borrowers of financial resources. As regards Italy, the regulatory framework is quite well-defined and stable (Table 4.4), and in the specific case of leasing even tends to reflect regulations found in the majority of other European countries.[18]

---

[17] On this issue see considerations and legislative/regulatory references in Tagliavini (2001).
[18] On this subject see the survey of tax regulations carried out by Carretta and Fiordelisi (2000). Also see Dessy (2001).

**Table 4.4.** Tax profile for borrowers of financial resources based on the Italian system as of 1 January 2004

| Source of financing | Type of tax | | |
|---|---|---|---|
| | IRES or IRE[19] | IRAP | IVA |
| Debt | Full deductibility of financial charges and expenses, except as regards thin capitalization rules for resources contributed by qualified stockholders. | Non-deductibility of financial charges. Full deductibility of the expenses. | Outside field of application. |
| Financial leasing | Full deductibility of "average installment" and expenses provided the leasing contract has a duration equal to at least half the asset's depreciation life for tax purposes. The exception is real estate, for which duration of leasing must be at least eight years. | Only full deductibility of the asset value and expenses, provided the leasing contract has a duration equal to at least half the asset's normal depreciation life for tax purposes. The exception is real estate, for which duration of leasing must be at least eight years. | All elements of the contract are subject to IVA. |

---

[19] Not distinguishing between IRES and IRE means that rules for tax deductibility for the three financing source categories are identical, although the tax treatment is different. Clearly, however, in the case of partnerships the impact on the income statement for tax purposes will be different depending on the average rate of IRE tax. The above rules are the same as those that were in force up to 31 December 2003, after which the previous IRPEG (corporate income tax) and IRPEF (personal income tax) were replaced by IRES and IRE.

**Table 4.4** (cont.)

| Equity | The tax effect is governed by changes in equity that took place between 30 September 1996 and 30 June 2001, according to the DIT mechanism. From 1 January 2004 the DIT mechanism was completely abolished and so now there is no tax benefit linked to equity financing. | No effect. | Outside field of application. |
|--------|--------|--------|--------|

Source: the author

With reference to borrowers, tax legislation differentiates between three types of financing source: debt (in whatever form), financial leasing and equity.[20] Debt financing benefits from a tax effect of 28.75%, namely, 33% for IRES (corporate income tax) net of 4.25% for IRAP (regional tax on productive activities). The tax structure for leasing, instead, cannot be defined a priori but depends on a series of factors, such as the type of underlying asset, duration, the borrower's IVA (value added tax) profile and month in which the transaction starts. This means that based on the case in point financial leasing can either have a much better or worse tax profile than debt financing. Lastly, equity financing benefited from the limited, partial effect of the DIT during the 1996-2001 period. However, the DIT was abrogated starting 1 January 2004 thus recourse to equity doesn't give companies any tax advantage. So, all things being equal, the latter is the most costly financing strategy.

Concerning the above, it should be emphasized that while tax variables in the Italian system are highly volatile, rules regarding deductibility of charges relevant to the source of financing and subdivision into the three categories – debt, leasing and equity financing – have essentially remained stable over time. Moreover, introduction by the legislature of a thin capitalization mechanism starting 2004 tends, on the one hand, to reduce the convenience of recourse to debt beyond a given level of financial

[20] For an exhaustive evaluation of tax effects on corporate financing decisions see Caselli and Gatti (2003).

leverage adopted by a company and, on the other, redirects use of stockholder resources away from debt and towards equity. This means the availability of three different categories (and de facto four including thin capitalization) produces interesting room for maneuver and financial planning, above all as regards the comparison between medium-term debt and leasing. Vice versa, there is no short-term maneuvering room, while recourse to equity financing is confirmed as not being structurally convenient given that it doesn't attract any form of tax benefit.

Overall, the tax treatment for financing sources as far as direct taxation is concerned draws on provisions found in the Tax Consolidation Act (TUIR) of 22 December 1986 (Presidential Decree 917) and later modifications, above all the 2004 Budget that introduced IRES and IRE taxes. In particular, application of rules governing deductibility of interest expense relating to financing contracts means there are effectively only two categories of financing from a tax standpoint: bank financing and leasing. In the case of bank financing, interest expense can be deducted and no specific reference is made to contractual form; as for leasing, specific rules provide for the deduction of installments paid by the lessee to the lessor.Furthermore, treatment for direct taxation purposes must be integrated by provisions governing IRAP tax. This tax was introduced in 1998 by Legislative Decree 466/1997, which indicated a different tax treatment for financing compared to the IRPEG (corporate income tax) regime in the Consolidation Act. In the specific case of leasing it must be remembered that elements of the contract paid by the lessee to the lessor are subject to IVA, inasmuch as leasing is considered to be a service and, if the call option is exercised, a sale of goods. As there are no specific provisions concerning IVA on leasing, tax treatment is in accordance with general rules that apply to providing services and sale of goods, while the applicable tax rate is determined by the asset underlying the contract (Presidential Decree 633 of 26 October 1972 and later modifications).

The analysis of tax treatment must therefore distinguish between bank financing and leasing, given that the tax implications and impact for the "borrower" are substantially different.

In the case of bank financing, the only significant element from a tax standpoint is interest expense, which the borrower can deduct from taxable income provided profits are sufficient. Regulations for direct taxation in force up to 31 December 1997 provided for the deduction of interest expense for IRPEG tax purposes (the tax rate at the time was 37%) and ILOR tax (local income tax, at a rate of 16.2%), meaning a total tax rate of 53.2%. From 1 January 1998, with the introduction of IRAP tax (a tax rate of 4.25% and the possibility to increase this by up to a maximum of 1% three years after its introduction), ILOR tax was abolished and interest expense was no longer deductible for purposes of calculating the new tax liability.

In the case of financial leasing, the deductible cost component is the installment paid periodically to the lessor and, if exercised, the asset's call option price, which for all intents and purposes represents the purchase price. The rules determining whether installments can be deducted are different in the case of IRES and IRAP tax. It should also be remembered that up to 31 December 1997, the rules were the same for ILOR and IRPEG tax.

From the IRES tax standpoint, deductibility must be calculated on a day by day basis relevant to the duration of the right. This means that every fiscal year the deductible amount for installments must be calculated according to the accrual accounting method, proportionate to the duration and independent of installments effectively paid or invoiced. In this sense the maxi-installment paid by the lessee at the beginning of the contract is "spread" evenly over all the remaining installments. If the lessee exercises the call option then the price paid has to be depreciated according to the normal rate for the asset concerned, as prescribed by the Ministry of Finance. From the IRAP tax standpoint only the "capital element" of the installments can be deducted. The deductible amount is determined by dividing the lessor's asset cost (calculated as the difference between the asset price and the call option price) by the duration of the contract in terms of days. Then for every tax year the deductible amount is this "daily" value multiplied by the relevant number of days for the year concerned. As regards the depreciation rate used for the asset after the call option has been exercised, this is the same as for IRES tax purposes.

It should be observed that in the case of both IRES and IRAP tax the legislator has subordinated deductibility of the cost elements to a constraint as regards the minimum duration of the leasing contract. For assets other than real estate, installments can be deducted provided the contract duration is not less than half the normal depreciation period established by coefficients stated in Ministerial tables. As for real estate, the minimum duration is eight years. In this latter case the legislation provides a considerable tax benefit as eight years is considerably less than half the normal depreciation rate for real estate, which on an annual basis is 3%. This represents the competitive edge of a real estate leasing transaction and can be used by the lessee to achieve the various objectives underlying the transaction itself.

Lastly, mention must be made of operating leasing, for which the legislature has applied the same basic approach used for financial leasing. There are, however, two important differences that represent an appreciable tax benefit:

- The constraint concerning minimum duration has been removed with reference to both IRES and IRAP tax.
- The calculation of cost deductibility for IRAP purposes is the same as for IRES tax.

This means that an operating leasing transaction in theory has a greater "tax acceleration" effect than financial leasing, especially when compared to debt financing. Clearly, however, in the case of operating leasing the lessee doesn't have a final call option right and so this transaction is of little interest if the company's business growth depends on owning the underlying asset.[21]

## 4.4.2 Sensitivity analysis for optimizing the leasing tax profile

A review of the regulatory framework for taxation as regards sources of financing highlights two significant factors that must be considered when assembling transactions to take full advantage of tax effects, namely, so that the net tax rate reduction is greater than the initial gross interest rate (TAEG – global effective annual interest rate).

Firstly, excluding the case of equity that offers no tax benefits for a company, there is no convenience a priori between debt-based financing as opposed to leasing. The convenience of one as opposed to the other must be verified case by case with reference to the structure of the transaction concerned.

Secondly, a financial leasing transaction's tax profile is more dependent on management and contractual factors and is therefore more flexible than debt financing. The main differences are the following:

- Financial leasing has three tax profiles (IRES, IRAP and IVA tax) and consequently depends on the lessee's overall direct taxation balance, compared to only one tax profile (IRES) for debt financing.
- Financial leasing cost (installment) deductibility is based on a non-financial criterion (spreading the initial maxi-installment over the entire duration of the transaction), as opposed to a financial criterion for deduction of debt financing cost (interest expense). Consequently, given the same TAEG, the net tax rate for a leasing transaction is first and foremost highly dependant on all the temporal factors that modify the

---

[21] Moreover, these increased tax benefits afforded by operating leasing have provided a strong stimulus to create "structured" transactions that give operating leasing the same characteristics as true financial leasing. This subject is covered in later sections dealing with synthetic leasing transactions.

deal's structure. Vice versa, in the case of debt financing, again given the same TAEG, temporal factors have no effect on the net tax rate.

- The duration of financial leasing transactions is by necessity tied to the depreciation period for tax purposes. This systematically generates a difference potentially in favor of leasing if financial costs associated with the leasing and debt transaction are the same.
- Real estate leasing transactions potentially have a greater tax benefit than debt financing deals given their shorter, eight-year duration.

Given these elements, a sensitivity analysis must be performed to define the framework of relationships between factors affecting the net tax rate for these financing transactions and the net tax rates themselves. This must be done in order to obtain a framework of functional rules to assemble structured deals that fully exploit the ability of tax leverage to create value from a tax-based finance standpoint.

The sensitivity analysis concerning the net tax rate for debt financing and leasing must be conducted with reference to two macro-factor categorie s:

- contractual variables
- tax variables

The first refer to financing contract (debt or leasing) factors and include the individual percentages represented by the maxi-installment, call option price and fees, the duration of the transaction and the start-date in the year.

Instead, the second refer to exogenous tax variables inherent in the transaction and endogenous ones associated with the debtor/lessee. The exogenous tax variable is the depreciation rate for tax purposes applying to the underlying asset, given that this is established by tax legislation. The exogenous variables are instead the contracting company's depreciation policy (normal or accelerated), IRES tax profile (in profit or loss), IRAP tax profile (profit or loss[22]) and IVA tax profile (in debit or in credit).

The method for calculating and evaluating the net tax rate for financial leasing and debt financing a model must be built to determine net tax flows for the transactions concerned. For a detailed review of the tables, which in fact are already consolidated in corporate finance, see the referenced works[23] and the review in the example shown in Section 4.4.2.1.

---

[22] The assumption of a pre-tax loss in the case of IRAP is extreme, inasmuch as it would imply a negative difference between the total for items in section A and items considered as deductible in section B of the statutory income statement.

[23] In this regard see the methodology reported by Caselli (1998).

The main points emerging from the sensitivity analysis of contractual variables (Table 4.5) and tax variables (Table 4.6) give a sufficiently precise, clear reference framework.

**Table 4.5.** Sensitivity analysis, given the same TAEG and assuming sufficient taxable profits, to evaluate the impact of contractual variables on the net tax rate for leasing and debt financing

| CONTRACTUAL VARIABLES | IMPACT ON NET TAX RATE OF LEASING | IMPACT ON NET TAX RATE OF DEBT |
|---|---|---|
| Maxi-installment | Increases slightly as the maxi-installment percentage increases. | - |
| Call option price | Increases slightly as the call option price percentage increases. | - |
| Fee percentage | Decreases as the fee percentage increases, in the face of a reduction in the maxi-installment percentage. | Decreases as the fee percentage increases, in the face of a reduction for financial costs. |
| Duration of transaction | Increases heavily as the duration of the transaction lengthens. | No impact |
| Start of transaction | Increases heavily the more the start-date for the transaction moves towards the end of the year. | No impact |

Source: the author

With reference to contractual variables, the joint leasing-debt financing evaluation in cases where there are sufficient profits highlights the strong sensitivity of net tax rate to all independent variables. Vice versa, debt financing is only dependent on the percentage amount of fees, from the standpoint of cross-subsidation compared with financial charges. If these results appear predictable based on the tax regulations in force, then certain basic results must be systematized in an organic reference framework.

The close dependence of the net tax rate for leasing on temporal variables (duration and start-date) is the result of a "non-financial" rule governing deductibility of installments. The results emerging highlight the strong positive tax impact if leasing exploits the minimum possible duration granted by legislation and the effect of a start-date in the early part of the year. The positive tax impact in these cases can be so considerable that it reduces the net tax rate to lower levels than those achieved using alternative sources of debt financing, even when the TAEG is lower. Vice versa, extending the duration and moving the start-date to later in the year tends to impact the company's cost of capital considerably, de facto meaning that leasing cannot be used for tax-based transactions. In the case of the maxi-installment and option call price, instead, the relationship to net tax rate appears blander, as although there is an increase in net tax rate if either of the two components are higher, the change is marginal. This means these two contractual elements can be modified and governed quite flexibly for financial planning purposes without impacting the company's cost of capital structure.

**Table 4.6.** Sensitivity analysis, given the same TAEG, to evaluate the impact of tax variables on the net tax rate for leasing and debt financing

| TAX VARIABLES | IMPACT ON NET TAX RATE OF LEASING | IMPACT ON NET TAX RATE OF DEBT |
|---|---|---|
| Underlying asset depreciation rate | Increases strongly with an increase in the underlying asset depreciation rate. | No impact |
| Depreciation policy selected by the company | Decreases strongly with a change from accelerated to normal depreciation. | No impact |
| IRES or IRE profile | Increases depending on if there is a loss for the year. | Increases depending on if there is a loss for the year. |
| IRAP profile | Increases depending on if there is a negative taxable base. | Increases depending on if there is a negative taxable base. |
| IVA profile | Neutral if the IVA account is usually in debit. Increases if the IVA account is usually in credit. | No impact |

Source: the author

With reference to tax variables, the overall results seem highly differentiated. The first issue concerns depreciation, seen from the standpoint of the rate and underlying policy. In the case of the rate, there is a very strong direct relationship with the net tax rate inasmuch as assets depreciated over longer periods show a progressively lower cost of capital for leasing. The same effect is essentially achieved by adopting normal as opposed to accelerated depreciation, given that the depreciation period is longer and therefore dilutes the tax benefit associated with ownership of the asset concerned. A second point to evaluate concerns the user's IVA profile. In the event of an IVA creditor position, this favorably affects the net tax cost of leasing as he IVA credit linked to the value of the underlying asset is split up over time. Lastly, a more obvious, general evaluation concerns whether there are profits or not, given that both in the case of leasing and debt financing a loss in one or more years will only serve to increase the cost of capital.

In conclusion, the comparative analysis of leasing and debt financing clearly indicates that financial leasing is much more preferable to debt financing when used for tax-based transactions, provided tax and contractual variables are used correctly to the company's advantage, given their impact on net tax rate. This means that sensitivity analysis can enable formulation of a set of operating rules to devise tax-driven effects when assembling structured leasing deals. These are as follows and, given the tax treatment in force concerning debt financing, can be extended from the Italian case to all other financial systems:

- The tax effect of leasing is maximized every time the minimum duration for the transaction as prescribed by legislation is exploited.
- The above effect is considerably greater if the transaction is organized to start in the early part of a tax year.
- Assets with lower depreciation rates enable leasing to exploit the effect of the minimum duration to a much greater degree. At international level, assets that generally having lower rates are those typically found in structured leasing deals and, in any event, the real estate sector always has the lowest rate.
- Any favorable ad hoc legislative measures concerning minimum duration, such as in the real estate leasing case in Italy, generate particularly attractive synergies for assembling structured operations.
- If the lessee has an IVA balance in credit and a normal depreciation policy profile, then this amplifies the tax benefit produced by leasing transactions.

### 4.4.2.1 An example for purposes of sensitivity of the net rate for leasing and debt financing

This sensitivity analysis is based on leasing and debt transactions for an amount of 900,000 euros, each having a duration of four years and starting 1 February 2004. The assumption in both cases is payment at the time the formal contract is stipulated of 3,000 euros (0.33% of the capital sum) to cover relevant costs. The transaction concerns purchase of machinery for which legislation establishes an annual depreciation rate of 12.5%. The purchaser is a joint stock company that is sufficiently profitable, has a monthly IVA debit balance and as a policy has adopted the accelerated depreciation method. The effective annual cost (TAEG) in both cases is 8%. The leasing contract provides for payment of a maxi-installment equal to 10%, followed by 47 monthly installments of 19,800 euros and a final call option price of 1%. On the other hand, the loan contract provides for repayment over 48 months with monthly installments of 21,853 euros. The graphs developed by simulation take into account the Italian tax framework in force as of 1 January 2004. Each simulation is carried out under equal conditions, namely, based on the same input data.

**Fig. 4.3.** Maxi-installment case

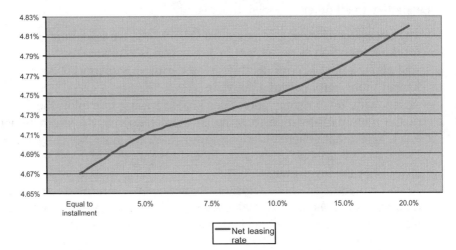

Source: the author

**Fig. 4.4.** Option call price case

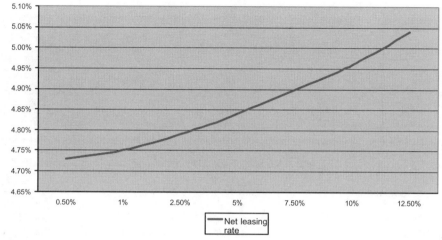

**OPTION CALL PRICE CASE**

Source: the author

**Fig. 4.5.** Fees case

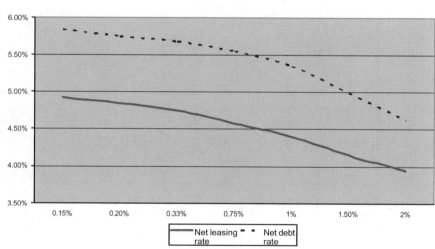

**FEES CASE**

Source: the author

**Fig. 4.6.** Duration case

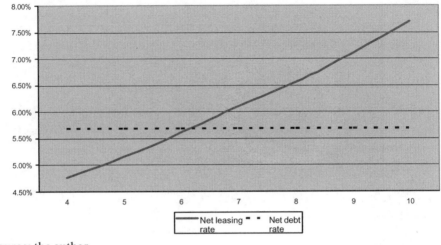

Source: the author

**Fig. 4.7.** Start-date case

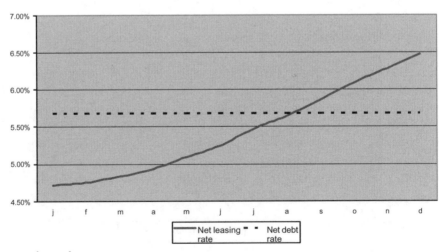

Source: the author

**Fig. 4.8.** Depreciation rate case

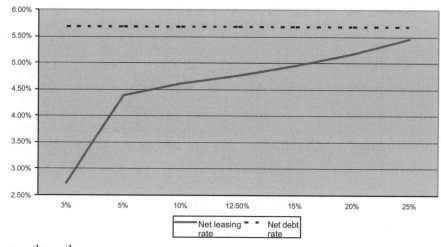

Source: the author

**Fig. 4.9.** Depreciation policy case

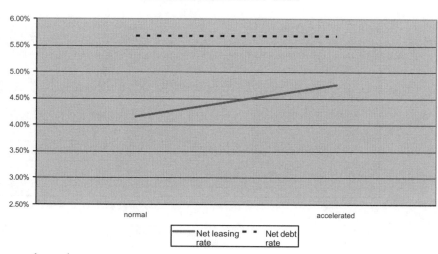

Source: the author

**Fig. 4.10.** IVA profile case

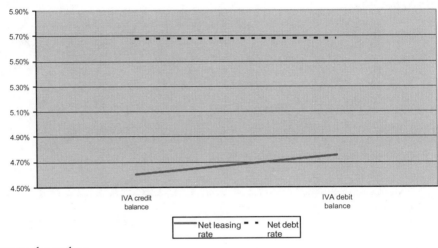

Source: the author

**Fig. 4.11.** IRES profile case

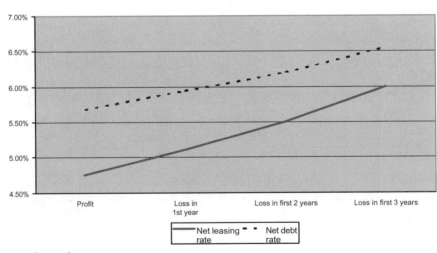

Source: the author

**Fig. 4.12.** IRAP profile case

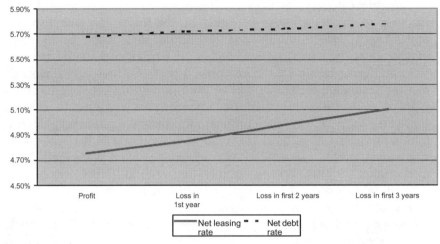

Source: the author

## 4.5 Assembling structured leasing transactions

### 4.5.1 A reference classification framework

Assembling structured leasing transactions can involve using the three basic elements, applying different methods to differing degrees, above all in the light of the tax evaluation the various parties to the transaction make in relation to their own objectives in terms of cost and return. For these very reasons, as mentioned at the beginning of this chapter, it is easier to outline the aims for assembling a structured transaction than to offer a comprehensive definition and analytical overview of how it is organized. However, a basic classification framework can be offered that, while not exhaustive, classifies elements recurring most frequently in the international market in certain macro-categories. It also captures the specific nature and objectives of transactions that occur in the market itself.

From this point of view structured leasing transactions can fall within one of three categorie s (see Figure 4.13):

– standardized or leveraged transactions

– synthetic transactions (so-called synthetic leasing or synthetic structured leasing)
– asset management transactions

The first category includes leasing deals basically structured around recourse to financial leverage.[24] This, so the lessor can both exploit the physiological effects multiplying the return as a result of recourse to indebtedness, and expand the number of participants in the transaction from the lessor-lessee axis to comprise a pool of third-party financers. In fact the leveraged technique can be used in any market situation for any type of transaction, provided the size justifies recourse to a pool of financers external to the original transaction. However, leveraged transactions tend to be used above all in those markets that, given certain conditions, offer specific tax advantages to leveraged leasing transactions.[25] This occurs mainly in two different situations: in international cross-border leasing, and when trusts are used.

The first case refers to the German, US and UK markets where use of cross-border leasing offers specific tax advantages to the lessor, making the transaction more attractive both for the foreign lessee and for potential financers of the leveraged transaction, who can "participate in" the increased tax benefits produced by the deal. At international level the classification used for these deals refers respectively to the terms GELL (German Leveraged Leasing), USPL (US Pickle Leasing) and BDDL (British Double Dip Leasing).

In the second case reference is again made to the US market as well as the Japanese market, where interposing a trust between the lessor and lessee doubles the tax benefits for the deal to the advantage of the parties concerned. In this case the terms used at international level are Trust Leasing (or Pickle Trust Leasing, if a trust is used in conjunction with a cross-border transaction) and JALL (Japanese Leveraged Leasing).

The reference structure for the second category of leasing transactions is instead based on using a dedicated SPV in the transaction.[26] This means the asset underlying the deal is held by the SPV, which therefore becomes the owner. The SPV then proceeds, on the one hand, to organize the leasing transaction with the lessee and, on the other, to put together the

---

[24] For an overview of leveraged-type leasing transactions see Euromoney, "World Leasing Convention, 2002", London, Euromoney Publication, 2003.
[25] From which the term "standardized" classification is derived, given that transactions are based on standard tax frameworks.
[26] On this subject see, in particular, Vogt (1999).

funding to purchase the asset itself. Recourse to synthetic leasing transactions is essentially guided by two factors:

– a search for countries in which to domicile the SPV enabling greater tax benefits to be obtained than in the country of origin;
– the optimzation of tax benefits by transforming financial leasing into operating leasing.

**Fig. 4.13.** A possible classification of structured leasing transactions

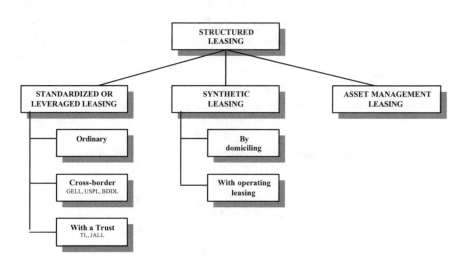

Source: the author

In the first case the SPV's income statement will comprise three basic elements: depreciation of the asset underlying the transaction, financial costs for servicing the debt and installments received from the leasing contract. The degree of net income not only varies based on the spread applied between the leasing and the financing transaction interest rates but above all will depend on criteria governing deductibility of costs and recording of revenues. It will therefore be in the lessee's interest to find the country offering the most favorable relationship between cost deductibility and revenue recording in order to reduce taxation and attract financers for funding the SPV.

In the second case the aim of recourse to the SPV (apart from objectives already mentioned for the first case) is to utilize an operating leasing rather than a financial leasing contract, so increasing the tax benefits from the transaction. To achieve this the SPV stipulates an operating leasing as opposed to financial leasing contract with the lessee, whereas the lessee acquires a call option on the shares of the SPV, de facto obtaining the right to become the owner of the asset as in the case of financial leasing transactions.

Lastly, the third category of structured leasing transactions refers to asset management, namely, the use of leasing as a tool to mobilize wealth, in terms of an asset that can potentially underlie a leasing contract. In this case the aim is value creation by using tax leverage.[27] The concept behind asset management transactions is to use the leaseback technique to accelerate the tax benefit, achieved by financial leasing as opposed to merely owning the asset, and to create available financial wealth. The joint presence of these two effects therefore means leasing transactions, mainly those concerning real estate, can become part of a creative, many-faceted asset management operation in which the overall architecture can also include setting up an SPV as in synthetic-type transactions.

### 4.5.2 Standardized or leveraged structured leasing transactions

As the term suggests, by assembling this type of structured leasing transaction the lessor makes considerable use of financial leverage. This basic principle can give rise to three different solutions with a growing degree of complexity: normal leveraged leasing, cross-border leveraged leasing and leveraged leasing using a trust (see Figure 4.14).

What these three cases have in common is the reason that induces the lessor to coordinate and manage the leasing transaction together with other financers. The latter can either be banking and financial parties who form a pool as used in medium and long-term financing deals, or the market in a wider sense in cases where the lessor issues bonds linked to a specific deal. The second technique is clearly only possible in the case of big-ticket deals that can justify the syndication and market placement costs. From this standpoint, these are the reasons producing a convergence of interests between the lessor and financers:

– The lessor increases the return on the deal by using greater financial leverage. As the market average for the debt component is 80-85% of the value of the deal, this enables the lessor to reduce utilization of

---

[27] On this subject see Caselli (2004).

internal sources to the minimum as the non-financed component is covered by the lessee's maxi-installment payment.

– Financers benefit from a dual guarantee of reimbursement given that installments are channeled directly from the lessee to financers and there is a lien on the asset in the event the customer should default, or alternatively a guarantee provided by the lessor.

– The dual guarantee received from the lessor by financiers means the cost of financing can be reduced.

– Financers achieve a more favorable risk-return ratio on the investment made.

**Fig. 4.14.** Model for standardized or leveraged structured leasing transactions

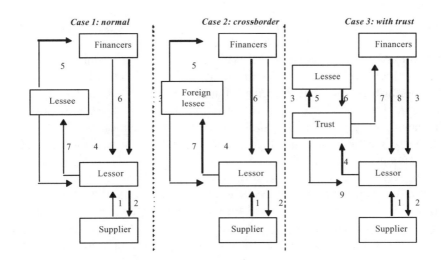

Source: the author

Moreover, apart from tax benefits the transaction generates for the lessee, the convergence of financer-lessor advantages benefits the lessee too as the lessor can apply a smaller spread to the funding.

In the normal transaction (see Figure 4.14, case 1), the lessor purchases the asset from a supplier (1) paying the price (2) utilizing financing provided by the financers (3) in the form of a direct loan or funding obtained from the market. Once the lessee obtains the asset from the lessor (4) payments are channeled to the financers (5), who in turn pay the lessor (6) installments net of the cost due for servicing the debt. At the end of the transaction the lessee (7) can exercise the call option on the asset and so obtain ownership.

The model for the cross-border transaction is identical to the normal deal (see Figure 4.14, case 2) except that the lessee is domiciled in a different country than the lessor and supplier of the asset. It follows that, apart from general benefits described for the lessor, lessee and financers, tax legislation in certain countries can give the lessor – or even the supplier of the asset – additional tax advantages introduced as support for the country's export business. As mentioned previously, the lessor can currently obtain additional tax advantages in the case of the USA (US Pickle Leasing), Germany (German Leveraged Leasing) and the UK (British Double Dip Leasing). These advantages become an element in negotiations between the parties concerned in order to optimize the lessor, lessee and financers' return-risk-cost profiles.

The model for the trust-type transaction, instead, interposes a trust vehicle between the lessor and lessee (see Figure 4.14, case 3). This means the trust receives the asset from the lessor (4) and channels payment of installments to the financers (7), who then pay a net installment to the lessor (8), exactly as in the case of the normal model. The difference from the normal model is that the trust subleases the asset to the lessee (5) in exchange for periodic installments (6) that the trust utilizes to pay the channeled leasing contract installments (7). Interposition of the trust is obviously worthwhile if tax legislation in the country in which the deal originates gives the trust a tax advantage utilizable when subleasing, or if the lessee has a greater tax benefit by paying the leasing payments to the trust rather than to the lessor. As of today the most attractive cases for this type of deal are found in the USA (Trust Leveraged Leasing) and Japan (Japanese Leveraged Leasing). Furthermore, in the US market deals can also be assembled that combine the cross-border technique found in Pickle Leasing with the tax benefits generated by using a trust.

### 4.5.3 Synthetic-type structured leasing transactions

Assembling a synthetic-type structured leasing transaction requires setting up a dedicated SPV that then becomes the pivot of the entire operation, given that it stipulates the leasing contract directly with the lessee (see Figure 4.15).

The overall model for a synthetic deal is based on first setting up an SPV that then purchases the asset (1) from the supplier, paid (2) by utilizing financial resources raised with the financers (3). As occurs in leveraged cases, the financers can fund the debt capital by a direct loan made through a pool or by issuing bonds. Moreover, as opposed to the leveraged case the financers can grant a limited part of the resources in the form of equity, either autonomously or together with the lessee, where the aim is to increase the commitment to and control over the deal. Then the SPV stipulates a leasing contract with the lessee and delivers the asset (4), receiving periodic installments (5) that are used by the SPV itself to repay the financers (6). At the end of the transaction the lessee may, if it wishes, exercise the call option on the asset owned by the SPV (7) or on shares in the SPV, so becoming the owner.

**Fig. 4.15.** Model for synthetic-type structured leasing transactions

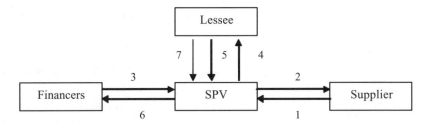

Source: the author

The reasons behind using the SPV are tax-based, given that the lessee can select the most advantageous country from a tax treatment standpoint, where a favorable difference can be created between installments received by the SPV and depreciation of the asset it owns. By creating this differential the lessee can reduce the cost element for the leasing contract while remunerating the investment guaranteed by the SPV's financers.

In addition to the above, an operating leasing contract can also be used and this increases the lessee's tax benefit as a result of a shorter contract duration. This is achieved by stipulating a normal rental as opposed to a financial leasing contract between the SPV and lessee, and the simultaneous stipulation of a call option between the SPV and lessee on the SPV's shares. When the rental contract ends the lessee can exercise the option and so become the owner of the SPV and, therefore, the underlying asset.

This second technique, apart from considerable tax advantages for the lessee, is particularly relevant when the company using the asset wants to set up an off-balance sheet transaction with a view to applying IAS principles or, more simply, to improve its structural margin thanks to a transfer of debt from the company to the SPV. In these terms, creating a tax advantage is accompanied by a significant window-dressing effect as regards the balance sheet, which can have a positive impact on the company's rating and, therefore, cost of money.

### 4.5.4 Asset management-type structured leasing transactions

Use of structured leasing transactions for asset management purposes is based on the sale and leaseback model in which the leasing vehicle is used to create liquidity and greater tax advantages than those deriving from ownership.

**Fig. 4.16.** Model for asset management-type structured leasing transactions

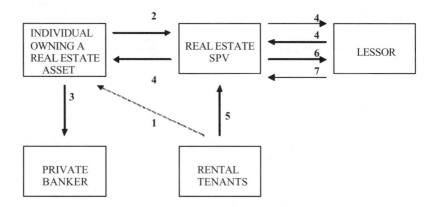

Source: the author

This effect is much more appreciable, the greater the tax benefit for leasing and when the underlying asset is part of the investment portfolio of the individual potentially interested in the deal. The result is that most asset management-type structured leasing deals are focused on the real estate sector and for an amount similar to that found in high profile private banking.

The structure of these transactions starts in the private sphere (for instance, a businessman's family) where a real estate asset is producing rental income (see Figure 4.16).

Rentals are paid by tenants to the owner (1) and the owner pays the highest marginal IRE rate on this income and cannot deduct any costs associated with managing the real estate investment. Consequently there is a very low annual net return on the real estate investment, without considering the risks and outgoings associated with any necessary extraordinary maintenance.

Recourse to a leasing transaction can either be handled through one of the owner's companies that can manage real estate as part of its charter or, more often the case, by setting up an ad hoc SPV as a vehicle specialized in real estate management. The owner therefore sells the real estate to the SPV (2) at market value. This enables the owner to achieve the first objective, namely, availability of liquidity to dedicate to more profitable investments compared to the modest return received previously (3). In order to raise the necessary funding the SPV sells the real estate it has purchased to a bank (4) and simultaneously stipulates a leaseback contract for at least eight years for an amount equal to the market rate. The effect for the SPV is particularly interesting, for the following reasons.

- First, the rentals received by the SPV (5) are channeled to the lessor and therefore used to pay a significant part of the leasing installments (6).
- Secondly, the considerable acceleration provided by the leasing contract generates a significant amount of deductible costs, which heavily reduce the SPV's tax liability.
- Thirdly, management costs for the real estate become deductible items for the SPV.

At the end of the leasing contract the SPV becomes the owner of the real estate (7) and continues to receive the rental payments (5). The original owner therefore achieves a second objective: management costs for the real estate are deductible and the value of the SPV increases, first because the tax liability is reduced and then through purchase of the real estate. An overall financial evaluation of the transaction leads to the observation that over the duration of the leasing contract the original owner's wealth has at least doubled, inasmuch as there is an availability of financial resources equal to the market value of the real estate and, when the leasing transaction ends, ownership of real estate with a nominal value equal to its market value.

## 4.6 Conclusions and growth prospects for the structured leasing market

The analysis in the preceding sections has highlighted the size and structure of the structured leasing deal market from the standpoint of demand and offer profile and, more generally, the competitive scenario at international level. In this sense what has emerged is that while the leasing contract has conventional and consolidated requirements, its use in the case of big-ticket assets, above all real estate, appears to be complex, growing and innovative. A significant aspect in this regard is market segmentation, which has led to the leasing instrument being used in various structured forms, such as leveraged leasing, synthetic leasing or asset management. In more general terms, while different from country to country, it can be said that structured leasing is in the strong growth stage of its lifecycle, even though there are clearly niche segments that must expand (for example, to-be-built leasing), above all in Italy.

Market growth prospects for structured leasing are closely linked to comparative developments in the various markets as regards elements fuelling demand and factors obstructing growth. Depending on which prevails, the structured leasing market will either see further growth or a decline in the use of this instrument.

Three macro-trends can be identified that help define a scenario and map out possible alternatives with a reasonable degree of accuracy.

The first is linked to the tax variable. It is inevitable that growth of both in-country and extra-country structured leasing will depend on changes to tax treatment affecting decisions concerning the structure of company liabilities and investments. This relationship has both a direct and indirect effect. Over the short term, a significant change in tax treatment for real estate financing deals can, as a direct consequence, strongly increase or decrease the size of the market. Over the medium term, innovative financial intermediaries then structure deals in a new way, looking for new market opportunities to replace those that have disappeared. This generates a dialectic exchange between fiscal policies and the creative ability of innovators that progressively modifies the weight and composition of the various structured leasing market segments.

The second, instead, refers to the private banking and family office issue. The considerable weight of real estate assets in the portfolios of high net worth clients and families of business people stimulates the creation of instruments for the management and investment of wealth. If, on the one hand, closed funds and securitization can represent useful tools for this purpose, on the other, real estate leasing has high potential. This is not only because of the simplicity of the technique itself but also the possibility to accumulate tax benefits by exploiting extra-country tax differences. In this sense it is reasonable to assume there will be strong growth in the real estate leasing market over the coming years driven by those operators who manage large real estate investment portfolios.

Lastly, the third macro-trend refers to international leveraged and synthetic-type transactions. The effective match between the leasing instrument and requirements of large real estate deals (in developing countries and others too) is a factor representing a substantial and structural stimulus for market growth. This stimulus, moreover, can only be exploited and sustained by financial intermediaries with a solid reputation in the international market, with a strong networking skill as regards the know-how required to organize complex deals and, above all, the ability to manage and share the asset risk.

# 5 Leveraged Acquisitions: Technical and Financial Issues

Vincenzo Capizzi

## 5.1 Introduction

Leveraged acquisitions constitute an important category in the area of structured finance, namely those that result in leaving the acquired company with a debt ratio that is higher than what it was before the acquisition.

There are a number of studies, adopting research perspectives differing in amplitude and in the ambit of different disciplines, that have studied this subject. At the level of business and management economics, these operations hold considerable interest in the Italian entrepreneurial context, given the possibilities that are open to small and medium enterprises owned by families, in terms of the resolution of company conflicts and the management of problems related to family succession. Another motive of interest, further, is represented by the capability of leveraged acquisitions to allow managers to change their status in companies in which they work, assuming an entrepreneurial role.

At a strictly financial level, leveraged buy-outs have been the subject of wide discussions relating to problems of financial structure and financial/economic performance of firms. If, to one side, the higher debt that distinguishes such operations, allows the exploitation of the effect of financial leverage on the earnings of the firm, on the other hand, these operations increase the financial risks of the firm itself, subjecting the management to pressures that are difficult to sustain, as it has to proceed by means of the unlevered cash flows produced by the firm, to guarantee the repayment of the debt and the payment of the charges for the servicing of the debt, coherent with the business plan agreed upon by the credit intermediaries. Consequently, the literature is concentrated particularly upon the determination of the ideal characteristics that need to be possessed by a firm, for it to be a good candidate for a leveraged acquisition, and also, on estimating the value for the shareholders of such an acquisition.

At the organizational level, the operations in question are often seen as a means of resolving conflicts of interest between the various stakeholders of the business, and, in particular, realigning the objective functions of managers and those of the minority shareholders. By means of a management buy-out, in fact, some managers themselves end up becoming minority shareholders in the acquired business.

At the legal level, the use of the leveraged buy-out in Italy has given rise an intense debate on its legality. In February 2000, the Fifth Penal Section of the Court of Cassation has explicitly declared that the outline of financing of the operations of Leveraged Buyout, born in the United States, is not importable in Italy because it is in contrast with the Italian law (sentence 5503 /2000). In spite of the firmness with which the Court it has declared the illegitimacy in Italy of the institution of the leveraged buy-out, the debate on the legality of such operations has not been resolved. And only recently, with dlgs. 6/2003, that the problem of the legitimacy of the LBO operations seems to have found a definitive solution. The Government has intervened with an act of the Parliament (L.366/2001) clarifying the ambit inside of which the institution of the leveraged buy-out can be considered legitimate

The phenomenon of the leveraged acquisitions is, therefore, complex and lends itself to being observed through various perspectives. The contribution that the authors mean to supply with the present work is to offer as complete a vision and critique as possible, of this family of instruments, in the knowledge that a partial approach to the topic could lead to simplistic conclusions or, eventually, vitiated from preconceived notions and judgments of value. At same time, another objective of ours is to decisively contextualize the instrument of the leveraged buy-out – born in the USA, as noted, and developed subsequently in United Kingdom – to the Italian reality, evidencing some perspective of use and applicative problems.

The rest of the work is structured as follows. Section 5.2 deals with the specifics of leveraged acquisitions with respect to the more traditional operations of extraordinary finance, furnishing a complete review of the various motivations for the same. Section 5.3 examines the various types of leveraged buy-outs and analyses the various ways in which it is technically possible to structure these operations. The next section deals with the financial aspects of a leveraged buy-out, underlining: a) the valuation methods most coherent with the logical assumptions behind similar operations in extraordinary finance; b) the elements that need to be considered during the forecasting of a sustainable financial structure; c) the various types of capital that can be raised from subjects interested in realizing these operations. Section 5.5, finally, presents an analysis of the Italian market for leveraged buy-outs, showing the sizes and volumes of realized transactions, key players in the market and the characteristics of target firms.

## 5.2 Leveraged acquisitions: major goals and characteristics

Leveraged acquisitions refer solely to a class of operations in extraordinary finance in the ambit of the larger "family" of merger and acquisition (M&A) activities. With the latter expression is qualified those operations that have the effect of producing permanent changes in the ownership structure of one or more enterprises.[1] Among the more diffuse types of operations on the ownership assets of the firm, one includes: fusions, bestowals and splits, exchange of shares, divisions and split offs, equity carve-outs, public offers of purchase and exchange, restructurings of businesses in crisis and quotations in officially regulated asset markets (IPO).

Leveraged acquisitions – hitherto also indicated by the expression leveraged buy-out, dealing with the most widespread category of such transactions – profoundly affect the ownership structure of the companies involved, but in contrast to other M&A activities, have certain unique characteristics. In the first place, these operations usually require the constitution of a "vehicle company" (also termed special purpose vehicle, new company or simply newco) for the transit of the ownership; from a technical point of view, it is this entity that, after being capitalized by the subjects interested in making the acquisition (termed the proponent subjects), and the industrial and financial partners involved with the proponents, will launch the offer for the company to be acquired (termed the "target firm"), or through a public offer for purchase, in the case that the target firm is quoted or, otherwise, through private negotiations. Therefore the fact cannot be avoided that, in contrast to the traditional activities of M&A, in the present case the acquisition happens "off balance sheet" for the proponent subject; it can be seen that the only accounting effect for the proponent is represented by the subscription to the capital of the newco. The capital raised through debt securities, the connected

---

[1] Refer for a more ample treatment of M&A services to: Capizzi (2003), Conca (2001), Confalonieri (2002).

package of collateral guarantees and covenants are, instead, pertinent to newco.

Secondly, it needs to be pointed out that the equity raised by the newco represents only a minor part of the complex of resources that are necessary for the conduct of the operation. The major part of the capital is, in fact, supplied by the debt securities by a pool of banks and financial intermediaries. This implies that, being very "pushed" by the recourse to indebtedness (and therefore to the exploiting of financial leverage), these operations are characterized by a higher intrinsic structural risk than is normally observed in the market for the reallocation of ownership of firms. And it is also possible to define leveraged acquisitions as particular types of M&A activities that leave the acquired firm with a debt ratio (debt capital/risk capital) higher than before the acquisition.

Thirdly, if one reflects upon the circumstance that, de facto, the newco specifically created for the realization of the acquisition is an "empty box" containing, at least initially, exclusively the risk capital raised by the proponents and by other firms interested in the operation, one would realize that the debt capital necessary for completing the amount required to allow the exit of the target from the previous ownership, is supplied from the banking system as a function of the capacity of the target firm in generating cash flows. This implies, firstly, that the banks finance the acquirer on the basis of the residual debt capacity of the acquired firm and its consequent capacity to repay the debt and the servicing charges for the same.[2] In second place, it is clear that the choice of the target firm has to be carefully considered by the proponents, seeing that, they would be responsible for the repayment of the financial obligations of the acquisition. In other words, not all the firms that could be objects of an M&A operation are good candidates for a leveraged acquisition. Without trying to generalize, and above all with reference to operations that are decidedly personalized, it is all the same evident that there are certain minimal prerequisites that the target needs to possess, if one things

---

[2] In the section dedicated to the modality of realising an MBO, it will be seen that from a technical point of view, the initial financing supplied to *newco* is obviously conditioned upon the subsequent realization of the acquisition on part of the same. At the end of the operation, it is normally expected that there is an immediate repayment of the financing, this time registered to the operating company resulting from the fusion of *newco* and the target.

of structuring an operation of this kind.[3] In the first place, it is important that the target firm shows a favourable agreement with respect to asset solidity: This signifies, among other things, that the firm should not have a financial structure that is laden with progressive debt. In the second case, the target should be capable of producing through its own operation, cash flows that are sufficient to punctually repay the debt and associated debt-servicing charges. This implies, as can be guessed, the capacity of the firm to make use of a solid and defensible competitive position, by virtue of the efficacy of its own competitive strategy or the profile of attractiveness of the market in reference. Thirdly, it is important to verify if the assets of the company are single plants or equipment or corporate divisions, if the necessity arises, suitable to be transferred, not being strategic, without compromising their current activity: These assets, moreover, could also be used as financial collateral in agreement with the banks. Finally, the presence of a highly motivated managerial team, possessing professional and operational competence is essential; management quality, according to widespread opinion among institutional investors in risk capital, is the most important factor contributing to the success of the entire operation.

It is evident that all three of the specifics just discussed with reference to leveraged acquisitions, namely – role of the vehicle company, high level of leverage and centrality of prospective cash flow in order to evaluate the feasibility of the operation – represent the defining elements of operations in project financing, leasing for large infrastructural works, securitization, even if, obviously, these cases are different than that of the acquisition of a firm, by using a corporate vehicle (newco). The accomplishment of a real investment, the construction and management of a public work, the securitization of a credit portfolio, and so on. For these reasons, in accordance with the operative approach characterising the most important local and global investment banks, leveraged acquisitions have been placed within the area of structured finance.

Before getting into the details of the various types of concretely realizable leveraged buy outs, and the various techniques of accomplishing them, it is worth treating in advance the typical objectives and advantages, for which it would be reasonable to put into place such an operation; moreover, with reference to the Italian context – characterised by a strongly fragmented entrepreneurial structure, in which there is a preponderance of small and medium, family-owned businesses.

---

[3] See Vender (1986), Pencarelli (1993), Ferrari (2003).

In this regard, it is possible to synthesize, in the following manner, the typical objectives of leveraged acquisitions:

1. to limit the patrimonial responsibility of the proponents to the subscribed share capital in the newco, with all the consequences that derive from it to the financial policies which remain at the formers disposition;
2. to accommodate the acquisition of a firm by a team of managers who do not have sufficient finances to conduct the transaction autonomously;[4]
3. to resolve the existing conflicts between the shareholders of the target firm, which do not allow the implementation of a unified strategic design, without having to "empty" the company through a split;
4. to rationalize the assets of small and medium, family-owned businesses, with a fragmented shareholder base, encouraging a "recompaction" around a subgroup of the proprietary family;[5]
5. managing, in the context of the types of enterprises mentioned earlier, problems of generational succession, maintaining at the same time, the autonomy of the target firm;
6. to enhance the image and the reputation – and thus, also the creditworthiness – of the target firm through the involvement in corporate team, of various types of financial intermediaries (banks, merchant banks, share financiers, closed end mutual funds, venture capitalists etc.)

It is clear that, with specific reference to the Italian context, the motivations that are most important are the last four, given the specificity of the national industrial system, characterised as mentioned earlier by the centrality of small and medium sized family owned enterprises. These firms, over the years, can experience a widening and diversification of the shareholder base, coherent with the "biological" evolution of the family ownership, so as to produce at a certain point: conflicts between the members and divergence of views regarding the prospects of future development of the firm; unclear family succession dynamics; limited contractual power in comparison with some key players (clients, suppliers, financial intermediaries). These problems, united with a lesser grade of managerialization and therefore separation of ownership and control, render, as can easily be guessed, the leveraged acquisition an

---

[4] In this case, as can be seen in the succeeding paragraph, it deals with the management buy out (MBO).

[5] In this case the type of leveraged acquisition is called family buy out (FBO).

instrument that is in some cases, crucial to the survival of a firm with similar characteristics.

## 5.3 Leveraged acquisitions: types and techniques of realization

As has already been anticipated, in part, there are a number of operations in extraordinary finance that are technically qualifiable as leveraged acquisitions, those, in good measure, differ mainly in relation to the identity of the proponent subjects, or rather in the nature of the interests for which these have been planned and brought into being. With regard to the literature, and the professional praxis, the following terminology and acronyms are in use:

- leveraged buy-out (LBO): deals with the most generic and typical category of such transactions, in which, on the one hand, there is a significant presence of financial intermediaries and institutional investors in the shareholding of the newco and on the other hand, there is not a significant presence of the subjects characterised in the variants of the LBO described as follows;
- management buy-out (MBO): the proponents are a group of managers of the target firm, who at the end of the operation, change roles, from managers to manager-entrepreneurs;
- management buy-in (MBI): in this case, the team of managers, who are proponents of the initiative are external to the target firm, often of the dimensions more compatible with the limited financing possibilities of the proponents;
- buy-out management buy-in (BIMBO): in this case, the nucleus of the proponent subjects, is composed of some managers operating within the target firm, who are in a position to involve in the initiative, other managerial resources from outside;
- family buy-out (FBO): this happens when a group of shareholders inside the owning family, take over the share of other members who are not interested in the maintenance of their investment in the target. If a part of the owning family decides to "exit" from the firm in reference to try to buy another corporate entity using a leveraged buy out, it is called a family buy-in (FBI);

– workers buy-out (WBO): this deals with a type widespread in the United States, which envisions that the acquisition is realized by dependents of the target, through the intervention of pension funds and the use of employee stock ownership plans;[6]
– corporate buy-out (CBO): in this case the acquirer is a company desirous of growing through external means without, inserting the acquired company directly into its corporate family. It is clear, on the other hand, that the transaction would be "visible" and connectible with the acquirer at the time when the latter would be considered a part of the group (and, naturally, concentrated upon the analysis at the level of the consolidated balance sheet).
– Fiscal buy-out (FBO): deals with an operation that comes into being with the precise aim of creating a "fiscal shield" through the reduction in the incidence of direct taxes on the income of the acquirer. In contrast to the other types of LBO operations, in this case a newco is almost never created, given the principal motivation behind the FIBO is the creation of tax savings on part of the acquirer.

It is an opportune moment to specify how, in practice, it is difficult to find any one of the above mentioned operations in its "pure" form; it happens more often that "combinations" of these operations take place. Again referring to the Italian context, it is quite common for example, to find leveraged acquisitions that have elements of an MBO on the one hand, and an FBO on the other. The stimulus for the operation could, in fact, be a specific desire to rationalize the ownership structure held by a part of the owning family of the firm; and then probably that the financial intermediaries condition their own participation in the initiative by a list of prerequisites, the first among which is the presence a management (internal or external) of unquestioned quality and competence and its involvement in the risks of the initiative – in order to reduce the risks of opportunistic conduct – through a subscription of a shareholding interest in the newco.

Coming now to consider the techniques of realization of an LBO, leaving aside the nature of the acquiring subject, the most interesting approach to follow seems to be that of synthesizing in a chronological order, diverse phases in which it is possible to divide the transaction.

---

[6] On this point see Ferrario (1991) and Stewart Bennett III (1998).

Firstly, the process starts with the identification and the selection of the target company on the part of the proponent subjects. It is clear that, in the case of the MBO, FBO and WBO this phase is automatic, from the fact that, for various reasons it is the one that the proponent subjects have a high degree of involvement.

In second place is the identification of the financial intermediary – or the team (internal or external) of professionals – that will assist the buyer as advisors. And it is the advisor that plans and implements the technical and contractual structure of the transaction, doing it so as to select the solution most coherent with the objectives of the proponents.

Thirdly, once the type of structure of the LBO has been defined, a business plan is made, a document that summarises the evaluations about the sustainability of the industrial model related to the new company that will rise from the transaction, and also the financial feasibility of the transaction, keeping in mind the financial charges of debt servicing and repayment given the proposed leverage. Naturally, it could also be that the proponent subjects already have a solid and rational business plan, which would certainly lessen the workload of the advisor – and the corresponding remuneration.

Fourthly, a pool of investors is identified – of an industrial or financial nature – to add to the initiative, and involve along with the proponent subject in the share capital of the newco. It is in this phase that the activities of the advisor, usually a subject endowed with contacts and relations, capable of involving the number of investors indispensable to the success of the operation, assume relevance. This work, as can be guessed, becomes more important with the size of the obstacles, in terms of capital available with the proponent subjects.

Fifthly comes the identification and capitalization of the newco that, as stated, represents the vehicle used for the realization of the acquisition; this could involve an already existing company within the group to which the proponent subjects belong but suitably "emptied" of its operating assets, or, more often, a company appropriately constituted for the occasion.

Next, one proceeds to the negotiation of the lines of credit needed for the replenishment of the capital that, united with the capital of newco, allows the payment of the proposed price – which is accepted by the ownership of the target firm – for the realization of the transaction. As can be seen successively, the techniques by which the newco comes to be financed are variegated and imply a diverse level of involvement at the outset of the operation, and correspondingly, a diverse risk-return profile. The financial grant, will be guaranteed, at least in part; typically the credit institutions request that the shares of the target firm, or the real assets of the same would be considered as collateral. It is not uncommon, moreover, that in this phase, the pool of banks place at the disposal a bridge loan of a short term and non-guaranteed, subordinate obviously to the realization of the acquisition, and also of a greater amount to that which is successively accorded at the close of the transaction, so as to allow the shareholders of the newco a certain flexibility with regard to the payment of the share capital subscribed at the time of its constitution.

At this juncture, it is possible to follow, in the structure of the transaction on the basis of a multiplicity of operative modalities, referring to two major types, that will be discussed as follows.

### 5.3.1 Merger Technique (or "KKR")

A major operative modality – known as the "merger" or "KKR", from the name of the American bank (Kohlberg, Kravis and Roberts) which had first given birth to such types to LBO – foresees that the newco acquires the totality (or a qualified majority) of the share capital of the target firm (as seen in Figure 5.1).

Successively, the newco proceeds with a merger by incorporation of the target; in case, less frequently, of the fusion of the newco within the target, it is termed as a reverse merger.

At the end of the transaction, meaning the proposed fusion, there is an extinction of the original financing accorded to the newco and the simultaneous opening of new financing contracts, entered into by the company resulting from the fusion, which are normally guaranteed by the shares and/or the operating assets of the same. In practice, the debt of the newco, is transferred "downstream" to the acquired company, which thus becomes the source of the cash flows through which the acquirer can repay the assumed liabilities. From a technical point of view, a similar objective can be attained by acting in such a way that, the company resulting from the merger, once it has been appropriately refinanced by the same pool of banks, "buys" the debt contracted by the newco. This financing, further assisted by a package of guarantees, more ample than the preceding one, is less burdensome on the company, to the advantage of the free cash flows available to the shareholders. It is clear then, that, if one wanted to further reduce the total cost of the debt, one could take into consideration the opportunity of returning to the capital markets, buy the issuing of debt securities for use in repaying the bank finance mentioned earlier. As always ensuring that there are no doubts on the quality of the investments anticipated in the business plan, and consequently, conditions exist for the issue of securities in question, to receive a high rating from the specialized agencies.

**Fig. 5.1.** LBO "merger" technique

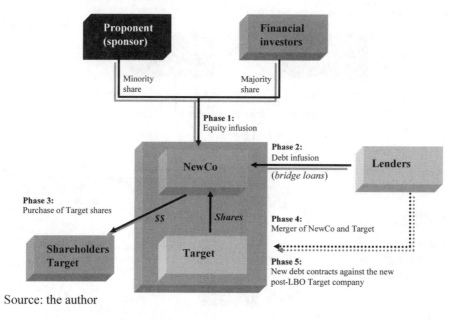

Source: the author

## 5.3.2 Asset sale technique (or "Oppenheimer")

The alternative technical modality, called "asset sale" or "Oppenheimer", also in this case named after the bank that first used this method, provides for the purchase of some assets or business divisions of the target firm, to be incorporated into newco, which from an empty box is transformed into a functional company. A variant of this scheme provides the splitting off, from the target firm, of the assets that constitute the object of the transaction, and their conferment onto the a freshly constituted firm newco (2) – the shares of which could stand guarantee, at least in part, for the financing given to the acquiring company, newco (1) (as seen in Figure 5.2). In this way, it is possible at least partly, to avoid the objections raised by those who, invoking article 2560 of the civil code, could see the asset sale technique as an expedient for "emptying" the target firm of its operating assets, prejudicing the interests of its creditors, as well as of its minority shareholders.

**Fig. 5.2.** LBO: "asset sale" technique

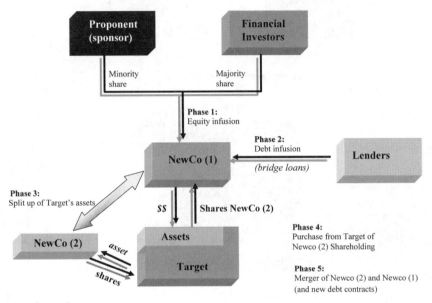

Source: the author

The newco (1) proceeds with the acquisition from the target of the shareholding (usually total) in the newco (2) and successively merges by incorporation of the latter.

Also in this case, at the end of the operation, one proceeds with the stipulation of new contracts (guaranteed) entered into by the new company resultant from the fusion of newco (1) and newco (2).

It is not necessary, naturally, that one must apply the two techniques just illustrated, in their original version. Nor is it necessary to acquire the total share capital of the target firm, or does one need to proceed with the merger of the newco and the target.

---

### Box 1: The Piaggio SpA case

The box 1, shows a concrete example related to the acquisition in 1999 of Piaggio by a group of institutional investors headed by Morgan Grenfell; in the case in point, it is evident that the newco (Piaggio Holding Spa) and the acquired company (Piaggio & C Spa) were maintaing in existence, also for the reason of widening the shareholderbase of the same newco.

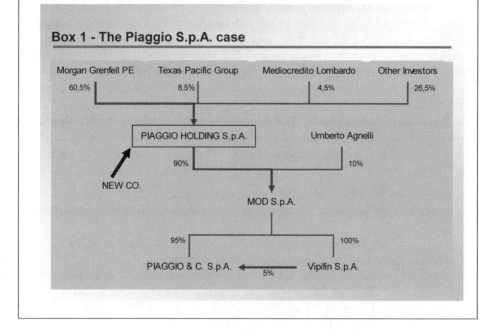

---

## 5.4 Leveraged acquisitions: financial issues

As noted earlier, the activity of planning and structuring performed by the advisor is critical, which requires the capacity to hypothesize – in a rigorous, rational and realistic manner – a mode of development of the target firm characterized by the creation of a significant value for the new shareholders in reference. The first element that needs to be considered carefully is how to ensure the survival of the target with the heavy debt burden and characterized by a level of financial leverage above that which is physiologically acceptable for working in a certain economic context – as a norm identifiable with the weighted average taken contemporaneously, of a sample of firms representing the sector of activities.

In this regard, it is evident that, the capacity for the repayment of the assumed debt, not to mention the remuneration of the same through the payment of financial expenses, is based, on the one hand, on the operating cash flows (unlevered) produced by the firm, following the change of management, its business strategies and policies; on the other hand, it is also conditioned by the possibility to unload assets and/or non strategic areas of business or, at any rate, not held held instrumental to the development of the selected core business. Thus emerges the importance of the business plan, which is the document, prepared by the advisor on the basis of the directions provided by the proponent subjects, which needs to address clearly, the aspects just mentioned, so as to make clear the advantages, in monetary terms, of each of the subjects participating in the operation: the proponents, the financial partners of newco, the credit intermediaries and the providers of debt capital. More particularly, a business plan created for an LBO, concentrates upon the following areas:

1. analyses on the historical development of the firm;
2. analysis of the corporate environment and internal organization of the target firm;
3. analyses of the business strategies in which the target firm is involved;
4. analysis of the competitive environment in reference;
5. predisposition of the logical scheme of the transaction (deal structure);
6. location and valuation of the possible forms of disinvestment, post-fusion;
7. analysis of the prospective financial dynamics of the target and the estimation of the prospective unlevered cash flow;
8. construction of a sustainable financial structure;
9. individuation of the equity value available to the members of the target from the anticipated transaction and merger, after the financial creditors have been repaid and the rate of return on the share investment (the IRR);
10. predisposition of the final offer memorandum, which would be the basis of reference for the negotiation and closing of the transaction.

If it is clear that, under a valuative profile, the logical sequence a transaction is based on the relation at the "industrial level (starting from 1 to 8) of the business plan – financial level (from 8 to 9) of the business plan – measurement of the equity value and the IRR of the investment", it should not surprise one that the methods of analysis and valuation that appear indispensable, inasmuch as they are coherent with the logic just described, are of a financial type, centred upon the present value of the future cash flows, first of all the discounted cash flow analysis (see Figure 5.3).

**Fig. 5.3** The "functional logic" of Discounted Cash Flow Analysis

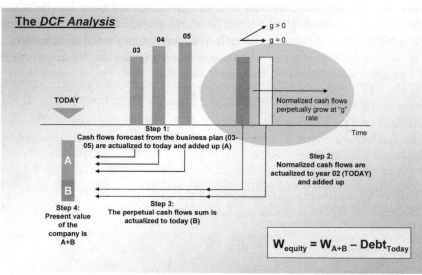

Source: the author

These methods, in fact, which make the value of the firm (entity value) and economic capital (equity value) depend upon the series of prospective cash flows (unlevered and levered respectively) produced by the firm subject to valuation, are the most suitable for capturing the value that can be generated by the firms, that though being heavily in debt, have a favorable market position, an effective business strategy, a solid reputation and therefore, expected to produce increasing cash flows over time. In this sense, the value of the target resulting from the application of earnings based, asset based and mixed methods could be penalized in so far as:

- they favor non monetary quantities;
- are based on historical or actual data, but difficult to project;
- treat in an asymmetric manner the payment to be guaranteed to the creditors and that to be offered to the shareholders;
- do not take into account the financial value of time.

It is not by accident that leveraged buy outs have originated in contexts – primarily Anglo-Saxon – in which it is clear that the value of a business is determined on the basis of its expected cash flows, discounted by a rate expressing the weighted average cost of capital. If this were not the case, it would be difficult to start a high debt initiative, and for a brief period characterized by an absence of monetary remuneration for the shareholders.[7]

Referring back to the vast literature, extant in corporate finance as regards to a systematic treatment of discounted cash flow analysis[8], it seems useful in this place to make some considerations in the theme of the construction of the financial structure, which undoubtedly represents one of the aspects most peculiar – and critical – to the realisation of an LBO transaction.

In this regard there is a series of elements that needs to be considered carefully by the advisor:

- the amount of equity, at least initially, at the disposal of the proponents (above all with particular reference to the case of MBO), is often a limited fraction of the total resources necessary to make the acquisition of the target;
- also considering the contribution of equity that can be furnished by the merchant banks, venture capitalists, closed funds and banks, the financial structure of the operation cannot prescind a substantial recourse to debt. It deals also, as seen in Section 5.2, with one of the aspects characterising leveraged acquisitions with respect to M&A operations in general;
- given the nature of the operation, the risk of the initiative and the "pressure" generated by the debt capital on the unlevered cash flow, it is difficult to

---

[7] For analysis of the methods of business valuation, see: Masari (1998), Guatri (1998) and Gatti (2002).

[8] See Massari (1998) Copeland et al (2000), Damodaran (2001) and Capizzi (2003).

make reference exclusively to the traditional bank debt (the so called senior debt);
- having seen the size of the amounts in play, and, once again, the risk of the initiative, it is rare that a single credit intermediary can supply the debt capital necessary for the conclusion of the initiative;
- in any case, with respect to traditional financial transactions, the ordinary debt provided is not, as a rule, fully covered by guarantees;
- it needs to be taken into account that, there are precise normative limits to the maximum amount of financial resources that can be raised through either bond issues (art 2410 of civil code) or the issue of limited voting shares (art 2351 of civil code).

The ability, therefore, of the advisor to structure a financial plan which is coherent with the elements and the obstacles just described, is essential and at the same time the plan must allow the precise formulation of a diversified range of techniques of financing capable of guaranteeing the entire coverage of capital required.

**Fig. 5.4** The "typical" financial structure of a management leveraged buy-out

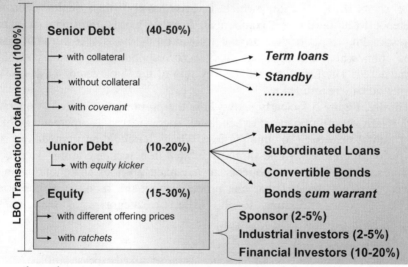

Source: the author

Figure 5.4, without claiming to generalize, based on the empirical observations with reference to the Italian market for leveraged buy-outs, illustrates the typical financial structure of an LBO operation and, more particularly, a management leveraged buy out.[9]

In the first place, for the reasons stated above, it is necessary to involve a pool of financial investors holding the debt capital in the initiative. The technical form with which the ordinary finance is supplied will therefore be a syndicated loan, typically a term or standby loan.[10]

Secondly, it is important that the advisor is able to make a balanced distribution of debt between senior debt (ordinary bank loans, privileged repayments in case of insolvency and business failure) and junior debt, that is, between technical forms of ordinary debt and "mezzanine debt"; this last expression, as noted, qualifies the so-called hybrid instruments of fundraising, which include such forms of financing (for example subordinated debt, convertible bonds, bonds cum warrant) that share some of the characteristics of debt capital, found in an intermediate position in terms of the risk-return profile.[11] The role of subordinated debt, also is crucial, incorporating specific options with a well defined value market value (warrants, conversion rights, so-called equity kickers meaning options that are incorporated within a bond which allow the bondholders to subscribe to shares of the issuer at an exercise price established ex ante), which is less "costly" than senior debt with reference to its pure credit component; In other words, the financial charges corresponding to junior debt are determined on the basis of lower than market rates upon which the financial charges corresponding to ordinary debt are parametered. The benefits produced by this to the "unlevered" cash flows of the period can be intuited.

Thirdly, Figure 5.4 clearly shows how the proponents realize the operation with relatively little financial expenditure, if considered as a percentage of the total capital necessary for this purpose. Their shareholding immediately after the fusion, therefore, will be similarly limited in percentage terms. To succeed in guaranteeing to the proponents an adequate level of shareholding in the newco, it is not unusual that one proceeds with the fixing of differentiated prices of issue attributing to the different categories of participants.[12]

---

[9] See: Aifi (various years).
[10] See Capizzi (2003) for types of financing instruments, and expense profiles.
[11] See Capizzi (2003).
[12] See Ferrari (2003) for numerical exemplification.

Moreover, to reduce the incentives for opportunistic behaviour that could damage the majority financial stakeholders, and also, to allow the proponents, after a certain time period, to succeed in increasing their own share of the equity capital of the firm, it is important to be able to stipulate certain contractual mechanisms – which establish a relation between the performance that the firm is able to reach in a pre-defined time horizon and the share quota held by the management –.

Fourthly, one need always to keep in mind how a financial structure like that shown in Figure 5.4 could be "unstable" and a source of financial risk; which means that that the level of leverage should be taken back to physiological values by the end of the time horizon assumed in the business plan (typically 4-7 years). The reaching of a similar result also allows the company to follow its own activity in the future, realizing new investments and obtaining the capital loans necessary for its development at a reasonable cost.

In conclusion, it needs to be stressed how, once the financial structure, adjudged sustainable for a given transaction, has been projected, it is basically then the capacity of the advisor to implement, that which is previewed in the business plan: verifying the order of the phases of subscription and return of the capital on part of the shareholders of newco (often assisting them in the phase of retrieval of the same capital through new financial operations), obtaining the initial financing for newco, managing the negotiations with the ownership of the target firm (and, eventually, the launch of an open offer, in case the target firm is quoted), realising the fusion, renegotiating/reactivating new financing contracts entered into by the company resulting from the fusion, assisting continuously the new ownership and management in order to make them achieve what was previewed in the industrial plan. Being an advisor to a team of sponsors interested in achieving a leveraged acquisition is, therefore, a complex activity which requires the possession of capability and competence (professional and relational) of a high degree, and that, also, explains the high incomes characterizing the financial intermediaries most active in this area of business.

## 5.5 The Italian market for leveraged acquisitions

### 5.5.1 A panorama of the European market

Before an in-depth analysis of the evolution of the Italian market for leveraged buy-outs (LBOs), it seems opportune to make a brief overview of the present European situation, in order to better understand the specificity and the potential of this type of action in the national context.

In order to make the subsequent analysis, one needs to make the assumption of the aggregation of the data relating only the nations on the Continent of Europe, excluding therefore, the United Kingdom. The basis of the methodological choice, rests on the fact that, given the size of the English share of the market, being equal to that of the United States, it needs to be considered as an aggregate in itself, and not included in that of Europe.

A second specification of a methodological nature regards the database and the sources of the official statistics taken as reference for the subsequent analysis and elaboration. To this purpose, given the complexity of the operations that are the object of analysis in the present section, and the not yet complete convergence of opinion in the doctrinal and professional context regarding the exact "boundaries" of the buy-out transactions, with respect to the broader market for mergers and acquisitions, one has chosen to rely upon, firstly, the "official" sources of periodic statistics on the LBO market – the European Private Equity and Venture Capital Association (EVCA), The Italian Association of Institutional Investors in Risk Capital (AIFI) and the Centre for Management Buy-Out Research (CMBOR) of the University of Nottingham – and, secondly, to certain samples of an occasional nature, which, moreover, base their observations on empirical analyses characterised samplings of non-homogenous transactions as regards their composition and time frame of reference.[13]

Starting from a synthetic view regarding the size of the transactions that are the object of the analysis, and taking into reference a five-year time period (Figure 5.5), the buy-out market of Continental Europe has recorded a different growth pattern in the years 1998-2000 and in the successive period; in the first sub-period, there was rapid increase in the total value invested in leveraged acquisitions, which had reached, in the end of the year 2000, a

---

[13] See: Banca Commerciale Italiana (1990), Fasati and Paleari (1996), AIFI (2001).

record value of 32.6 billion euro. Successively, following a decline in the economy as a whole, along with the well noted political tensions in the last trimester of 2001, there was a gradual decline in the total value of the transactions effectuated; a decline which brought about an inferior market value of the transactions as compared to the year 2000 (31.3 billion as compared to 32), assessed on the values of 1999. In the course of 2002, however, the European private equity players were able to combat the difficult macroeconomic conditions steering the market to a new record total investment of 38.7 billion euro.

**Fig. 5.5** Evolution of the European and Anglo-Saxon markets for LBOs (1998-2000)

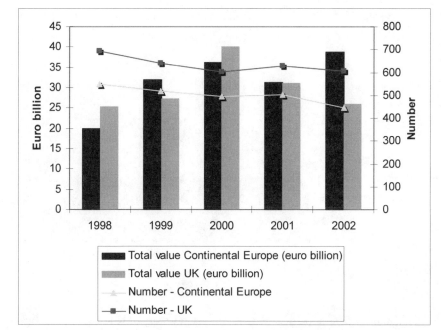

Source: author's elaboration on CMBOR data – University of Nottingham (various yrs)

This is even more significant, if compared to just the market of the United Kingdom. In fact, after a substantial equilibrium in the course of 2001, the Continental Europe data were higher than the U.K., which, after years of spectacular growth, culminated in 2000 with about 40 billion euro invested, and then showed a heavy decline in buy out investments, which settled to around 25 billion euro.

As regards the number of operations made, its possible to observe a negative trend which ahs brought the Continental market from about 550 buy-outs in 1998 to 447 in 2002 (a decline of 18.7%) Also the English market (14.3% in the same time period) replicates the negative dynamic observed in the European market., even though the values have been decidedly higher because in the course of 2002 itself, about 600 operations were realized which was slightly less than the previous year, but in line with the values observed in 2000.

**Fig. 5.6** Average size of investments made in 2002 (million euro). Continental Europe Vs. UK

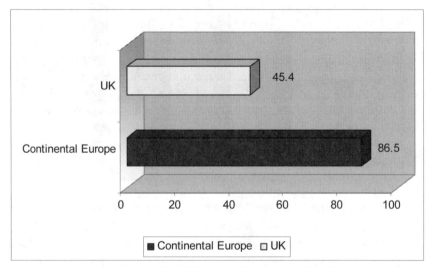

Source: author's elaboration on CMBOR data – University of Nottingham (various yrs)

Trying to "intersect" what has emerged from the analysis of the two types of data just shown, it is possible to deduce that the medium to large size operations form the "backbone" of the Continental market (60% of the total invested comes deals that have a value greater than or equal to 500 million euro), while the UK market is based on a larger number of transactions, but of smaller unit size. These observations, find confirmation in the data regarding the average value of buy-out operations that have been registered in the last year (Figure 5.6): In fact, in the UK, the average amount invested in a single deal was around 45.4 million euro, in the Continent the same quantity has been significantly higher (86.5 million euro).

**Fig. 5.7** Average size of MBOs and MBIs (million of euro). The Continent Vs. UK

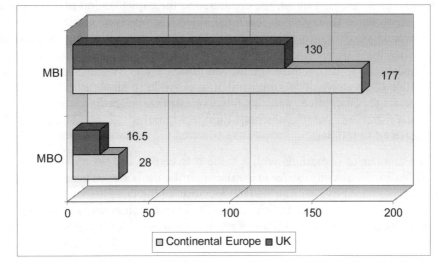

Source: author's elaboration on CMBOR data – University of Nottingham (various yrs).

A similar size difference observed between Europe and the UK, was confirmed by data disaggregated by buy-out type, distinguishing in particular between operations of MBO (management buy-out) and MBI (management buy in). In 2002, as has been observed in previous years, the average values be it of MBOs[14] or MBIs[15] was higher in Continental Europe with respect to that recorded in the United Kingdom: MBOs score a total value of 28 million euros

---

[14] In an MBO the acquisition of the target happens from the internal management of the same, helped by specialised intermediaries.

[15] In an MBI the management that makes the operation is not internal to the firm.

in Continental Europe and 16.5 million euro in the UK. The difference is even greater in the case of MBIs (which also include IBOs[16] or investor buy-outs): 177 million euro in Continental Europe versus 130 observed in the UK (Figure 5.7)

The motives for which MBIs are in the long run more frequent than MBOs is quite clear: It is in fact more difficult that, at a certain point, the managers of a firm desirous of changing their own status within the entity in which they function, to assume the role of an entrepreneurial nature, have, on their own, the financial resources sufficient to give life to a leveraged acquisition: This, as seen, involves, first of all, the creation and the capitalization of a newco. It is more probable that one can reach the objectives involved in the initiative if other managerial figures either industrial partners external to the target firm, and when this happens the operation becomes technically counted as an MBI.

Concentrating particularly on the information and statistics provided by CMBOR (University of Nottingham) it is possible to show a series of other "interesting" qualitative and quantitative aspects regarding the principal characteristics of the Continental European market as on 31 Dec 2002 synthesized as follows:

- the number of operations with a value between 25 and 50 million euro has fallen by 50% with respect to 2001, while the deals larger than 250 million have increased by one fourth; The operation of the largest size has been that related to the acquisition of the French electronic components firm Legrand, with a total value of 4,9 billion euro, by a consortium of investors led by the German venture capital firm Wendel and the noted US investment bank KKR;
- The public to private operations, namely those operations that, as a final effect, produce the exit of the firm from official listing on the bourses, maintaining a significant weight in terms of investment value. It is sufficient to note that the buy-out that has brought about the delisting of the Irish firm Jefferson Smurfit, has represented, with 3,2 billion euro, the third largest operation of 2002.
- The hi tech sector has shown, also for 2003, an increment with respect to the previous year, confirming the trend of uninterrupted growth continuous

---

[16] In an IBO the operation is conducted directly by the institutional investors in risk capital.

for ten years in this area; in particular, during 2002 there were 123 operations effectuated against 119 in the preceding year.

Passing to an analysis, disaggregated by country in the Continental market (Figure 5.8), the analysis which will be seen in-depth in the following pages for the Italian context, it is possible to not how, till the end of 2001, the German market, also denoting the first signals of crisis, resulted in being the most developed market with 7.8 billion euro of investments, followed by France, following a negative trend of growth since 1999, reached 6.1 billion. The Italian market was in difficulties which, among the major Continental European countries active in the buy-out sector, till 2001, lost its position as compared to Holland and Sweden, showing a value similar to nations such as Belgium, Spain and Switzerland.

**Fig. 5.8** Trends in invested resources (million euro) in buy-outs in the principal countries of continental Europe (1999-2002)

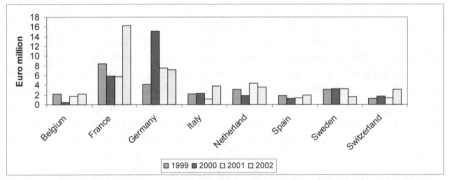

Source: author's elaboration on CMBOR data – University of Nottingham (various yrs).

During 2002, the crisis sparked in the preceding year continued to influence the German market leading to a marked decline in the total amount of the buy-out operations, from 7.8 billion euro in 2001 to 7.5 billion in 2002. On the contrary, France was the protagonist, in the same year, of an extraordinary growth which more than doubled the total volume of investments reaching in 2002, the remarkable figure of 16.7 billion euro. In a similar fashion, Switzerland, Italy, Spain and Holland have seen growth in terms of total invested resources, in their domestic markets, managing to reach in the year just completed their maximum values.[17]

With reference, in conclusion, to the number of transactions made, 2002 saw a predominance of France (122 deals) followed by Germany (96 deals) Holland (59 deals) and Italy (37 deals).

## 5.5.2 The trend in the Italian LBO market

Concentrating specifically on the Italian buy-out market – utilizing as the principal source of data, the AIFI database – one immediately notices the significant growth registered in the past years, starting from 1995. A similar trend of growth, though interrupted temporarily in 2001, for reasons mentioned in the previous section, has influenced both the number of operations (redoubled in the course of the 5 year period considered), as well as the value of the investments effectuated (grown by more than 6 times in the course of the same time period).

The contraction of 2001, moreover has regarded above all the total number of transactions made (-43.4% with respect to the previous year), given that the value of the investments, though lower (-25.6% with respect to the end of 2000), has remained appreciably higher than that of 1999. Regarding this, it would be useful to underline how, in terms of volumes invested, the buy-out segment being characterized by a remarkable dynamic of growth in the years 1998-02, given that its percentage weight of the total value of investments in the market for venture capital and private equity – which includes, according to the AIFI categories, also the "early stage", "expansion" and "replacement" segments – has jumped from 26% to 59% by the end of 2002.

Getting down to the details, it is possible to observe how, in the period 1998-02, there were 262 deals concluded, for a total market value invested[18] of

---

[17] It is important to note that the data up till now shown relating to the European market are the result of numerous studies conducted annually by CMBOR. The data specific to the Italian market are furnished by AIFI - to avoid confusion it is important to make a methodological clarification. The CMBOR results are from direct research on the principal actors. The analysis conducted on the number of firms acquired (not on the number of acquisitions made by a single investor) and consider the total value of the acquisitions including the debt capital.

[18] Where not specified , the term "market value" indicates the total amount of equity, semi-equity, and mezzanine debt brought by institutional investors for the acquisition

5,047 million euros (Figure 5.9). More particularly, the number of buy-out operations has moved from 38 in 1998, for a total market value of 242 million euro, to 76 for a market value of 1,330 million euro in 2002. The major part of the growth, however, was obtained in 1998-00: +463% in terms of total market value of the realized investments and +39.5% in terms of number of transactions concluded. The two years following was characterized initially by a contraction in activities, due to political and economic difficulties, at the national and international levels, that characterized 2001; however, already in the following year the trend was resumed, due to which 2002 closed posting a record total both in terms of the number as well as total market value of the investments in buy-out operations.

**Fig. 5.9** Dynamics of the buy-out market (1998-2002)

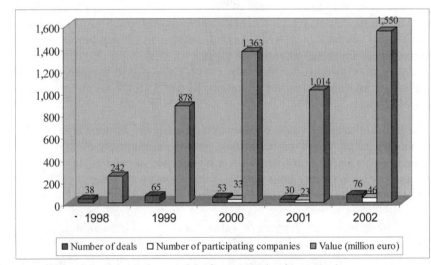

Source: elaboration of the author on data from AIFI (various years)

Though dealing with a perception difficult to demonstrate empirically, one cannot but connect the boom in the market observed in 2002 with a greater trust, on part of practitioners and specialized operators, in the normative

of the firm. This value is less than either the total value of the acquired firm or the total price paid.

context of reference following the launch of reforms in company law, amply discussed in other parts of the present text.

If one then refers to the data relating to the number of participating companies (available only from 2000), it is interesting to note how, in the course of 2000-02, there has been an appreciable increase in the number of firms becoming objects of interventions (+39.4%).

To this proposition, it would be useful to note how, in the course of the same temporal horizon, there has been an increase in the gap between the number of operations concluded and the number of target companies involved. Such a phenomenon could be read as a signal, on the one hand, of the fact that with the passage of time, the "collegiality" of the operators in the sector, participating jointly in the same buy-out, succeed in dividing the risk of a single investment and largely diversifying their portfolio of shareholdings; on the other hand the phenomenon in question is clearly connectible to the increase recorded in the last years of the so called "mega deals", namely those with large unit values, which therefore require the formation of syndicates of institutional investors in risk capital, other than syndicates of credit intermediaries for the supply of debt capital.

Moving now to consider, as always with reference to the period 1998-02, the average invested value per operation, Figure 5.10 shows an important and two-fold aspect:

– the trend in average value of investments analyzed in their entirety shows, after an initial phase of enormous growth, culminated in 2001 with an average size of 44.1 million euro, a perceptible decline (-31.7% compared to the preceding year) falling to 33.7 million euro in the end of 2002. This data is however, affected by some conspicuous investments. For example, the 1999 data is influenced considerably by the operation of Piaggio and Fiat Lubricants, with respective values of 403 and 223 million euro.[19] On the values relating to 2000, impinges the acquisition of Mark IV, for an amount of equity invested in excess of 300 million euro. In conclusion, on the data for 2001-02, there have been various deals larger than the average (the "mega deals" cited earlier), to the realization of which have participated pools of operators, Italian and International, among which it is worth

---

[19] Without considering the acquisition of Telecom Italia by Olivetti, which at 31.3 billion euro represents till now the largest LBO realised in Italy.

mentioning the acquisition of Alfathern (around 100 million euro) and Fisia Italimpianti (280 million euro);[20]
- the same investigation, made this time excluding the mega deals, shows a marked and stable growth trend, that in spite of a slight decline in 2001 (-12,5% with respect to the previous year), has brought the average size of the buy-out operation from 8,1 million euro in 1998 to 18.5 in 2002, with an increment of 56% between the beginning and the end of the period considered.

**Fig. 5.10** Average invested amounts in buy-out operations (with and without mega-deals)

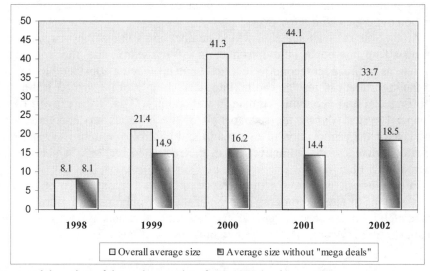

Source: elaboration of the author on data from AIFI (various years)

The motives for the considerable growth in the Italian market for buy-outs, shown by the data just considered, are undoubtedly a reflection of the profound changes in the socio-economic fabric of our country. This trend of development has been influenced by, firstly, the particular structure of the

---

[20] In 2003 the acquisition of Autostrada through the vehicle company Newco28 through a 7 billion euro IPO will be entered into the AIFI data.

Italian economy, characterized by the presence of numerous small and medium enterprises, those that represent fertile ground for acquisitions sustained by institutional investors in risk capital following increasingly frequent problems concerning the difficulties of generational succession.[21]

Not randomly, according to the evidence of a significant empirical study conducted by AIFI in collaboration with prestigious university centers and business schools, the principal motivations for the cession of businesses to institutional investors – present in over 50% of the cases – is a result of the generational changes, following from the necessity to move away from activities considered "non-core" and the search on the part of managements for greater independence. In the end, other factors that have brought about the cession of the firm or a branch of the same have been: a particular financial crisis situation, conditions of favorable price offers, and also the opportunity to exploit synergies with other firms.[22]

Among the causes for the growth in number and value of buy-outs, it needs emphasizing moreover, the introduction of the euro, and the consequent variations in the macroeconomic context have provided a considerable impetus to the investment of foreign capital into Italy, in light of the greater stability of the financial and economic climate in the country. Again, the growth of our financial system during the second half of the Nineties has encouraged the market for the reallocation of ownership and control of enterprises, thanks to greater efficiency and attractiveness in the regulated markets, which became increasingly able to offer a valid form of disinvestment.

In conclusion, as always with reference to the Italian market for buy-outs, it is important to cite the process of privatization of public sector firms started, concretely, in the second half of the Nineties, that has brought about the realization of investments, though few in number, of huge amounts.[23]

---

[21] Also see Caselli (2002) and Confindustria (2002) for an analysis of the financial/economic characteristics of the Italian entrepreneurial system.

[22] See AIFI (2001).

[23] For a reason or purpose of example, of particular interest for the dimensions and the volumes it employs to you can turn out the acquisition of Seat Yellow Pages from part of a group of financial investor and industrialists, for which they have employed more than 1,500 million euro.

## 5.5.3 The main players in the Italian LBO market

After the overview just conducted, of the development of the buy-out market in Italy, it seems useful to make an analysis of the principal financial actors in this segment of the market, with specific reference to the situation just emerged during the course of 2002.

The main category of operators characterizing the buy-out market is undoubtedly represented by "institutional investors in risk capital", that is those subjects that stably and professionally make investments assuming shareholding in the risk capital of non financial companies. The objective of these subjects is to cede, after a pre-defined time interval, the shareholding acquired – through a private negotiation with other financial intermediaries (private sale) or through the placement of the firm financed by the market (public sale) – in order to extract from it a capital gain that guarantees, in total, a rate of return on the investment which is coherent with the risk profile and thus with the initial expectations. If the definition just supplied has an undoubtedly general character, and can thus be adapted to a wide range of operators, that which can technically qualify and distinguish the financial intermediaries operating in the buy-out space, is represented by their "investment philosophy", which means, their orientation with reference to a series of variables such as: a) the breadth of the time horizon desired for the investment, that can vary from the short to the medium-long term; b) the percentage share of the risk capital assumed in the participating firm, which could either be a choice of a strategic nature but however, susceptible to the discretion of the same intermediary or due to normative obstacles which could be levies on certain types of operators (for example, the "limits of separation" imposed by the Unified code of laws in banking and credit matters upon Italian banks); c) the mode of monitoring the investments adopted, which could from time to time, provide for flows of information of a qualitative and quantitative nature, periodic check ups of the participating firms, positions of responsibility in the organs of governance of the participating firms; d) participation in the definition of strategic and managerial choices of firms, which, obviously, will be a function of the industrial or financial nature of the buy out investor and moreover, of the specific knowledge and competencies of the sector and management; e) the agreed scheme of remuneration, which could favor relatively stable flows of dividends rather than mechanisms of various types, that lends to the correspondence of remuneration with the increase in the nominal value of the shareholding.[24]

In detail, the institutional investors operating in the buy out sphere, as counted in the official statistics, lend themselves to the following typology.

1. Closed end mutual funds: in Italian law, closed ended funds are financial intermediaries that, through the sale of shares, raise resources from the public, formed mostly by other institutional investors (pension funds, insurance firms, banks etc.) and from private "experts" (namely those who have a consistent reputation and domain knowledge), and then investing the resources, for the medium/long term, in securities of promising firms, opening an important financial channel for unquoted companies that need risk capital for their development. To do this, the capital of the mutual fund comes to be administered by a savings management company (SGR), which determines the strategies and the investment policies of the same fund;[25]

2. Italian commercial banks and merchant banks: as regards the banks, it is necessary to emphasize that only from a few years, that is from the coming to force of the Unified Text of laws in banking and credit matters (D.lgs 385/93), national banks have been able, respecting predetermined quantitative limits, to assume shareholding in the risk capital of non-financial firms.[26] With the term "financiers of shareholding", are indicated those particular types of domestic operators, who, on the Anglo-Saxon model of merchant banks, undertake professional activities in the area of risk capital, other than activities of intermediation and consulting in the corporate finance segment, of structured finance, of asset management and risk management;

3. Foreign banks and investment banks: under this label, have re-entered all the foreign intermediaries that have been present in our country for years. It

---

[24] See Capizzi (2003).

[25] For a more systematic treatment of closed funds see Capizzi (2002).

[26] Previously, the Instructions of the Bank of Italy (Cicr deliberation, 6 February 1987) concurred with the credit institutions and to the institutes it centers them (the credit institutions turned out already qualifies one to the assumption of participation in industrial enterprises, with the relative limitations, from the Bancaria Law of the 1936) to operate in the activity of institutional investment in understood them of risk of enterprises not the financial institutions solo through the societies of intermediation purposely constituted, the so-called societies of intermediation financial institution (Sif).

deals, in particular, with the investment, merchant banks of anglo-saxon variety, of affiliates of foreign banks that operate in Italy through connected companies and closed end funds under foreign law, managed on their own or in collaboration with Italian partners. These operators, especially closed pan-european funds (operators with a super-national range of action), by virtue of either their greater experience in the risk capital market, or in some cases, the different normative context under which they can perform their institutional activities, and lastly, due to the enormous capital raising capacity, represent in terms of the amount of resources supplied, the subjects most active in the Italian market;

4. Government-owned investors and cooperative operators: these operators perform buy-out operations in order to sustain depressed geographical areas or disadvantaged industrial sectors, or more generally, with the objective of supplying economic and occupational aid to especially backward regions. It deals, therefore, primarily with financial intermediaries that, though operating in the are of institutional investment in risk capital, set themselves objectives partly different from those of the operators discussed till now, objectives that influence, in a relevant manner, the selection of the target firm, the duration of the holding (in most cases for long periods) and the modality of monitoring investments;

5. Specialized operators in venture capital and private equity: deals with operators having specific competencies that participate in the capital of small/medium enterprises, often of recent constitution, in order to help them in the difficult seed/startup phase. In the major part of the cases, the venture capital player, like the other business angels[27] or the "incubators of companies[28]", concentrate their own activities in sectors that are technologically advanced (hi tech), which record the highest percentage of business failure, but also, for obvious reasons, the highest rates of return.

As can be noted, in this synthetic panorama of the major protagonist operators of buy-outs in the Italian market, there are excluded some financial intermediaries that, instead, play an important role in other countries. It is the

---

[27] With the term "business angels" indicates those private investors , having own financial means, of a good network of acquaintances and managerial abilities, they decide to invest in one new activity, above all start up technologies.

[28] The "incubators of enterprises" are specialized operators in a position to supplying fresh resources and managerial support to young enterprises, helping them to survive and to grow during the period of "early stage", in which they are mainly vulnerable.

case, above all, of pension funds, particularly developed in the anglo-saxon markets but not yet completely taken-off in our country, also because of the noted but not entirely resolved structural deficiencies, that for years has afflicted the national providential system. It's however, foreseeable that in the next few years, pension funds will become an increasingly relevant subject in the venture capital and private equity market in general, and in the area of buy-outs in particular.

**Fig. 5.11** Evolution of the operators in the buy-out segment (2000-2002)

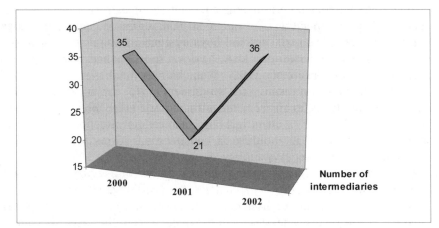

Source: elaboration of the author on data from AIFI (various years)

At this point, passing to a more specific analysis of the recent evolutionary paths regarding the qualitative and quantitative composition of the operators in the market, it is immediately worth showing how, during the last year, there has been a marked increase (+71%) of the number of operators in the buy-out segment, passing from 21 (2001) to 36 (2002). A similar value aligns itself, in fact, to that observed in 2000, when the institutional investors in risk capital active in buy outs were 35 (Figure 5.11), and moreover in coherence with the total dynamic seen earlier, with reference to the number and volumes of investments realized in the buy out space.

**Fig. 5.12** Percentage distribution (on number of deals made in 2002) by category of investor

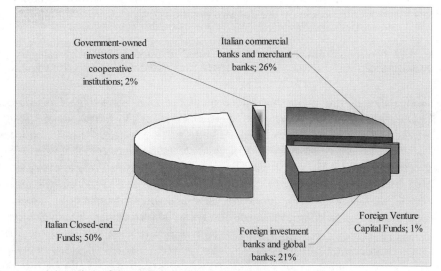

Source: elaboration of the author on data from AIFI (various years)

Going into further detail, and making reference to the number of operations brought to conclusion in 2002 (Figure 5.12), it is noted that the most active operators were the closed end domestic funds, those that realized, by themselves, half the transactions officially censused, confirming themselves by then, as the key actors in the market. On their shoulders, we find the banks and the financiers of shareholding, protagonists of 26% of the number of realized buy outs and the foreign operators, with a share of 21% of the entire market. Lastly, with marginal shares we find the regional/public/cooperative actors (2%) and not surprisingly the venture capital players (1%).

As regards the distribution of the institutional investors active in buy outs, by volumes invested, the market in 2002 as always, is found to be even more concentrated than previously observed (Figure 5.13).

In fact, in this case, nearly all the investments – a good 94% – is concentrated in the hands of a unique category of institutional investor: the investment banks and overseas operators, market leaders with 71% of the total invested, and the Italian closed funds, present with a share of 23%. In a marginal position, we find the banks and Italian shareholding financiers, which absorb 4% of the invested amount and the regional/ public/ cooperative actors (1%). The data related to the last two categories of operators, confirm what was observed in the preceding graphic where, even on the basis of numbers of deals these operators occupy the last two positions.

**Fig. 5.13** Percentage distribution (of total value invested in 2002) by category of investor

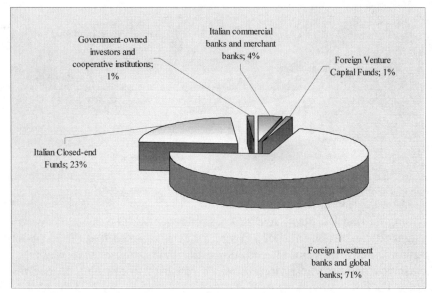

Source: elaboration of the author on data from AIFI (various years)

One consideration that emerges from such a non-homogeneous distribution of number and value of buy-outs realized by the principal actors in the market is, that the national operators (closed funds and above all, banks) are better equipped to cover the PMI market, by virtue of their greater operative possibilities in terms of territorial coverage; the foreign operators, on the other hand, are more focused on operations with a higher unit value (the mega deals), those which are, obviously, realized less frequently. The achievement of a certain threshold size, is among others, also related to the need to repay the structural costs that are undoubtedly more heavy, as characterized by the foreign investment banks.

**Fig. 5.14** Market share (in relation to volumes invested) of the intermediaries active in buy-outs comparison 1998-2002

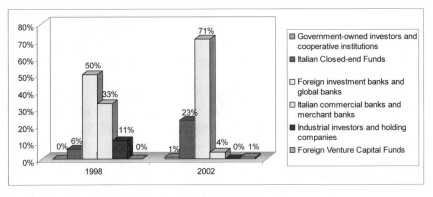

Source: elaboration of the author on data from AIFI (various years)

Continuing to refer to the intermediaries involved in buy outs, it is interesting to note how, between the start and ending of the period considered, 1998 and 2002 respectively, there has been a significant change in the distribution of the market share among the categories of investors considered till now (Figure 5.14). In fact we can note that the international operators maintain their leadership in the market: their relative share has even increased in the period considered, moving from 50% in 1998 to 71% in 2002. In the same time, the banks and the Italian shareholding financiers have seen a significant fall in their importance, passing from a share of 33% to 4%. Even worse has been the result of the buy out activities performed by industrial/ financial firms in the industrial matrix[29], that from a share of 11% of the

---

[29] Generally deals with companies held - singularly or in joint-ventures – by industrial subjects that have the objective to assume participation in enterprises of recent constitution, with high growth potential. In such a way, the large enterprise succeeds in financing the technological innovation, to defend the original business from the threat of substitutive products and to explore specific segments of market, in order to create itself of the "windows" on new and attractive business, without internalizing investments it characterized by an elevated and thus incompatible profile of risk and therefore with the managerial policies agreed with the market and the financiers of the same.

market in 1998, have practically disappeared in the course of 2002, having preferred to concentrate their attentions on the areas of seed and start-up financing. A diametrically opposite tendency has been shown by Italian closed funds, which have moved from 6% to 23%, being able to reach the second place in the Italian market. Finally, in the course of 2002, one can note the presence of two types of operators that at the beginning of the period, were absent from the buy out panorama: the regional/public/cooperative operators and the venture capital players, that respectively, however, do not exceed 1% of the total invested.

Finally, it is opportune to emphasize that, other than the institutional investors in risk capital, there exists another category of actors, important to the efficient and regular functioning of the buy out market, constituted by the subjects that perform a role of an essentially consultative nature and, with their activity of planning and coordination, represent in most cases, the true architects of a transaction. This could deal with banks and/or other intermediaries, whose actions do not necessarily involve a supply of capital, or could deal with a consulting company or a team of professionals of varied backgrounds.

### 5.5.4 Characteristics of the target firms

Also in terms of the characteristics of target firms, it is possible to note how in the past few years, their size has increased steadily.

In this regard, it is important to clarify, that the officially available statistics do not allow the reference to the of analysis made in the present section to the same temporal horizon taken for reference, in the preceding section. In any case, the documentary analysis conducted by the Author, along with a series of discussions with exponents of the more authoritative institutional investors in risk capital, appears to confirm the continuation of the structural trends identifiable in the 1995-1999 period and illustrated as follows.

**Fig. 5.15** Distribution of the buy-outs by value of the target firm (million euro)

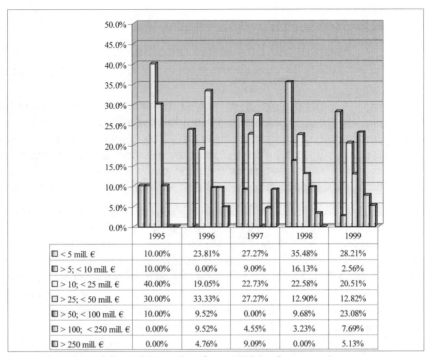

| | 1995 | 1996 | 1997 | 1998 | 1999 |
|---|---|---|---|---|---|
| ☐ < 5 mill. € | 10.00% | 23.81% | 27.27% | 35.48% | 28.21% |
| ☐ > 5; < 10 mill. € | 10.00% | 0.00% | 9.09% | 16.13% | 2.56% |
| ☐ > 10; < 25 mill. € | 40.00% | 19.05% | 22.73% | 22.58% | 20.51% |
| ☐ > 25; < 50 mill. € | 30.00% | 33.33% | 27.27% | 12.90% | 12.82% |
| ☐ > 50; < 100 mill. € | 10.00% | 9.52% | 0.00% | 9.68% | 23.08% |
| ☐ > 100; < 250 mill. € | 0.00% | 9.52% | 4.55% | 3.23% | 7.69% |
| ☐ > 250 mill. € | 0.00% | 4.76% | 9.09% | 0.00% | 5.13% |

Source: elaboration of the author on data from AIFI (various years)

Above all, analysing the data contained in Figure 5.15, relating to the distribution of buy-out operations by the value of the target firms, made in 1995-1999, it is possible to note that the operations with a value in excess of 100 million euro (mega deals), did not exist in 1995, while in 1999 represented 13% of the total.

It is noted, that the high volatility one is can find in the value related to the classes of operations that have a unit size greater than 250 million euro, is due, as can be imagined, to the relatively small frequency with which buy-outs come to closure in this size class.

**Fig. 5.16.** Sectorial distribution of target firms: comparison 1994-1999

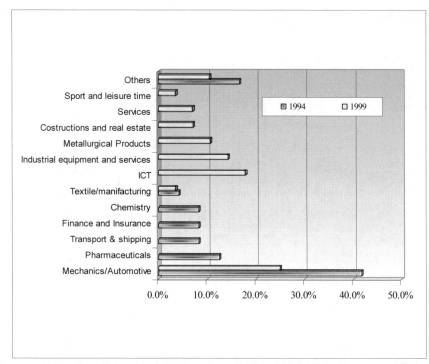

Source: elaboration of the author on data from AIFI and KPMG (various years)

It needs to be emphasized, moreover, the growth in the number of operations in the 50 to 100 million euro range, that moved from 10% of the total in 1995 to 23% in 1999. In the same manner, emerges also a more even distribution of buy out operations on the entire gamut of possible target firms. In fact in 1995, the large majority of majority of operations was concentrated in the small and medium sized firms – 90% was represented by firms of a value less than 50 million euro – in 1999 the situation was much more balanced with firms having a value not more than 50 million euro forming around 64% of the total.

The data just shown, among others, can be placed in strict relation to that shown in Figure 5.10, where it clearly emerges that, if taken into consideration with the more significant analyses without the mega deals, there is a consistently positive trend in the average amounts invested in buy-out operations.

Parallel to the growth in number and value of the effectuated operations, also the sectorial distribution of the target companies, though remaining still within more traditional sectors, has had changes, over the years, on the basis of the main evolutionary tendencies characterizing our business system.

**Fig. 5.17.** Geographic distribution of the target firm

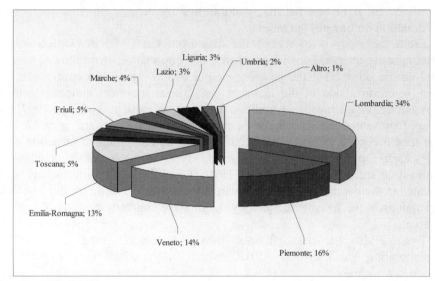

Source: AIFI (2001).

From Figure 5.16, in particular, it is possible to note that, with reference to 1994, the mechanical/ electromechanical sector represented more than 40% of the buy-out operations realized in our country. At the same time, with the exception of the pharmaceutical sector, there have not been any sectors of particularly innovative content represented, while as always, the traditional sectors, important among which are the transportation, and finance/insurance and chemicals sectors, all with a weight of 8.3% of the total.

In 1999, on the other hand, facing a resizing of the percentage weight of the mechanical/electromechanical sector (25%), and a significant presence of buy-outs in the metallurgical sector (10%), is evidence of acquisitions made in completely new areas than in the past, with a larger technological presence. In particular, there has been a notable concentration of operations in the ICT (Information and communication technology) sector, in the ambit of which, during 1999, there were 18% of buy-outs realized. Significantly in terms of the movement of attention of institutional investors towards more innovative activities, the share of the products and services to industry (14%), services in general (7.1%) and the sport and leisure (3.6%). The operations made in the clothing sector remained stable, going from 4.2% in 1994 to 3.6% in 1999.

The trend that emerges from the analysis just made, utilizing the data furnished by AIFI and KPMG, is confirmed by the use of other sources of information on buy out operations.

From the analysis of the of the data from the CMBOR, University of Nottingham, emerges, on the one hand, the importance of traditional sectors and on the other hand the growing weight of new areas and innovations. In fact, in confirmation of the fact that institutional investors concentrate their buy out activities, mostly in traditional sectors, as usual referring to 1999, the areas represented the most have been manufacturing in general with 18% of the total investments made, followed by paper and shipping construction with 10% each. On the other hand, though, testifying to the increased attention in innovative sectors, in the course of 1999, 9% of the buy out operations were located in the computer sector (software and hardware), while for the first time operations in the Internet technology sector were counted, reaching 3% of the market.

Finally, also the data obtained from the research made by AIFI in collaboration with INSEAD – LIUC, which analyses 101 buy out operations made in a wide temporal arc (1988-2000), what has been noted earlier, namely that the manufacturing sector has catalyzed a majority of the investments, representing around 38% of the sample studied, followed by the chemicals sector (8%) and that of consumer goods (7%). At the level of the sectors with high technological content, the research confirms the incidence of the electronic sector (7%), medical bio-tech (4%) and information technology (1%), showing also the fact that the acquisition of hi tech firms on the part of institutional investors in risk capital is, however, a phenomenon that has started to affirm itself only in recent years and is still growing.

A final and significant piece of information which can be useful to note in this text, refers to the geographical distribution of target firms and utilizes the same sample of transactions as cited above. (Figure 5.17) The regions most represented are those of Northern Italy, which can be related to 84% of the total transactions. In Lombardia and Piemonte are seen the most number of acquisitions at 34% and 16% respectively – followed by Veneto (14%) and Emilia Romagna (13%). Results are absent from the southern part of Italy while in the center of the country we find operations in Lazio (4%), Toscana (5%), Marche (3%) and Umbria (2%). The market leaves therefore interesting spaces for development in future years, above all with reference to national operators, those that as noted earlier, who lend themselves better to capture business opportunities that can originate from relations maintained with small and medium enterprises within the entire national territory.

# Appendix – LBOs in Italy: Institutional Issues

Simona Zambelli[1]

## A.1 Introduction

Recently, the Parliament introduced a new Corporate Governance Law aimed at regulating, among other things, the Leveraged Buyout process (LBO) in Italy, appearing to legalize the LBO technique under specific conditions (Legislative Decree 6/2003, applicable as of January 1, 2004). This might spur the future development of LBO transactions within the Italian private equity market and hopefully diminish the uncertainty surrounding the legal validity of LBOs.

The legitimacy of Leveraged Buyout transactions (LBO) in Italy has been strongly debated during the last decade. The controversy surrounding several buyout transactions realized in Italy over that period[2] has led part of the doctrine and jurisprudence to believe that the overall Leveraged Buyout scheme was designed with the only purpose of eluding the Italian Law, especially with reference to the provisions regarding the purchase of own shares by a company (articles 2357 – 2358 Civil Code – c.c.).[3]

The debate has intensified after a recent decision by the Italian Supreme Court (Corte di Cassazione, February 4, 2000, n. 5503) which has declared the Leveraged Buyout scheme illegal. This Decision has increased the uncertainty about the legal consequences of LBOs in Italy, probably preventing investors from adopting this financial scheme.[4]

---

[1] Simona Zambelli wrote this section on the basis of previous publications. A more detailed analysis on the institutional issues related to the legitimacy of the LBO scheme in Italy is included in: Zambelli (2005), Zambelli (2004), Zambelli (2002).
[2] Examples of LBO transactions that have intensified the debate are the following: Farmitalia case (Milan Tribunal, May 14, 1992 and Milan Tribunal, June 30, 1992); Pepperland case (Milan Tribunal, May 4, 1999); Manifattura di Cuorgnè case (Ivrea Tribunal, August 12, 1995), D'Andria case (Supreme Court, February 4, 2000). For details on the economic and legal implications related to the above cases see: Zambelli (2005). For information on the doctrine and jurisprudence related to the above cases see: Fava and Fuschino (2003), Bruno (2002).
[3] This particular interpretation is known as "substantial thesis". The major authors embracing this view are: Montalenti (1996, 1990), Morello (1995), Apice (1990).
[4] See: Capizzi (2004), Aifi (2001).

In reality, LBO is just a financial tool. Like other tools, it can be used properly or misused. In our opinion, this does not justify the Court to reject it in absolute terms since, when properly used, it allows a company to access alternative source of finance. Moreover, LBO may have a positive effect on the return on equity (ROE) and the Firm Value, by lowering the weighted average cost of capital (wacc).

After the introduction of the new corporate governance law, the crucial question is the following: Is the debate on the legitimacy of LBOs finally over? This section intends to answer this question. In particular, the purpose of this section is twofold:

1. to discuss the reasons why LBOs were considered illegal in Italy;
2. to highlight the legal requirements for the legitimacy of LBOs, in view of the recent Company Law Reform (Legislative Decree 6/2003, applicable as of January 1, 2004).

For the purpose of this section, a buyout is defined as an acquisition of the equity capital of a firm (called target) by another company (called newco). The term Leveraged Buyout on the other hand describes a particular technique used to accomplish the acquisition. It is characterized by the fact that the acquisition of the target company is financed with a large amount of debt relative to the asset value of the acquired company. The debt financing is arranged by the newco and is secured by the assets of the firm that is being acquired (target). The financing is obtained under the expectation that it will be repaid with the cash flows generated by the acquired company or by the sale of its non-strategic assets. Following the acquisition, the newco and the target merge. The combined firm has a higher leverage ratio (total debt/total assets) than the target firm had before. LBOs differ from other leveraged acquisitions because the debt is effectively secured by the acquired company and not by the buyer. Hence, the target firm pays the economic price of its own acquisition. [5]

The scheme of the typical LBO transaction can be summarized through the following steps:

– Phase 1: Creation of a new company (newco)

A group of buyers establishes a new company (newco) with the aim of acquiring a specific firm (target). The initial buyers are in many instances the management of the target company (Management Buyout) or an outside management team (Management Buyin);

---

[5] See: Capizzi (2004), Bertini (2000), Altman and Smith (1993), Grande Stevens (1990), Gambino (1990), Cantoni (1989).

- Phase 2: Debt financing

In order to obtain the funds necessary to accomplish the acquisition, the newco generally requires debt financing (leverage). This debt usually takes the form of bridge financing and is collected from specialized financial institutions (mainly banks);

- Phase 3: Acquisition of the target

Once the bridge financing provided by lending institutions has been obtained, the newco acquires all the target's shares;[6]

- Phase 4: Merger

The acquisition is followed by the merger of the target with the newco. As a consequence, the debt obtained by the newco is merged into the target's liabilities.[7] After the merger, the bridge financing is generally replaced by a medium or long-term debt, secured by the assets of the merged company. The target company has to repay the debt obligation with its future cash flows. In this sense, the target firm bears most of the economic costs of its own acquisition. Hence, the success of an LBO depends on the financial characteristics of the target company, especially in terms of growth potential and ability of its management team.

The high degree of leverage which characterizes most post-LBO firms has at least two effects. On the one hand, the presence of a high level of debt puts pressure on the management team and acts as an incentive. On the other hand, it increases the firm's default risk. The latter tends to be especially high in case of a turnaround Leveraged Buyout, in which the target firm is already in financial distress before the LBO transaction. In this situation, it is essential to have a highly motivated management team with proven experience and skills.[8]

---

[6] For LBOs completed in Italy so far, the Newco has always acquired 100% of the capital of the target company. This simplifies the merger procedure following the acquisition. After the incorporation of the target into the NEWCO, the target's shares are cancelled. See: Aifi (2001), Mills and Seassaro (1990).

[7] See: Confalonieri (2004), Savioli (2003), Spolidoro (2000).

[8] One of the most successful examples of such a turnaround LBO in Italy is the acquisition of Ducati Motor by the Texas Pacific Group (TPG) in 1996. Texas Pacific Group is a private equity company based in San Francisco. TPG bought Ducati Motor in 1996 through a leveraged buyout alongside Deutsche Morgan Grenfell (now Deutsche Bank). Before the buyout transaction, Ducati was owned by the Cagiva Group, a private manufacturing conglomerate. In 1996, the Cagiva Group suffered a serious liquidity crisis which also affected Ducati's business, reducing Ducati's motorcycle production, sales and financial performance. Ducati

This section is organized as follows. The next paragraph discusses the debate on the legal validity of LBOs and analyzes the case judged by the Supreme Court decision (Corte di Cassazione, February 4, 2000, n. 5503). The third section describes the recent legal reform of Leveraged Buyouts, introduced by the new corporate governance law (Legislative Decree 6/2003).

## A.2 The debate on the legal validity of LBOs before the new corporate governance law

Over the past few years an intensive juridical debate about the legitimacy of LBOs in Italy has developed. Divergent opinions between scholars (doctrine) and Italian courts (jurisprudence) have characterized the discussion.[9] At the core of this dispute was the interpretation of the final result of a Leveraged Buyout transaction. The result of the LBO scheme has been considered similar to what would happen if the target firm made a loan or provided a guarantee to the newco for the purchase of its own shares.[10]

Let us analyze in greater details the reason why the LBO scheme was considered illegal by part of the doctrine and the jurisprudence.[11] The

---

came close to being declared bankrupt. Texas Pacific Group recognized the growth potential of Ducati's line of business and, following an accurate evaluation of Ducati's business plan, decided to acquire the company through a leveraged turnaround transaction. Subsequent to the acquisition, Ducati implemented a successful turnaround program that substantially increased the production of motorcycles and unit sales. Lastly, Ducati went public in March 1999.

[9] Examples of cases that are commonly considered part of the existing jurisprudence on LBOs in Italy are the following: Tribunal of Milan, May 14, 1992; Penal Tribunal of Milan, June 30, 1992; Tribunal of Ivrea, August 12, 1995; Tribunal of Milan, October 27, 1997, Supreme Court Decision 5503/2000. These cases do not show a clear and uniform trend in the jurisprudence. The number of variations on the basic LBO scheme encountered in practice is large, while each court decision examines only the particular operations of the case at hand. A detailed analysis of the doctrine and jurisprudence concerned with LBOs is presented in: Zambelli (2005), Fava and Fuschino (2003), Bruno (2002), Varrenti (2001), Picone (2001), Angelini (2001), Frignani (1996), Desideri (1993), Preite (1993), Belviso (1993); Mills and Seassaro (1990).

[10] For more information from a legal point of view, see: Montalenti (1996, 1990), Morello (1995), Apice (1990).

[11] See: Montalenti (1996).

debate on the validity of a typical LBO transaction was mainly focused on the interpretation of two provisions of the Civil Code (c.c):

– Article 2357;
– Article 2358.[12]

Article 2357 defines a set of conditions according to which a company can repurchase its own shares. A company can repurchase its own shares only within the limits of the available net profits and only in case they are fully paid (see par. I). Furthermore, the purchase must be approved by the shareholders' meeting and the par value of the shares shall not exceed 1/10 of the entire share capital (see par. II, III). These limits also apply to purchases realized through an intermediary or a fiduciary company (par. V). In case of a violation of these restrictions, the shares exceeding the specified limits must be sold within one year from their purchase. If this does not occur, the shares shall be cancelled and the book value of the share capital shall be reduced by a corresponding portion. Otherwise, a Court must intervene and order the reduction of the share capital (par. IV).

The main intention of the lawmaker is to protect the target's paid-in share capital, avoiding a weakening of the guarantees granted to the target's creditors. In fact, if a company buys back its own shares using funds other than current profits, the result is a partial restitution of equity capital to shareholders. Consequently, by draining funds from the company and increasing the leverage ratio, pre-existing loan obligations become more risky, to the obvious detriment of the firm's creditors.

According to a particular interpretation of the law[13], the result of an LBO transaction is considered similar to a situation in which the target company acquires its own shares through the intermediation of the newco, eluding the restrictions specified by article 2357.[14]

This interpretation of article 2357 does not seem justified from an economic viewpoint, given the rationale behind the article as outlined above.

First of all, in a simple share buy-back by the target company (even through the intermediation of a third party) the final ownership structure

[12] See: Busani (2003), Fava and Fuschino (2003), Bruno (2002), Accini (1996), Preite (1993), Varrenti (2000).
[13] This interpretation is defined as "substantial thesis " by the Italian doctrine. See: Cottino (1999); Montalenti (1996, 1990); Morello (1995); Apice (1990).
[14] Farmitalia case was accused to elude the provisions of article 2357 c.c. (Decision of the Tribunal of Milan, May 14, 1992). For a review of the related jurisprudence, see: Zambelli (2005), Fava and Fuschino (2003), Bruno (2002), Picone (2001), Scodditi (1993); Sorrentino (1992).

does not necessarily change. LBO transactions, on the other hand, are fundamentally characterized by a change in ownership structure. The ultimate owners of the combined entity are the owners of the newco. Hence the economic goal of an LBO is fundamentally different from the goal of a simple share buyback.

Second, depending on the specifics of any deal, creditors may or may not be in favor of the buyout transaction. Does the protection of investors and other parties with pre-existing contracts justify the application of article 2357 to LBO transactions? Under the current Italian Law, creditors have the possibility to oppose any LBO transaction that appears to lower the value of their claims.[15] This "veto right" of creditors opens up the possibility of mutually beneficial agreements between creditors, target company and acquirer, which a restrictive interpretation of article 2357 would rule out.

Article 2358 prohibits a company from making loans or providing guarantees for the purchase of its own shares, either directly or indirectly through the intermediation of a third party (financial assistance rule). Before the introduction of the New Corporate Governance Law, a violation of this provision was punishable under criminal law with a sentence of up to 3 years of prison (according to article 2360 c.c., 1$^{st}$ paragraph, number 2)[16].

The rationale behind article 2358 is twofold:

- To protect the equity of the target company in the interest of creditors, similarly to article 2357. The legislator wants to avoid a deterioration of the target firm's capital structure;
- To avoid abusive behavior by the target's directors, e.g. to prevent them from taking over the company fraudulently through a hidden acquisition of its own shares. If the actions described in article 2358 were permitted without restrictions, the directors could misuse the funds of the company by making loans or providing guarantees to an outside party (trustee). This implies that, through the intermediation of that party, the directors could indirectly take over the company and influence the shareholders' meeting.[17]

---

[15] Article 2503 of the Civil Code.

[16] This article has been eliminated by the Legislative Decree 6/2003, applicable as of January 1, 2004.

[17] For more information, see: Cottino and al. (2004), Angelini (2001), Montanari (2001), Zambelli and Jenter (2001), Cartolano (2000), Molino (2000), Picone (2000), Morano (1992).

The above article represents the most-often invoked provision against the validity of LBOs in Italy.[18] As a consequence of the merger, in fact, the target's assets serve as a guarantee for the payment of the debt previously contracted by the newco. According to a particular interpretation of the law (known as "substantial thesis"), the result of an LBO transaction is to elude the provisions specified by article 2358, because the target company in the end provides a guarantee for the purchase of its own shares. The newco in turn is interpreted as an intermediary acting on behalf of the target company. According to this particular view, the result of an LBO transaction is similar to what would happen if the target firm made a loan or provided a guarantee to the newco for the purchase of its own shares.[19] This would be prohibited by article 2358 c.c.

Recently, the Italian Supreme Court has reinforced this view (Supreme Court's Decision n. 5503/2000, D'Andria case).

## A.2.1 The Supreme Court's decision n. 5503/2000

A recent decision of the Supreme Court (February 4, 2000, n. 5503) stated explicitly that "the LBO scheme cannot be imported into the Italian system because it is in contrast with article 2358 of the Civil Code".[20]

The above statement has been severely criticized by the doctrine.[21] In our opinion, the decision of the Court is driven by a misunderstanding in the definition of the characteristics of this type of transaction.

As noted, this decision does not seem justified from an economic viewpoint. There is no ex-ante equivalence between LBO transactions and the acquisition of own shares through an intermediary.

First, in an LBO, the debt guarantee by the target company comes into effect only after the merger has been completed, i.e. after the ownership of the target company has changed.

Second, creditors will not be defrauded as long as they have the ability to object to any Leveraged Buyout which reduces the value of their claims.

---

[18] A famous case accused to elude the provisions of article 2358 c.c. is represented by: Manifattura di Cuorgnè ( Decision of Ivrea Tribunal, August 12, 1995). For more information see: Zambelli (2005), Fava, Fuschino (2003).

[19] See: Cottino (1999), Montalenti (1996, 1990), Morello (1995), Apice (1990).

[20] Supreme Court's decision, V penal section, n. 5503, February 4, 2000. For more information see: Filigrana and Cartolano (2000), Molino (2000), Picone (2000), Varrenti (2000).

[21] See: Accini (2001), Filograna, Cartolano (2000).

Furthermore, in the case of listed companies, LBOs are publicly announced and do not allow managers to take control of their own firms in a hidden manner.

In order to evaluate the general relevance of this decision for LBOs, it is important to analyze the facts of the case that induced the Court to make the above statement (D'Andria case – Box 1).

---

**Box 1. The D'Andria case (Supreme Court, February 4, 2000, n. 5503)**

A conglomerate of companies entered into a financial crisis and collapsed into bankruptcy. The administrator of the group was accused of fraudulent bankruptcy under the provisions of the Italian bankruptcy law. The administrator had, through the course of his business activities, financed the acquisition of several companies. Some of these acquisitions had been financed using promissory notes guaranteed by the target companies. In the Court's opinion, he knew he could not honor these promissory notes since it was evident that he did not have the necessary funds to accomplish his stated goals. Since several acquisitions involved a guarantee provided by the target companies, the Court saw an evident violation of article 2358 Civil Code as described above. After being accused of fraudulent bankruptcy, the administrator received an arrest order (July 7, 1999). He appealed against this arrest order and its defendant argued that the transactions in question followed "a modern but absolutely legal scheme of self financing, similar to a leveraged buyout", carried out in the U.S. Only in response to this specific argument did the Supreme Court intervene and declared the LBO schemes illegal in Italy.

---

In our view, the case considered by the Supreme Court could not represent a general and strong precedent for the Italian legal system.

First, the facts of the case considered by the Supreme Court in the decision at hand did not represent a reliable basis for resolving the issue of LBO validity in Italy. The Supreme Court made the above statement on LBOs only indirectly, or better incidentally, with reference to a criminal law case of fraudulent bankruptcy. The issue of the legitimacy of LBO transactions was not the actual problem of the case and emerged only incidentally during the appeal.

Second, the defendant improperly described the financing transactions mentioned before as a Leveraged Buyout. A closer examination of the financial transactions in conflict with article 2358 c.c. casts doubt on whether the case can even be considered close to an actual LBO transaction. In the case at hand, there is little doubt that the financial instruments used were illegal, and that the promissory notes where issued without the expectation that there would be sufficient funds to honor them.

For these reasons, it seems unjustified to conclude that the facts of the case represent an appropriate picture of standard LBO transactions. The latter can be implemented in widely different forms, and whether or not any given transaction conflicts with article 2358 c.c depends on the specific circumstances and details of each deal. Finally, article 2358 c.c. describes a transaction scheme which is not used for most LBO transactions. It assumes explicitly that the target company plays an active role in the acquisition process, providing ex-ante guarantees or loans to the newco in order to facilitate the purchase of its own shares. This is what happened in the case considered by the Supreme Court. The target companies provided bank guarantees in favor of the newco in order to obtain the capital needed to proceed with their own acquisition. A part from this particular situation, which is indeed prohibited by article 2358 c.c., it is difficult to see LBO transactions in general as illegal as long as the target assumes a passive role and does not give formal ex-ante guarantees to the newco. [22]

As mentioned, LBO is just a financial tool and the legal validity of each LBO deal has to be evaluated on a case by case basis, taking into account the specific facts and circumstances that characterize each transaction.

The decision by the Supreme Court, rather than solving a problem, has increased the uncertainty about the admissibility of LBOs in Italy. Empirically, the number and the amount of LBO transactions have significantly decreased during 2001 (Table A.1). [23]

**Table A.1.** Number and amount (€ millions) of Buyouts transactions in Italy (2000-2001)

|  | Number of Buyouts transactions | Amount of Buyouts transactions (€ millions) |
|---|---|---|
| 2000 | 53 | 1,363 |
| 2001 | 30 | 1,014 |

Source: AIFI

---

[22] For more information see: Zambelli (2005), Accini (2001), Filograna and Cartolano (2000), Bontempi (1993), Frignani (1989), Varrenti (2001), Mills and Seassaro (1990).

[23] See: www.aifi.it

According to the database collected by the Italian Venture Capital Association (AIFI), the number of buyout transactions in Italy has passed from 53 (in year 2000) to 30 (in year 2001).[24]

An important factor contributing to this dramatic decrease has been the negative economic trend affecting the Italian private equity market. However, according to data collected by AIFI, the decline in the number of LBO transactions has been more pronounced than the one in the number of start-up and expansion deals. It seems reasonable to suspect that the uncertainty surrounding the legitimacy of this type of transaction and its legal consequences has prevented investors from adopting this financial scheme.

## A.3 The legitimacy of LBOs in Italy light of the new corporate governance law

Recently, the Italian Parliament has introduced a new regulation which reforms the Corporate Governance rules (Legislative Decree 6/2003, applicable as of January 1, 2004) and, among other things, intends to clarify that LBO transactions cannot be considered invalid if they respect specific legal conditions (see art. 2501 bis Civil Code ). More precisely, article 2051 bis states that mergers between a leveraged vehicle (newco) and the acquired company (target), where the target acts as general guarantee for, or the source of reimbursement of, shall now be permitted subject to certain requirements.[25]

First, the board of directors of each merging company has to write a particular report indicating:

- The business reasons justifying the entire LBO transaction (included the merger process);
- The business and financial plan describing the objectives of the merger and the financial resources that the directors expect to obtain as a result of the merger.

Second, it is necessary to prepare a merger plan describing the financial resources that are necessary to repay the debt contracted by the newco. The merger plan must contain, among other things, a description of the share exchange ratio of each firm and the financial resources that will be used by

---

[24] For details on Italian LBO transactions in 2001, see the previous chapter, written by Capizzi. See also: Capizzi (2004), Aifi (2001).
[25] See Cottino and al. (2004).

the merged company to satisfy its obligations. Third, an external auditor's report is also necessary in order to validate the content of the merger plan. Finally, the latter has to be integrated with a report prepared by financial experts, in order to confirm the fairness of: the business and the financial plan; the share exchange ratio; the director's report.[26]

This reform has definitely reduced the ambiguity surrounding the legal validity of LBOs in Italy, and has eliminated the risk for managers of the merged company to receive a sentence of up to 3 years of prison, according to the previous provision of art. 2630 c.c.[27] Hence, we expect an increase in number and volume of LBOs transactions in Italy.

However, the debate is still open with reference to:

1. The difficulty to justify the merger with a valid business reason;[28]
2. The legal consequences of LBO transactions that occurs through a reverse merger (when the newco is incorporated into the target company). In this case, the debate on the legitimacy of the whole transaction remains open. The goal of the whole transaction seems the acquisition by the target of its own shares, without respecting the provisions specified in article 2357 c.c. and article 2358 c.c.;[29]
3. The criminal law consequences, in case of bankruptcy of the merged company. According to the recent Legislative Decree 61/2002, new bankruptcy events and criminal law articles have been introduced and they might be applicable to LBOs, when it is demonstrated that the LBO transaction has caused the financial crisis of the target company (art. 2628 c.c, art. 2629 c.c, art. 2634, art. 223 Bankruptcy Law);[30]
4. The fiscal implications connected to the deducibility of interests related to the Debt Financing contracted by the newco. According to the Thin Capitalization Rule, introduced by the Legislative Decree 344/2003 (which has changed the Consolidation Act of Income Tax – TUIR), the tax shield connected to the Debt Financing received by the newco might dramatically diminish.[31]

At present, opinions with respect to the above aspects appear to be contrasted. We shall wait for new Jurisprudence.

---

[26] Financial experts are chosen within a particular Register of Auditors.

[27] See Iannaccone (2002).

[28] "It may prove difficult to ascertain a valid business reason for a merger in the case of a typical LBO carried out by professional investors such as private equity players, where a leveraged *newco* vehicle has been established solely for the purpose of the transaction", La Torre and Rio (2002).

[29] See: Zambelli (2005), Confalonieri (2004), Musco (2002), Manzini (2000).

[30] For more information see: Zambelli (2005).

[31] See Confalonieri (2004).

## A.4 Conclusions

In this section we have described the juridical debate on the validity of LBOs in Italy, which has intensified after the Supreme Court has affirmed the invalidity of LBOs in Italy through its decision n. 5503/2000. Two articles of the Civil Code have been invoked by the doctrine and jurisprudence against the validity of LBO transactions:

– Article 2357 (restricting the purchase of own shares by a company);
– Article 2358 (prohibiting financial assistance for the purchase of own shares by a company).

The Supreme Court Decision n. 5503/2000 has been strongly criticized, mostly because it has increased the uncertainty surrounding the legitimacy of LBOs in Italy, instead of resolving it. This decision, assumes implicitly that the target company plays an active role in the acquisition process, providing ex-ante guarantees or loans to the newco in order to facilitate the purchase of its own shares. This is what happened in the case considered by the Supreme Court. However, there is no ex-ante equivalence between LBO transactions and the acquisition of own shares through an intermediary. In our opinion, it seems premature to generally declare that the LBO scheme is illegal in Italy. In an LBO, the debt guaranteed by the target company comes into effect only after the merger has been completed, i.e. after the ownership of the target company has changed. Creditors will not be defrauded as long as they have the ability to object to any Leveraged Buyout which reduces the value of their claims. In a simple share buyback by the target company (even through the intermediation of a third party) the final ownership structure does not change. LBO transactions, on the other hand, are fundamentally characterized by a change in ownership structure. The legal validity of each deal depends on the specific circumstances and characteristics of each transaction and has to be decided on a case-by-case basis.

Recently, the Italian Parliament has introduced a new regulation aimed at reforming the corporate governance rules (Legislative Decree 6/2003, applicable as of January 1, 2004). This new Corporate Law Reform, among other things, specifies the requirements for the legal validity of LBOs.

Notwithstanding the new corporate governance rule, the legal debate on LBOs doesn't seem completely solved, mainly with respect to the fiscal and criminal law consequences.

# References

AA VV (1999) La cartolarizzazione dei crediti in Italia. Caratteristiche tecniche, aspetti legali e fiscali e vantaggi per le banche e per le imprese. Bancaria Editrice, Rome

AA VV (2001) La cartolarizzazione nelle imprese non finanziarie. Egea, Milan

Accini G P (1996) Profili penali nelle operazioni di leveraged – management buyout. Giuffrè, Milan

Accini G P (2001) Operazioni di leveraged buyout ed un preteso caso di illiceità penale. Rivista delle società

AIFI (2000) Manifesto. Milan

AIFI (2001) L'impatto economico delle operazioni di buyout. Collana Capitale di Rischio e Impresa Quaderno 11

AIFI (various years) Capitale per lo sviluppo. Guerini & Associati, Milan

AIFI, Insead, Università Cattaneo Castellanza (2001) The economic impact of management leveraged buy-out. Research paper, Milan

Albisetti R (2001) Il project finance. Etas Libri, Milan

Alfano F, Corona A, Lupi (2002) Una valutazione della performance dell'Italia nel settore delle TLC alla luce dei risultati della Settima Relazione della Commissione Europea sullo stato di attuazione del quadro normativo. Telecommunications Guarantee Authority, Rome

Altman E I, Smith A (1993) Ristrutturazioni per mezzo di leveraged buyout. Economia & Management

Amatucci F (1998) Applicabilità del modello del project finance in sanità. Meconsan 6

Amatucci F (2002) Il project finance nelle aziende pubbliche. Egea, Milan

Angelini D (2001) Aspetti finanziari del leveraged buy-out e problemi di qualificazione giuridica. www.tidona.com

ANPA (1999) Secondo rapporto sui rifiuti urbani e sugli imballaggi e rifiuti da imballaggio

ANPA-ONR (2001) Rapporto rifiuti 2001

Antolisei F (2002) Manuale di diritto penale. Leggi complementari. Giuffrè, Milan

Apice U (1990) Il leveraged buyout in Italia. Intervento all'incontro di studio curato dal Centro Studi di diritto fallimentare, Rome

Artale G, Pampana A, Rasola C (2000) Guida alla securitization: i vantaggi, gli strumenti e gli adempimenti della nuova legge. Bancaria Editrice, Rome

Ascari R, Albisetti R (1996) Project Financing: new trends of World Bank Activity. World Bank Publishing, Washington DC

ASSR – Agenzia per i Servizi Sanitari Regionali (2002) Bilanci delle aziende ospedaliere per l'anno 2000. Il Sole 24 Ore Sanità December

Baldi M, De Marzo G (2001) Il project financing nei lavori pubblici. Ipsoa, Milan

Banca Commerciale Italiana (1990) I leveraged buy-out: esperienze internazionali e prospettive per l'Italia. Tendenze Reali 39

Banca Intesa (2002) Liberalizzazione del settore elettrico e mercati finanziari. Monetary Trends 81

Barzaghi L (2002) Operazioni di LBO: un modello di valutazione. Amministrazione & Finanza 4

Belviso F (1993) Il leveraged buyout al vaglio dei giudici italiani. Rivista diritto d'impresa

Benfenati I (2003) La responsabilità penale dell'amministratore di fatto nei reati di bancarotta fraudolenta ex art 223 Legge Fallimentare. www.filodiritto.com

Bennet Stewart G III (1998) La ricerca del valore. Una guida per il management e gli azionisti. Egea, Milan

Bernardi M (2003) Legittimità delle operazioni di leveraged buy-out. Diritto e Pratica delle Società

Bernstein A J (1993) A lesse's guide to structuring the cross-border aircraft lease. In: Hall S (eds) Aircraft financing. Euromoney Publication, London

Bertini B (2000) LBO e MBO: problemi operativi e tendenze giurisprudenziali in Italia ed in Europa. Contratto e Impresa

Bhattacharya A K, Fabozzi F (1997) Asset-backed securities. Frank J. Fabozzi Assoc.

Boeri T, Cohen R (1998) Analisi dei progetti di investimento. Teoria e applicazioni per il project financing. Egea, Milan

Bond Market Association, International Swaps & Derivatives Associations (2002) Securities industry association. Special purpose entities (SPEs) and the securitization markets

Bontempi M, Scagliarini G (1999) La securitization. Giuffrè, Milan

Brealey R A, Cooper I A, Habib M A (1996) Using project finance to fund infrastructure investments. Journal of Applied Corporate Finance 9-3

Bruno N A (2002) Il leveraged buyout nella casistica giurisprudenziale. Università LUISS Guido Carli, CERADI, Rome

Burton M, Nesiba R, Lombra R (2003) Financial markets and institutions. Thomson South-Western

Busani A (2003) Leveraged buy-out. In: Forestieri G (eds) Corporate e Investment Banking. Second Edition, Egea, Milan

Butti G, Chiosi M (2003) Al via la liberalizzazione del settore gas: quali i principi e le prospettive?. Ambiente e Sicurezza 3

Calvello S (1990) Leveraged buy-out. Contratto e Impresa

Campanini L (2002) Finanziamento degli investimenti nel settore dei rifiuti solidi urbani. Convention Financing investments in the solid urban waste sector, Banca Intesa, Milan

Caneva P (2001) Cartolarizzazione. Considerazioni per una valutazione economica. Banche e Banchieri 1 p 65

Cantoni G (1989) Il leveraged buy-out come forma tecnica di acquisizione. Aspetti reali e finanziari. Finanza, Marketing e Produzione

Capizzi V (2001) L'attività di advisoring: le condizioni dell'offerta. In: Zara C (eds) Le banche e l'advisoring nella finanza straordinaria. Bancaria Editrice, Rome

Capizzi V (2002) The constitutions of a venture capital company: the case of a Italian closet-end fund. In: Caselli S, Gatti S (eds) Venture capital in the Euro system: market structure, strategies and management. Newfin, Università Bocconi, Milan

Capizzi V (2003) Gli intermediari finanziari e i servizi a supporto delle acquisizioni aziendali. In: Forestieri G (eds) Corporate and investment banking. Second Edition, Egea, Milan

Capizzi V (2003) Il costo del capitale e le operazioni di investment banking. Egea, Milan

Capizzi V (2003) Le attività e i servizi originate dalle ristrutturazioni e dai riassetti societari. In: Forestieri G (eds) Corporate and investment banking. Second Edition, Egea, Milan

Capizzi V (2004) Le operazioni di leveraged buy-out in Italia: aspetti tecnici e finanziari. Newfin Ricerche

Capizzi V, Ghelfi A (2004) Management buy-out: an agency theory approach. Working paper presented at III CEMS Academic Conference, Bruxelles

Cappellini G, Gatti S (1997) Il settore del project finance in Italia – Situazione attuale e prospettive future. Economia e Management 6

Caputo Nassetti F, Fabbri A (2001) Trattato sui contratti derivati di credito. Egea, Milan

Carretta A, De Laurentis G (1998) Il manuale del leasing. Egea, Milan

Carretta A, Fiordelisi F (2000) Il leasing operativo. Caratteristiche giuridiche, economiche e gestionali nei mercati europeo e statunitense e prospettive di sviluppo in Italia. Bancaria Editrice, Rome

Cartolazzo M (1989) L'avanzo ed il disavanzo di fusione: profili economico-contabili, civilistici e tributari. Bollettino tributario

Caselli S (1996) Lo sviluppo del leasing nei paesi dell'est Europa. Newfin, Università Bocconi, Milan

Caselli S (1998) La valutazione del costo. In: Carretta A, De Laurentis G (eds), Il manuale del leasing. Egea, Milan

Caselli S (2002) Corporate banking per le piccole e medie imprese. Bancaria, Rome

Caselli S (2003) La struttura del mercato italiano dei servizi di corporate e investment banking. In: Forestieri G (eds) Corporate and investment banking. Second Edition, Egea, Milan

Caselli S (2004) Lo sviluppo delle sinergie fra corporate e private banking: le opportunità di mercato nella relazione fra la famiglia e l'impresa. In: Caselli S, Gatti S (eds) Banking per il family business. Newfin, Università Bocconi, Milan

Caselli S, Gatti S (2003) Il corporate lending. Bancaria Editrice, Rome

Cathcart A (1996) Done deal for Ducati. Cycle World 35-11

Cesarini F (2003) Le operazioni di finanza immobiliare. Bancaria Editrice, Rome

Chrappa C (1999) Big ticket residual value problems surfacing. Equipment Finance Journal 5

Clifford Chance (1994) Project finance. IFR, London

CMBOR (various years) European management buy-outs: annual review

Colagrande F, Fiore L, Grimaldi M, Prandina D (1999) Le operazioni di securitization. Edizioni Il Sole 24 Ore, Milan

Comitato per la vigilanza sull'uso delle risorse idriche (2001) Relazione annuale al Parlamento sullo stato dei servizi idrici per l'anno 2000, Rome

Conca V (1991) Le acquisizioni. Egea, Milan

Confalonieri M (2004) Trasformazione, fusione, conferimento, scissione e liquidazione delle società. Il Sole 24 Ore, Milan

Confindustria (2002) La competitività dell'Italia. Il sole 24 Ore, Milan

Copelan T, Koller T, Murrin J (2000) Valuation. John Wiley & Sons, New York

Cottino G (1999) Le società. Cedam, Padova

Cottino G, Bonfante G, Cagnasso O, Montalenti P (2004) Il nuovo diritto societario. Zanichelli, Bologne

D.L. 27 novembre 2001, Operazione di cartolarizzazione dei crediti e proventi appartenenti allo Stato derivanti dai giochi del Lotto e dell'Enalotto. G.U. Serie generale 283

Dailami M, Hauswald R (2001) Contract risks and credit spread determinants in the international project bonds markets. World Bank Institute, Washington DC

Damilano M (2000) La securitization dei crediti. Giappichelli Editore, Turin

Damodaran A (2001) Corporate finance. Theory and practice. John Wiley & Sons, New York

De Angeli S, Oriani M (2000) La securitization dei crediti bancari. Franco Angeli, 2000

De Masi C, Massi A (1999) Finanziamento private alle opera pubbliche e progettazione. Giornale di diritto amministrativo 2

Department of Trade & Industry (2001) Communications liberalisation in the UK, London

Desideri S A (1993) Il LBO tra liceità e illegalità. I limiti all'acquisto di azioni proprie. Fisco

Dessy A (2001) Sistema fiscale e leverage aziendale: esperienze a confronto. Egea, Milan

Diamond S (1985) Leveraged buy-outs. Dow Jones Irwin, Homewood

Draetta U, Vaccà C (1997), Il project financing: caratteristiche e modelli contrattuali. Egea, Milan

Equipment Leasing Association (2001) 2000 – Survey of industry activity. Washington DC

Equipment Leasing Association (2002) 2001 – Survey of industry activity. Washington DC

Equipment Leasing Association (2003) 2002 – Survey of industry activity. Washington DC

ESF Securitisation Report (2001) European securitization issuance soars to another record in 2001

Esty B C (2002) Returns on project-financed investments: evolution and managerial implications. Journal of Applied Corporate Finance 15-1

Esty B C, Megginson W L (2002) Creditors' rights, enforcement and debt ownership structure: evidence from the global syndicated loans market. Mimeograph, Harvard Business School

Euromoney (2001) World leasing convention 2000. Euromoney Publication, London

Euromoney (2002) World leasing convention 2001. Euromoney Publication, London

Euromoney (2003) World leasing convention 2002. Euromoney Publication, London

European Commission (2002) Economic portrait of the European Union 2002. Eurostat, Brussels

EUROSTAT (2002) New decisions on deficit and debt: securitization operations undertaken by general government. Statistical Office 80 July

EVCA (various years) EVCA yearbook. www.evca.com

Everhart S S, Sumlinski M A (2001) Trends in private investment in developing countries. Statistics for 1970-2000 and the impact on private investment of corruption and the quality of public investment. IFC Discussion Paper 44

Fabozzi F (1999) Issuer perspective on securitization. McGraw-Hill

Fabozzi F, Nevitt P K (1996) Project Financing. Euromoney Publication, London

Fassati A, Palari S (1996) Le peculiarità dei buy-out in Italia negli anni Novanta. Notiziario economico della Banca San Paolo di Brescia 3

Fava P, Fuschino P (2003) Il leveraged buyout. La Tribuna, Piacenza

Felicetti C (2002) Public private partnership in sanità: l'esperienza italiana. Finlombarda Convention Finanza e Sanità, Milan

Ferrari P (2003) Gli intermediari finanziari e le operazioni di leveraged buy-out. In: Forestieri G (2003) Corporate and investment banking. Second Edition, Egea, Milan

Ferrario M C (1991) Management buy out. Isedi, Turin

Ferro Luzzi P (2000) La cartolarizzazione: riflessioni e spunti ricostruttivi. Bancaria 1 p 24

Filograna E, Cartolano F (2000) Un falso precedente in tema di leveraged buy-out. Foro Italiano

Finance & Leasing Association (2001) Annual Review 2000. London

Finance & Leasing Association (2002) Annual Review 2001. London

Finance & Leasing Association (2003) Annual Review 2002. London

Fisher G, Babbar S (1999) Private financing of toll roads. RMC discussion papers 117, World Bank Publications, Washington DC

Forestieri G (2003) Corporate and investment banking. Second Edition, Egea, Milan

Forestieri G (2003) L'investment banking: origini e sviluppo. Egea, Milan

Forestieri G, Tasca R (1994) Il mezzanine finance. Egea, Milan

Fox J, Tott N (2000) The PFI Handbook. Jordan Publishing Ltd, London

Freshfields, Bruchaus, Deringer (2002) The Italian Power Market

Frignani A (1989) Il leveraged buy-out nel diritto italiano. Giurisprudenza Commerciale 1

Frignani A (1996) Factoring, leasing, franchising, venture capital, leveraged buyout, hardship clause, countertrade, cash and carry, merchandising, know how, securitization. Giappichelli, Turin

Galletti D, Guerrieri G (2002) La cartolarizzazione dei crediti. Il Mulino, Bologna

Gambino A (1990) Il leveraged buy-out in Italia. Diritto Fallimentare

Gatti S (1998) Il settore delle grandi opere nella regione del Sud Est Asiatico. Economia & Management 5

Gatti S (1999) Manuale del project finance. Bancaria Editrice, Rome

Gatti S (2002) Dove si trova il valore delle aziende? Vantaggi e svantaggi delle metodologie a confronto. Mimeo, SDA Bocconi, Milan

Gatti S (2003) Le operazioni di finanza strutturata: il project finance. In: Forestieri G (eds) Corporate and investment banking. Second Edition, Egea, Milan

Gatti S, Germani A (2003) Il project finance nel settore sanitario. Stato dell'arte e prospettive in Italia. Economia & Management 3

Genovese A (1997) L'invalidità dell'atto di fusione. Giappichelli, Turin

Gervasoni A (1996) Imprese e mercati finanziari. Guerini & Associati, Milan

Gitman L J (1997) Principles of managerial finance. Addison Wesley Longman Inc, USA

GME – Gestore Mercato Elettrico (2003) Il mercato elettrico: regole ed opportunità per gli operatori

Grande Stevens F (1990) Il leverade buy-out in Italia. Diritto Fallimentare 1

Grant R, Gent D (1992) Asset Finance and leasing handbook. Woodhead Faulkner, Cambridge

Gualtieri P (2000) Taluni aspetti problematici attinenti la realizzazione dei programmi di securitization in Italia. Banche e Banchieri 2 p 93

Guatri L (1998) Trattato sulla valutazione delle aziende. Egea, Milan

Hands G, O'Riordan M (1999) Leasing, securitisation and principal finance in Europe. In: Drew P (eds) World leasing yearbook. Euromoney Publication, London

Iannaccone G (2002) Conference tax & Legal. AIFI, Milan

IFC (2003) IFC's experience with promoting leasing in developing countries 1990-2002. World Bank Publishing, Washington DC

Infrastructure Journal – Power news (2003) The Italian electricity market and the launch of its power exchange

International Finance Corporation (1996) Financing private infrastructure. The World Bank Publication, Washington DC

International Finance Corporation (1999) Lesson of experience 7 – Project Finance in developing countries. The World Bank Publication, Washington DC

JCR-VIS (2003) Securitization. Special Report

Jensen M (1989) Active investors, LBOs and the privatization of bankruptcy. Journal of Applied Corporate Finance 2-1

Kaplan S (1988) Management buyouts: efficiency gains or value transfers? Ph.D. thesis, Harvard University

Kaplan S (1991) The effect of MBO on operating performance and value. Journal of Financial Economics 29

Keating S (1996) Synthetic leasing moves into the mainstream. Asset finance and leasing digest May

Keating S (2003) UK leasing review 2001-2002. Asset finance and leasing digest supplement October

Kensinger J W, Martin J (1988) Project finance: raising money in the old-fashioned way. Journal of Applied Corporate Finance 3

Krieger L (1994) Management buy-outs. Butterworths, Londond

La Torre M, Rio R (2002) Italian government set to change LBO legislation. Southern Europe Unquote. Bancaria 2

Lasfer M A, Evis M (1998) The determinants of leasing decisions of small and large companies. European financial management June

Leaseurope (2002) Leasing activity in Europe. Key facts and figures. Leaseurope September

Leaseurope (2003) European leasing barometer. Leaseurope 4th Edition

Leaseurope (2004) European leasing barometer. Leaseurope 5th Edition

Legge n. 130 del 30 aprile 1999, Disposizioni sulla cartolarizzazione dei crediti. G. U. Serie generale 111

Leixner T (various years) Securitization of financial assets. Holland & Knight LLP, http:// pages.stern.nyu.edu

Leland H, Skarabot J (2002) Financial Synergies and the optimal scope of the firm: implications for mergers, spinoffs and off-balance sheet financing. Mimeograph, Haas School of Business, University of California

Lo Cicero M (1996) Project versus corporate financing. Rassegna Economica 4

Manzini G (2000) La fusione c.d. inverse, ossia l'incorporazione della controllante nella controllata. Contratto e Impresa

Marabini F (1996) Problemi sempre attuali del leveraged buy-out. Diritto del commercio Internazionale

Massari M (1998) Finanza aziendale. Valutazione. McGraw-Hill Libri Italia, Milan

Messingson W L, Kleimeier S (2000) Are project finance loans different from other syndicated credits?. Mimeograph, University of Oklahoma

Mills D, Seassaro F (1990) Italy. International Financial Law Review, February Special Supplement

Mills S (1996) Project financing of oil and gas fields development. Journal of International Banking Law 1

Ministero dell'Economia e delle Finanze (2002) Documento di programmazione economico-finanziaria 2003-2006, Rome

Molino P (2000) La Cassazione mette al bando il leveraged buy-out. Società, Bilancio e Contabilità

Monferrà S (1998) Il leasing internazionale. In Carretta A, De Laurentis G (eds) Il manuale del leasing. Egea, Milan

Montalenti P (1990) Il leveraged buy-out. Conference on leveraged buyout in Italy, Rome

Montalenti P (1991) Il leveraged buy-out. Giuffrè, Milan

Montalenti P (1996) I giudici italiani e il leveraged buy-out tra responsabilità della capogruppo e divieto di assistenza finanziaria. Giurisprudenza Italiana sez 2

Montanari A (2001) La ratio dell'articolo 2358 codice civile e la diffidenza verso il leveraged buy-out. Rivista Diritto Privato

Morano G (1992) Liceità o illegalità. Le società

Morello U (1995) Il problema della frode alla legge rivisitato. Fusioni, concentrazioni e trasformazioni tra autonomia e controllo, Milan

Musco E (2002) I nuovi reati societari. Giuffrè, Turin

Navone C (2002) I profili fiscali della securitization. Rassegna Tributaria 4

Nevitt K P (1997) Project financing. Cariplo Laterza, Milan

Nicolai M (2002) Finanza e risorse idriche. Paper at convention Finanza e risorse idriche, Finlombarda, Milan

Nomura Fixed Income and Research (2002) Thirty years later securitization is still good for America

Norsa A (1998) Riflessioni sul project financing – l'esperienza britannica e l'applicabilità in Italia. L'Ufficio Tecnico April

Novo M (1999) Gli aspetti legali del project financing. In: Gatti S (eds) Manuale del project finance. Bancaria, Rome

Pardolesi R (1989) Leveraged buy-out: una novità a tinte forti (o fosche?). Giurisprudenza Commerciale

Pennarelli T (1993) Leveraged buy-out e processi di successione nelle imprese familiari. Economia & Management 5

Perra L (1999) Rifiuti solidi urbani: una analisi economica dell'aspetto produttivo. Working paper, Proaqua

PFI (1997) PFI – Private Finance Iniziative – Come fare finanza di progetto per le infrastrutture, Milan

Picone L (2000) Liceità del merger leveraged buy-out? (Note at Cass. Pen, sec. V, 02-04-2000 n. 5503). Le Società

Picone L (2001) Orientamenti giurisprudenziali e profili operativi del LBO. Giuffrè, Milan

Porzio C, Spotorno L, Zorzoli S, Fauceglia G (2001), Securitization e crediti in sofferenza. Bancaria Editrice, Rome

Preite D (1993) I merger leveraged buyouts e gli articoli 2357 e 2358 c.c.. Giurisprudenza Commerciale

PWC (1997, 1998, 1999), Buyout survey Italy, www.pwcglobal.com

Rumi G (2001) Securitization. Edizioni Il Sole 24 Ore, Milan

Ruozi R, Caselli S, Gatti S, Monferrà S (1997) Il leasing nel project finance. Egea, Milan

Satin F, Soppelsa C (1996) Il reperimento del capitale di rischio. In: Gervasoni A (1996) Imprese e mercati finanziari. Guerini & Associati, Milan

Sattin F, D'Anzi (1998) Le operazioni di leveraged buy-out: esperienze internazionali e realtà italiana. Amministrazione & Finanza 20

Saunders A, Cornett M C (2004) Financial markets and institutions, a modern perspective. McGraw-Hill International Ed

Savioli G (2003) Le operazioni di gestione straordinaria. Giuffrè, Milan

Scoditi E (1993) Il caso Farmitalia fra leveraged buy outs ed acquisto di azioni proprie per interposta persona. Foro Italiano 2

Shah S, Thakor A V (1987) Optimal capital structure and project financing. Journal of Economic Theory 42

Sironi A, Iannotta G (2003) Il mezzanine finance. In: Forestieri G (eds) Corporate and investment banking. Second Edition, Egea, Milan

Smith A J (1990) Corporate ownership structure and performance. The case of MBOs. Journal of Financial Economics 27

Smith C W, Warner J B (1979) On financial contracting: an analysis of bond covenants. Journal of Financial Economics 7

Sorrentino R (1992) Dal Tribunale arriva il via libera al buy-out su Farmitalia C. Erba. Il Sole 24 Ore 05-16-1992

Spolidoro M S (2000) Effetti patrimoniali e rappresentazione contabile della fusione inversa. Le Società p 333

Spotorno L (2003) La securitization: strutture contrattuali e modalità operative. In: Forestieri G (eds) Corporate e investment banking. Egea, Milan

Standard & Poor's (2002) Project and infrastructure finance review

Tabarrini A, Tabarrini L (1999) Le nuove norme in material di lavori pubblici – Commento alla Merloni Ter, Maggioli, Rimini

Tagliavini G (2001) Il lease back. Etas Libri, Milan

Tagliavini G, Caselli S (1998) I canali distributivi del leasing. Newfin, Università Bocconi, Milan

Talete Creative Finance (2002) Rapporto annuale sul mercato italiano della cartolarizzazione 1999-2001. Internal publication

Talete Creative Finance (2003) Rapporto annuale sul mercato italiano della cartolarizzazione 2002. Internal publication

Tinsley R (2000) Advanced project financing. Euromoney Books, London

Unità Tecnica Finanza di Progetto (2001) Relazione annuale, Rome

Varrenti (2000) A follow up to the legal saga on leveraged buyouts: Italian supreme court holds LBOs transactions to be illegal. Corporate Finance, London

Varrenti A (2000) Leveraged buyouts in Italy: an update on a highly debated acquisition system. In: AA.VV. (eds) Corporate Finance, London

Vender J (1986) Il leveraged buy-out: una tecnica finanziaria per acquisire la proprietà di un'azienda. Finanza, Marketing e Produzione p 230

Vogt R (1999) Synthetic leasing. In Drew P (eds) World leasing yearbook. Euromoney Publication, London

Walton M (1999) UK lease taxation: a case for Europe. Leasing life October

Williamson O (1988) Corporate finance and corporate governance. Journal of Finance 43

Wright M, Robbie K (1991) Buy-ins and buy-outs. New strategies in corporate management. Graham & Trotman, London

Wright M, Robbie K (1999) Management buy-outs and venture capital into the next millennium. Edward Elgar, Cheltenham

www.abalert.com

www.borsaitalia.it

www.securitisation.it

Zambelli S (2002) A note on leveraged buyout transactions in Italy: economic and legal aspects. Working paper n. 171, University of Bologna

Zambelli S (2004) Le operazioni di merger leveraged buy-out: rilevanza economica per le policies aziendali e i problemi di legittimità. Newfin Ricerche, Milan

Zambelli S (2005) Il leveraged buyout in Italia: controversie e casi aziendali. Aracne Editrice, Rome

Zambelli S, Jenter D (2001) Financial and legal aspect of leveraged buyouts in Italy. The supreme court's decision n. 5503/2000. Lettera Newfin 3

# List of Contributors

Corresponding Address:

Professor Stefano Caselli
Professor Stefano Gatti

Institute of Financial Markets and Financial Intermediaries
"L. Bocconi" University
Via Sarfatti, 25 - 20136 Milan
Italy

stefano.caselli@uni-bocconi.it
stefano.gatti@uni-bocconi.it

**Stefano Caselli**
Associate Professor in Banking and Finance at "L. Bocconi" University, Milan, Italy. Professor at Banking and Insurance Department of SDA Bocconi, the Management and Business School of "L. Bocconi University", Milan, Italy. He's developing research activity, managerial education and strategic consulting in: corporate and investment banking, leasing and asset finance, credit risk management, SME's financing.

**Stefano Gatti**
Associate Professor in Banking and Finance at "L. Bocconi" University, Milan, Italy. Professor at Banking and Insurance Department of SDA Bocconi, the Management and Business School of "L. Bocconi University", Milan, Italy. He's developing research activity, managerial education and strategic consulting in: corporate and investment banking, project financing, corporate finance and company valuation.

**Vincenzo Capizzi**
Associate Professor in Banking and Finance at "A. Avogadro" University, Novara, Italy. Professor at Banking and Insurance Department of SDA Bocconi School of Management, Università Bocconi.

**Roberto Tasca**
Full Professor in Financial Markets and Intermediaries at "Università degli Studi di Bologna", Forlì, Italy. Professor at Banking and Insurance Department of SDA Bocconi, the Management and Business School of "L. Bocconi University", Milan, Italy. He's developing research activity in: bank management and corporate and investment banking.

**Simona Zambelli**
Assistant Professor of Banking and Finance, at University of Bologna, Forli School of Business. She is developing research activity, managerial education and consulting in: Private Equity & Venture Capital, Project Financing, Risk Management and Business Valuation.

Printing and Binding:  Strauss GmbH, Mörlenbach